A Fisherman's Guide to Maine

A Fisherman's Guide to Maine

KEVIN TRACEWSKI

COUNTRYSPORT PRESS
CAMDEN, MAINE

Copyright © 2004 by Kevin Tracewski

Cover and interior design by Janet L. Patterson

Printed by Versa Press Inc., East Peoria, Illinois

5   4   3   2

ISBN 0-89272-596-6

Library of Congress Control Number 2004105745

Countrysport Press
P.O. Box 679
Camden, ME 04843
A division of Down East Enterprise, publishers of Fly Rod & Reel *magazine,*
www.flyrodandreel.com

To request a book catalog or place an order, visit www.countrysportpress.com
or call 800-685-7962.

Front-cover photograph by Randy Ury

Contents

Acknowledgments

NOVELIST Charles Brower once said, "Few people are successful unless a lot of other people want them to be." Brower's statement is certainly true for this book. From the good Samaritan in Eagle Lake who took me fishing while my truck was being repaired to all the friends who have shared their favorite Maine angling spots with me, I owe thanks to "a lot of other people."

I am most indebted to my wife and best friend, Cheryl. She took many of the photos that appear in this book, and she has been at my side since we spent our honeymoon at site Number 21 in Rangeley Lake State Park twenty-five years ago. Without the complaint-free years of effort that she put into taking care of our house and kids while I was fishing, this book would not have been possible. My three children—Kristen, Kendall, and Tyler—deserve more credit than I can mention here; they spent their youths hiking into ponds and being bitten by blackflies while their friends were at an amusement park or the beach. Hopefully, some day they will look back at our adventures as fond memories.

Dozens of professional people made significant contributions to this book. Chandler Morse, a good friend and former graduate student at the University of Maine, produced the maps and spent a good deal of his personal time working on this project. I gratefully acknowledge his efforts. Sandra Hale, the artist who drew the portraits for the regional expert profiles, went out of her way to be certain that everything was just right.

I would like to thank three other people at the University of Maine. Betsy Paradis is a former special collections librarian who frequently undertook extra work to make life much easier for me. Kelly Edwards is a member of the Department of Biological Sciences who spent a considerable amount of his own time assisting me in copying, editing, and printing many of the pictures that appear in this book. Michelle Larson is a former student who helped edit each chapter's text.

Chris Cornell and Joe Arnette at Down East Books made my experience as a first-time author go as smoothly as possible.

I offer my gratitude to all of the hard-working regional biologists and game wardens in the Maine Department of Inland Fisheries and Wildlife. I can't recall a single instance in twenty years when one of these people failed to return a phone call or give me a straight answer. Forrest Bonney, Paul Johnson, Scott Roy, John Boland, Ron Brokaw, Greg Burr, Dave Basley, Frank Frost, and their colleagues are the unsung heroes of the Maine fishing scene.

Finally, I would like to thank the regional experts and the photographers who contributed to this book. Their generosity and trust exceeded my wildest hopes. It is heartwarming to discover that there are still many good people out there. Getting to know all of them was my favorite aspect of this project.

This book is dedicated to my mom and dad.
Their hard work and sacrifice are what put me in a position
to be able to enjoy the Maine outdoors.
My only regret is that neither of them lived to see this book published.

Preface

THE PURPOSE of this book is to provide an overview of the fishing opportunities that are available in Maine. It is arranged into eight geographical regions and covers all major freshwater habitats as well as selected marine fisheries. Because of my personal inclinations, the book is slanted toward fly-fishing for trout and salmon. I have, however, included information about spin-fishing and about warmwater species such as bass and pike.

Maine is a large state that offers a wide range of angling options; thus, each chapter begins with a brief overview of the fisheries in the region and a map that shows many of the waters that are discussed in the text. The maps are not drawn to scale nor are they intended for navigational purposes. Readers familiar with a given region will notice that only a limited number of waters are described. In a book of statewide coverage, it was impossible to include additional fisheries. For the most part, well-known places that provide reasonable opportunities to catch quality fish are emphasized. A few, specific omissions are intentional—I didn't think the fisheries could stand the increased pressure that might result from exposure in a widely distributed book. Most omissions, however, are due either to space concerns or because I never fished in a particular location.

Maine has a rich sport-fishing history—anglers have been coming here for one hundred fifty years. An attendant at the Rangeley Historical Society put this into perspective for me when he said, "As wagon trains were carrying settlers past many of the rivers out west that are now famous, sports were traveling to Rangeley and Moosehead to fish." It is my belief that an understanding of Maine's angling history and tradition can add to the enjoyment of fishing experiences. Therefore, early in each chapter I have included a look at the history of the particular region before discussing its present-day fisheries. Because the character of its people is what makes Maine special, I have also provided a profile of an important angling personality from each region.

I spent seven years working on this book—it took that long because I am not a full-time writer. I earn my living teaching biology at the University of Maine, and in that capacity I usually have a block of time in the summer to fish, write, or do whatever I choose to do—a luxury that real outdoor writers do not have. Looking back, I think taking seven years to write this book made it better. It allowed me to revisit places a number of times and to obtain a better selection of photos. It also gave me the opportunity to work on worthwhile (and time-consuming) side projects like the maps and regional expert profiles.

The background research I did for this book was similar to that of my scientific work. It involved spending hours in the library learning about the history of each region and reading numerous articles and books on Maine fishing. I considered including a bibliography with references and footnotes, but, because this book is intended to be a practical guide rather than a scholarly work, in the end, I decided to keep it simple.

Presently, most fishing in Maine takes place either on private property or paper-company land. People have unrestricted access to nearly all the waters of the state, and, although catch-and-release has gained popularity, most places still allow a few fish to be killed. Several years ago, the start of the new millennium was marked with comparisons between the lifestyles and issues of today and those of the past. It's likely that similar comparisons will be made between Maine fishing now and in the future. Perhaps a comprehensive book like this one will serve as a status report on the current condition of the resource.

Maine fisheries are facing a number of challenges from environmental intrusions like development pressure, acid rain, and the introduction of exotic species. These are difficult issues that will have an enormous impact on what our sport looks like in fifty to one hundred years. On some fronts, I fear that we might be fighting a losing battle. But Maine fishing means a great deal to me, and I plan to do whatever I can to help support it. Maintaining undisturbed habitats that can sustain wild fisheries is an important element in continuing the Maine fishing tradition. Therefore, I intend to place half of the profits from this book into a conservation fund to be used as seed money to raise capital for fishery habitat maintenance. Ultimately, if even a modest number of the people who love Maine fishing get involved, we can make a difference.

But the essence of fishing, to me, is not about conservation funds, fancy equipment, or matching the hatch. It's not even about catching fish. It's about people and places. Fishing has introduced me to many good friends and has helped to sustain those relationships over the years. It has also taken me to more beautiful places than I ever imagined possible. Without fishing, I probably would have never risen early and seen the day break over Allagash Lake, or traveled to faraway places such as Newfoundland, Wyoming, and Alaska. Without fishing as the backdrop, I also might not have had the chance to get as close as I have to my family.

My dad worked in a factory six days a week throughout my entire childhood. But he loved fishing and always found time to take me. We talked through many issues during the hours we spent together in a boat, and even during my troubled teenage years we never missed an opportunity to fish together. One Father's Day, I bought him a drawing of a man and a child fishing together in a small stream. For many years, I pictured those two people as me and him. But now that I am older and Dad has passed away, I see myself and my own kids in that drawing.

More than anything else, the real beauty of fishing is that it can be enjoyed by people of all ages. Hopefully, this book will help young people learn the basics of fishing as well as furnish seasoned veterans with a few new ideas. Doing so will provide both groups with a better opportunity to enjoy the wonderful state of Maine and, in the long run, might instill in these people a passion and respect for the outdoors that will be needed to protect it in the future.

Southern Maine

Early October is a prime time to fly-fish for salmon at Sebago Lake Station.

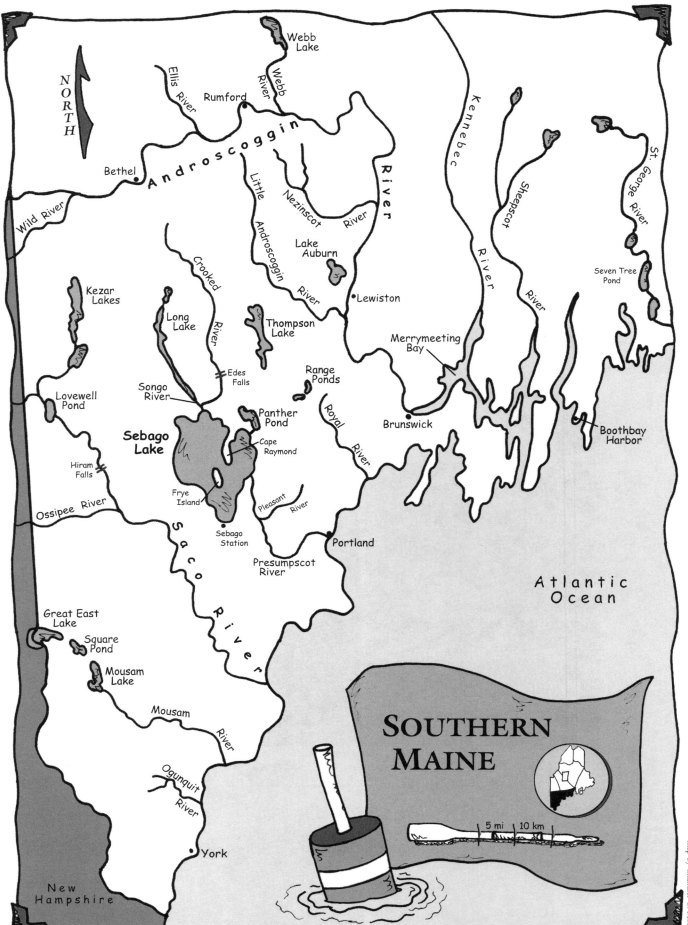

NORTH

Webb Lake

Ellis River

Webb River

Rumford

Androscoggin

Bethel

Wild River

Little Androscoggin River

Nezinscot River

Kennebec

River

Sheepscot River

St. George River

Lake Auburn

Crooked River

Kezar Lakes

Long Lake

Thompson Lake

Lewiston

Seven Tree Pond

Merrymeeting Bay

Range Ponds

Edes Falls

Songo River

Lovewell Pond

Panther Pond

Cape Raymond

Royal River

Brunswick

Boothbay Harbor

Sebago Lake

Hiram Falls

Frye Island

Pleasant River

Ossipee River

Saco River

Sebago Station

Portland

Presumpscot River

Atlantic Ocean

Great East Lake

Square Pond

Mousam Lake

Mousam River

Ogunquit River

York

New Hampshire

SOUTHERN MAINE

5 mi   10 km

map by Chandler C. Morse

Bucky Owen

illustration by Sandra Nesterode-Hale

BUCKY OWEN loves the Maine outdoors, and everyone who knows him well has a favorite story or two about his exploits afield. Be it fishing, hunting, hiking, biking, white-water canoeing, or crosscountry skiing, Bucky sinks his heart and soul into every activity and usually finds a way to end up with a favorable outcome.

Bucky Owen spent thirty years as a professor of wildlife ecology at the University of Maine where he studied species such as black ducks, woodcock, and bald eagles. In 1993 he was appointed Commissioner of the Maine Department of Inland Fisheries and Wildlife, and one of the issues that he was most concerned about was the decline in the quality of the state's coldwater fisheries, particularly wild, native brook trout.

Instead of accepting this situation as an inevitable consequence of an increasing population and remaining content with memories of the good old days of Maine fishing, Bucky, in characteristic fashion, took action. His primary goals were to upgrade the state's outdated fish hatcheries and to implement quality-fishing regulations that would significantly reduce the number of trophy trout and salmon that were killed in Maine waters each year.

Upgrading the state's hatcheries met with widespread approval, and the corporate sponsorship of hatcheries has facilitated improvements that benefited anglers throughout the state. The quality-fishing initiatives were much more controversial. Although most anglers recognized that the number of large fish being killed needed to be significantly reduced, few wanted to give up their share of the resource.

The debate over this issue was heated and raged on for months at public hearings held throughout the state. Frequently, Bucky bore the brunt of verbal attacks from people who didn't share his views. In typical fashion, he held his ground and responded with rational arguments that repeatedly returned to one obvious point: "When the best native brood stock is killed off, they can no longer contribute their desirable genes to future generations." By the time Bucky Owen left office in 1997, most of his quality-fishing initiatives had been signed into law and have become widely accepted as some of the most farsighted changes ever implemented by any Commissioner of Inland Fisheries and Wildlife.

Since his retirement, he has worked actively to facilitate the removal of unneeded dams. Removal of dams on the Kennebec River, Souadabscook Stream, and several waters in the North Woods has had an immediate impact on the fishing in those areas. But Bucky notes that even dam removal is becoming much more controversial. Currently, Bucky Owen is working with environmental groups such as The Nature Conservancy and the Forest Society of Maine to acquire land and easements to protect the integrity of large river systems, including the St. John, Machais, Dennys, Penobscot, Saco, and Kennebec Rivers.

Much of southern Maine is situated on the lowlands of the coastal plain and is, at least by Maine standards, heavily populated. The Saco and Androscoggin are two of the state's largest rivers and provide popular put-and-take fisheries for brown, brook, and rainbow trout at a number of locations. Similar hatchery-supplemented fishing opportunities can also be found on smaller rivers like the Ossipee, Nezinscot, Little Androscoggin, St. George, and Sheepscot. Although few opportunities to catch quality native brook trout are available in this region, healthy populations of warmwater species such as largemouth and smallmouth bass, perch, and pickerel are widely distributed.

The coldwater fishing scene in southern Maine is dominated by twenty-nine-thousand-acre Sebago Lake. Long known as a producer of large salmon, the state's second largest body of water draws legions of spring trollers to locations such as the mouth of the Songo River and Jordan Bay. Spawning salmon also run up the Crooked River in the fall and provide fly fishermen with an opportunity to partake of Sebago's bounty. In addition to salmon, the lake produces many togue—Maine lingo for lake trout—over five pounds and a wide array of warmwater species. Because Sebago Lake is only fifteen miles from Portland, Maine's largest city, it can get quite crowded on summer weekends. Nevertheless, shortly after ice-out when the fishing is best, Sebago Lake can be a great place for an angler to spend an enjoyable day.

For many years, the most overlooked species of game fish in southern Maine lived in saltwater. During the 1980s, however, around the time that President George Bush moved the summer White House to Kennebunkport, Mainers discovered that striped bass, bluefish, and mackerel would respond to their flies just as readily as trout and salmon and that these ocean-dwelling critters were usually a lot bigger. Since that time, there has been an explosion in saltwater fishing along the entire southern Maine coast.

History

The first European known to have sailed along the Maine coast was Giovanni Verrazano in 1524. During the one hundred years that followed, explorers from many nations embarked on voyages to this area. Initially, Europeans were lured here by reports of a shorter route to the Far East and by fictitious tales of

Sawmills were established in several southern Maine towns in the mid-1700s.

14

Maine State Museum

Granite quarries, like this one near Stonington, provided coastal Maine settlers with an alternative to farming and fishing.

Norumbega, a city whose streets were paved with gold. But, ultimately, it was the great bounty of the seas and forests that persuaded the powerful nations of England, France, and Spain to maintain their interest in this remote area of the New World.

By the early 1600s, a number of settlements had been established along the south coast between Kittery and Casco Bay. In 1639, Royal Governor Ferdinando Gorges officially declared that this territory would be called the Province of Maine. Most early inhabitants were either tenant farmers from Europe who wanted to own a piece of land or people trying to escape religious persecution. But making a life here wasn't easy; historians estimate that the combined effects of the harsh climate, lack of food, and conflicts with Indians caused half of these early settlers to die within their first five years of residency.

Travel between settlements was difficult and done mostly by footpath or boat. In an attempt to promote

colonization, a primary road that could accommodate horses and allow for delivery of mail was established between Boston and Portland in 1707. During the next century, a network of inns and taverns that provided travelers with food and lodging was also built. These developments prompted the construction of many new homesteads within proximity of the Boston–Portland road and established this region as the heart of colonial Maine.

Sawmills in York, Berwick, Wells, and Falmouth established lumbering as the first major industry in this area. Limestone and granite quarries also provided many jobs. Most people who settled here, however, made their living as farmers who cut and burned the forests, then grew crops in the fertile soil of the cleared land. During the peak of colonization that occurred during the fifty years following the Revolutionary War, thousands of acres of land were cleared annually. Early diaries describe smoke-filled skies that persisted for months over southern Maine and floods that carried large burdens of ash and soil into the area's streams.

In addition to causing these profound environmental disturbances, colonization also led to the introduction of exotic warmwater species such as perch, pickerel, and bass to southern Maine waters. The combined effects of these actions resulted in the destruction of most local brook trout fisheries by the time that Maine joined the Union in 1820.

The saltwater fisheries in this area held up much better to this initial barrage of human activity. Striped bass and Atlantic salmon were so plentiful that for many years colonial law stipulated that indentured servants could not be forced to eat them more than six times a week. Alewives and shad were even more abundant and were frequently netted in the spring for use as fertilizer. Writings from the 1700s indicate that to early settlers the astounding bounty of anadromous fish seemed inexhaustible. Less than a century later, these fish runs were almost completely eliminated by the dams and pollution of the Industrial Revolution.

Sebago Lake was one place that managed to avoid many of the hardships that plagued other waters and fisheries in southern Maine. Sebago Lake was one of the four original homes of landlocked salmon in Maine and historically was known as a lake that produced very large fish. The first written account of a Sebago salmon is in the 1825 diary of Nathaniel Hawthorne, who wrote, "On the way home from Frye's Island, Mr. Ring caught a black-spotted trout that was almost a whale. It weighed, before it was cut open, eighteen and one-half pounds." Another account from a few years later states, "Acres of water were boiling with smelts and salmon but a boat's length away, and very ordinary and everyday fishermen were reeling in from twelve to eighteen pound fish." Salmon up to twenty pounds were taken from Sebago through the early 1900s. By 1950, the weight of an average fish had dropped below four pounds.

Around 1960, salmon fishing in Sebago Lake reached an all-time low. As a result, the Maine Department of Inland Fisheries and Wildlife (MDIF&W) conducted a three-year study to explore the reason for this decline. They discovered that the widespread aerial spraying of a little-known insecticide called DDT had caused a dramatic drop in reproduction and growth rates of salmon. The MDIF&W study and others like it, backed by biologist Rachel Carson's history-making book *Silent Spring*, contributed greatly to the environmental movement that blossomed throughout the country a few years later.

Southern Maine Lakes Region

Sebago Lake has long been known for its world-class salmon fishing and is the focal point of the lakes region. Unlike the early days, however, when anglers traveled from Portland in riverboats on the Cumberland and Oxford Canal or arrived at Sebago Lake Station by railroad and slept in area farmhouses for one dollar a night, the lake is now surrounded by paved highways and has more services than it needs. Thompson, Kezar, Auburn, and a dozen other productive lakes lie within twenty miles of Sebago's north shore. And like Sebago, they can be reached by paved roads and have quite a few camps on them. Despite increasing pressure, most waters in this region still provide a quality experience for southern Maine anglers.

Sebago Lake

Sebago is an Abnaki Indian word that means "large open water." When you stand on the lake's shore and gaze across its forty-square-mile main basin you can see why it received this name. Salmon are the traditional target for most anglers on Sebago Lake, and though the size of the average fish has declined over the years, this lake still represents one of the best places in Maine to land a trophy. In 1972, biologists introduced togue into Sebago because they are well-suited for the lake's vast expanses of deep, cold water. Togue over ten pounds are now caught regularly.

Because of its size, the easiest way to discuss fishing on Sebago Lake is to outline the opportunities that are available within reasonable distances of the major access points. On the north end of the lake, a heavily

Spring salmon fishing from a dock on Long Lake around 1935.

Maine State Archives

used boat launch can be found just off U.S. Route 302 at Sebago Lake State Park. This area is popular because it is located at the mouth of the Songo River, which supports a heavy run of smelts and attracts large numbers of hungry salmon in the spring. On weekends during April and May, it's not unusual to find fifty boats working sewn smelts or tandem streamer flies back and forth across the dropoff at the mouth of the river. Early season trolling here can be an unproductive, bone-chilling experience if the fish aren't feeding—I have been skunked on several occasions. Nevertheless, anglers who are on the water early and put in their time are often rewarded with some of their biggest fish of the season.

Many Sebago Lake salmon are taken shortly after ice-out by anglers trolling smelt-imitating flies and lures.

dozens of fly patterns like the Miss Sharon, Senator Muskie, Bibeau Killer, and Green Wonder have been devised by prominent fishermen such as Art Libby, Bob Bibeau, and Carroll Cutting to fool Sebago Lake salmon. Live smelts, Rapalas, Mooselook Wobblers and Cecil's Smelts have also taken countless numbers of fish. Despite this disparity in terminal tackle, one rule of thumb that many people follow is that trolling speed should be slow immediately after ice-out and increase proportionally with the rise in water temperature. Once a thermocline becomes established, many anglers on the south end of the lake switch to deep-trolling for togue in the vicinity of the Camel's Pasture.

Another productive area for trolling is along the west side of Cape Raymond from the Notch that separates it from Frye's Island through the Dingley Islands. This area can be reached either from the state park or a launch site at Sebago Lake Basin that is located just off the White's Bridge Road. Legendary guide Art Libby fished this area for many years and felt that the key to success here was keeping your offerings close to shore. "Early in the season," Libby often said, "the smelt ain't out in deep water, and neither are the salmon." Over the years I've found this to be excellent advice, and I have caught many fish within ten feet of the shoreline rocks.

The best access to the southern part of the lake is from the boat launch at Sebago Lake Station. In the spring, salmon can be spread along the southwestern shoreline from the Lower Bay all the way to Ward's Cove. Over the years,

The most innocent-looking hotspot on the entire lake is the three hundred yards of shoreline adjacent to the dock at Sebago Station. This area is particularly good in the fall; several years ago, I landed three, twenty-inch salmon in a couple hours of fishing during the extended catch-and-release season in October. This section of the lake is characterized by a gradually sloping gravel beach and has no inlet or outlet, so to someone not familiar with its reputation it looks very ordinary. The first time I visited this spot, I walked out on the dock and took a quick look in the water, then left without even rigging my rod. According to biologist John Boland, "What makes this particular place special is it is where many hatchery-reared salmon are released, and each fall many of them return to spawn." Trying to pinpoint one fly that works best is difficult—I've seen fish taken on everything from small nymphs to large marabou streamers. Probably the most

Chip Tracewski

Although large togue are still caught regularly, small togue became so plentiful in Sebago during the late 1990s that the daily bag limit was increased to six fish to prevent the lake's smelt population from being decimated.

reliable method is to fish small attractors like the Pink Lady or Mickey Finn on a sinking line under low-light conditions.

Sebago Area Rivers

The Crooked is a moderate-sized river that flows into the north end of Sebago Lake near the state park. Each spring, smelts run into the lower section of this river and concentrate fishing activity from the U.S. Route 302 bridge down to the lake. One of the best-known opening-day spots in the state is located at Songo Locks, which is about a mile up from the lake at the confluence of the Crooked and Songo Rivers. Regardless of the weather, hordes of fishermen turn out to cast lures and baited bobbers out into the river's icy flow. Despite its popularity, I have never found fishing here to be very good until the smelt run peaks later in the month. April fishermen on the Crooked River also frequent several deep pools just above where it dumps into Sebago Lake. This area usually fishes best from a boat in the early morning hours, but it can be tough to work in strong wind and high-water conditions.

Maine Department of Inland Fisheries and Wildlife statistics indicate that nearly 35 percent of the salmon caught in Sebago Lake are wild fish that have been pro-

duced in the Crooked River. Thus, my favorite time to fish here is in the fall when large salmon leave the lake and head upriver to spawn. Since the water flow is not regulated by dams, the key to late-season success is timing your visit to coincide with a flush of rain that will trigger fish to move into the river. When you hit it right, salmon can be found anywhere in the twelve miles between the U.S. Route 302 bridge and Bolsters Mills. The river is sand-bottomed and fairly shallow throughout most of this area, so fish tend to congregate in deep corner pools that have some current moving through them. Frequently, I will use a bright marabou streamer to prospect likely looking water, then switch to smaller nymphs if fish are reluctant to take the larger fly. Since the Crooked is a narrow river whose banks are lined with deciduous hardwoods, fouling your fly with leaves and other floating debris is an annoying problem that you will often encounter during the fall season.

Two smaller tributaries on the north end of Sebago Lake are the Muddy River in South Naples and Panther Run in Raymond. Both of these rivers have early season fisheries that are dependent on a strong flow of water to draw fish into them from the lake. Each year, a number of salmon are taken by anglers who work streamer flies along the edges of the fast water below the Muddy

The Presumpscot River flows out of Sebago Lake and is a very popular southern Maine fishery.

River bridge and in the pools below the dam on Panther Run. Later in the season, Panther Run also receives a generous stocking of brook trout that usually provides a couple of weeks of fast fishing throughout the river.

The Presumpscot River is stocked in the fall with nice brook trout.

The Presumpscot River forms the outlet of Sebago Lake and represents the only season-long river fishery in the drainage. Most angling takes place within two miles of the lake in the Eel Weir bypass section of the river. This is a relatively new fishery—until 1992, virtually all of the outflow from Sebago Lake was diverted into a man-made canal for hydroelectric generation. Since minimum-flow rates were mandated as part of a Federal Energy Regulatory Commission dam relicensing agreement, the MDIF&W has had great success managing the upper Presumpscot River as a coldwater fishery.

According to biologist Francis Brautigam, "Because of its close proximity to the Portland area, the department's [MDIF&W] goal for this revitalized section of the Presumpscot River is to provide a high-quality coldwater fishing experience for the maximum number of anglers possible. And the best way to do this is through liberal stocking and fairly restrictive regulations." The river is stocked eight times a year, primarily with brook trout and brown trout that range from eight inches to eighteen inches long, and is open year-round to fly-fishing only. Despite heavy fishing pressure, this short stretch of river elicits many favorable comments from the anglers who fish here.

I usually visit the upper Presumpscot River in the fall after most of my favorite northern haunts have closed. October through early December is a great time to be on this river, and I have caught trout on dry flies here until well after Halloween. A gravel parking area on the south side of Route 35 is the main access point; a number of productive runs and pools can be reached by walking a short distance upstream or downstream from the access. Because of the river's crystal-clear water and the heavy fishing pressure it receives, the most effective way to catch its wary trout are with nymphs fished with a strike indicator or with small wet-flies and emergers.

Brook trout are also stocked in the spring below three other dams located on the next seven miles of the Presumpscot River. But, because minimum-flow require-

ments have not been mandated, during the summer these stretches of river become too warm and dewatered to hold trout. Biologist John Boland told me that the MDIF&W is working to establish minimum flows for these dams and hopes to eventually develop quality coldwater fisheries below them.

The final Sebago area river fishery of note is the Pleasant River in Windham. A two-mile stretch from U.S. Route 302 to the River Road is frequently stocked with oversized brook trout and brown trout and is restricted to catch-and-release fishing with artificial lures. Bucktail streamers like the Little Brook Trout and Warden's Worry, along with wet flies and nymphs, produce well for April fly fishermen. Small roostertails, Mepps Spinners and Al's Goldfish are popular with spin fishermen. Hatches usually begin by early May and provide dry-fly fishermen with plenty of action on fish that can be seen rising in the tailouts of many of the larger pools.

Other Sebago Area Lakes

Most of the other popular lakes in the Sebago region are "two-story" fisheries that provide salmon and trout for topwater trollers in the spring, then become primarily bass and other warmwater fisheries in the summer. Although these lakes are in several different watersheds, they are all located in the same area and support similar fisheries; therefore I have grouped them under a general heading.

To help narrow the nearly overwhelming number of choices, I asked biologist John Boland to list his favorite Sebago area lakes according to fish species. For both salmon and togue, he liked Thompson, Kezar, and Auburn Lakes. He added the Ossipee Lakes to his salmon list, and he liked Great East Lake for togue. Selecting brown trout fisheries was more difficult, but eventually Mousam and Crystal Lakes, along with Hancock and the Range Ponds, emerged as his top choices. Other popular, local salmonid waters include Moose, Trickey, Cushman, and Bryant Ponds. Because warmwater species are found throughout this region, Boland felt that highlighting just a handful of lakes might be a bit misleading. Eventually though, he picked Little Sebago, Long, Lovewell, and Androscoggin Lakes as his top bass, pickerel, and perch fisheries.

Conspicuously absent from this list is Square Pond in Shapleigh, which has a well-deserved reputation for producing large brown trout. Despite its shoreline development, this nine-hundred-fifty-acre pond regularly yields fish in excess of five pounds and in 1996 produced a state record brown that weighed close to twenty-four pounds. The main reason for the preponderance of large trout is that landlocked alewives were introduced as a forage fish in the early 1980s. Shortly thereafter, the state's trout-stocking program was discontinued because the public access site to the pond was lost. This produced an environment that provided the limited number of brown trout in the pond with a nearly unlimited food supply, which allowed them to grow at a phenomenal rate. But this situation is changing; the state recently purchased a site for a new boat launch and will probably resume stocking. For several years, though, it was interesting to see the size that ordinary brown trout could attain if left alone in a favorable environment.

The introduction of landlocked alewives also benefited several other local lakes that lacked enough smelts to support their coldwater fisheries. For example, less than five years after alewives were introduced into Kezar Lake, the catch rate for salmon nearly doubled and the length of the average fish increased by three inches. Similar improvements have been noted in Mousam Lake and in Hancock and Crystal Ponds. Based on these results, the MDIF&W will continue to evaluate lakes in this area that might benefit from the introduction of alewives. However, it is important for such introductions to take place in a deliberate, well-thought-out manner because there is always risk involved when transplanting species.

One of my favorite places in southern Maine to be at ice-out is Lake Auburn. Located just beyond the border of the state's third-largest metropolitan area, this twenty-three-hundred-acre body of water might seem like an unlikely spot for a quality fishery. But Lake Auburn has always had a healthy population of smelts that allow its togue and salmon to grow to bragging size. Because it serves as the water supply for the cities of Lewiston and Auburn, it is closed to ice-fishing and has a number of other restrictions.

White perch grow large in many southern Maine waters.

Lake Auburn is heavily fished starting at midnight of opening day when bank fishermen line up along Lake Shore Drive to plunk jack smelts and shiners along the edge of the receding ice. I usually wait until there is enough open water to launch a twelve-foot boat at the landing on Route 4, then I troll around Salmon Point up to the inlet in North Auburn. Live or sewn smelt fished slowly on a sinking line is usually the most reliable way to catch early season salmon and togue. But once the water warms a bit, tandem streamers like the Nine-Three and Umbagog Smelt, along with Rapalas and Mooselook Wobblers also produce their share of fish.

Southern Maine Rivers

There are a number of rivers outside the Sebago Lake drainage that provide good trout fishing. Many of these are seasonal fisheries that rely rather heavily on stocking, but some reliable hatches and good early and late season fly-fishing opportunities can be found here.

St. George and Sheepscot Rivers

Two of my favorite places to visit in the spring are the St. George and Sheepscot Rivers. Both are fairly small waters located in the rolling hills east of Augusta. My fondness for these rivers centers around their reliable hatches of Hendricksons (mayflies), which usually begin a couple of days on either side of Mother's Day—the second Sunday in May. During most years, catching this midday hatch provides me with my first glimpse of rising fish. After six weeks of flinging streamers with a sinking line, getting back to dry-fly fishing is always a welcome event.

The St. George is the better known of these waters. It flows nearly thirty miles from the outlet of St. George Lake in Liberty to the tidewater in Warren. Brown trout are the primary target for most fishermen—some of the deep pools in the hard-to-reach sections of the river can hold gorgeous browns up to twenty inches long. When the water level is good, the four-mile stretch between Searsmont and North Appleton is a great place to spend a day float-fishing from a canoe. The only serious white water is a two-hundred-yard run located immediately above

Late-season nymphing can be productive on the Payson Park stretch of the St. George River near Warren.

the Ghent Road Bridge. If you decide it looks too difficult, you can line your canoe down along the west bank. Of course, you can also catch plenty of trout simply by wading the shallow riffles and pocketwater near the bridges. But I find that the extra effort required to take a canoe through this section is worth it, because many of the best holding pools are away from the road.

Salmon, brook trout, and browns can be taken in the Sheepscot River.

Other St. George River hotspots include a one-mile section between Appleton and Sennebec Pond, the runs below the outlet of Sennebec Pond, the small stretch of moving water between Round and Seven Tree Ponds, and the deep holes between the Middle Road and Warren Village. Along with brown trout, these lower sections produce smallmouth and largemouth bass, pickerel, and white perch. White perch can be so numerous that during their spawning runs in early May people flock to popular locations like Ayer Park in Union to fill five-gallon buckets with these tasty fish.

The Sheepscot River contains brown trout, brook trout, and a few salmon in both its mainstem and West Branch. Much of the river is lined with dense vegetation and is tough to navigate with a canoe. A number of paved roads and trails crisscross the area from Palermo to Whitefield, so anglers willing to beat the bushes can usually find a productive place to fish.

The most popular section of the Sheepscot is the two miles of riffles and pools found below the Palermo Fish Hatchery. In many places, the river here is less than twenty feet across, yet because of its high productivity this stretch has produced a number of fat trout for me over the years. Hatches are reliable during May and June, and fish can often be taken on dry flies floated tight against a half-submerged log or undercut bank. When no fish are showing, a beadhead nymph with a small wet-fly as a dropper can be effective. The MDIF&W is so impressed with this section of river that they made it catch-and-release in 1997 and are managing it solely on the basis of natural reproduction.

A number of other places, including the hard-to-reach section of the Sheepscot's West Branch between Route 3 and the Dirigo Road and the area in the vicinity of Route 17, also produce consistent catches of trout. The lower Sheepscot from North Whitefield to the Head Tide Dam is generally deep enough to float with a canoe in the spring and a few trout are taken in the fast-flowing stretches. The number of bass, pickerel, and perch in your catch will increase as you move downstream.

Androscoggin and Saco Rivers

The two largest rivers in southern Maine are the Androscoggin and the Saco. Before the arrival of Europeans, both rivers played vital roles in the lives of the native people that lived along them. The name Androscoggin comes from the Abnaki word *Amascogin*, which means "fish coming in the spring." Prior to the dams and pollution that arose during the Industrial Revolution, both rivers supported heavy runs of anadromous fish such as Atlantic salmon, shad, alewives, and sturgeon. The Androscoggin and Saco Rivers remained badly polluted until measures mandated by the Clean Water Act (1972) began to take effect in the late 1970s. Today these rivers represent an important environmental success story, and they provide a variety of quality fisheries for anglers to enjoy.

Both the Androscoggin and Saco Rivers originate in the White Mountains of New Hampshire and travel more than one hundred twenty miles before reaching the sea. The Androscoggin is the better trout fishery because of its habitat and the inputs of cold water it receives from a number of tributaries. The upper twenty-five miles of the Androscoggin, from the New Hampshire border to around Rumford, is the longest stretch of trout water on either of these rivers.

The most popular time to fish the upper Androscoggin is the period after spring runoff subsides in late May until the water warms in July. During this time of year, browns and rainbows can be caught in most of the pools and riffles that are accessible from Route 2 or from the North Road. But the Androscoggin is a large river whose broad flood plain is frequently covered by farmland, which makes access and roadside fishing difficult. The best way to solve this problem is to float the river in a small boat or canoe. Launch sites are located in Gilead, Bethel, and Newry, but a canoe can be slipped over the bank in a number of other places. When the water is high enough, some people begin their trips in the lower reaches of tributaries like the Wild or Sunday Rivers.

Early in the season, flies such as Muddlers, Hornbergs, and the Little Brook Trout, along with lures like the Panther Martin, Little Cleo, or Rapala will all produce trout. Two reliable places to catch fish at this time of year are the deep pools associated with many of the river's islands or anyplace where the river flows around rock ledges. The ledges near the bridge that crosses the river at Gilead have been particularly productive for me. When the water temperature approaches seventy degrees, most trout will abandon their lies in the main river and move to the mouths of cooler inlet streams or spring holes. During the heat of summer, concentrations of fish can sometimes be found in the vicinity of tributaries like the Wild River, Wheeler Brook, and White's Brook. These trout are usually most active during low-light periods in the early morning or evening.

Smallmouth bass are much more numerous south of Rumford. Although thousands of trout and salmon are stocked here, I always think of this part of the river as a bass fishery. Like most other large, bass rivers in Maine, the action on the lower Androscoggin doesn't really pick up until after the spring runoff has subsided and the water temperature has pushed above fifty-five degrees. From June through September, the fifty miles of river from Dixfield to Lisbon Falls produces some of the best smallmouth bass fishing in the state. During certain times of year, striped bass and an occasional sea-run brown trout can be found below the Central Maine Power Company Dam in Brunswick. This area is best fished from a boat, which can be launched from the landing located just off U.S. Route 1 on the south shore of the river.

The Saco is generally a deep, slow-flowing river that in most places looks like bass habitat. But in addition to plenty of smallmouths, this river also provides anglers with some good trout fishing. The fifteen-mile stretch between Hiram Falls and the Route 25 bridge in East Limington is regularly stocked with both brookies and brown trout. Each spring many anglers work accessible places such as Hiram Falls, Steep Falls, and Limington Rips in search of these fish. Brown trout are smart, long-lived fish that can survive under less than optimal environmental conditions, and many of them here grow to bragging size. Occasionally, a five-pound brown will be caught by someone who is canoeing the river, or by a casual angler who happens to get lucky. But most of these large holdovers are taken by experienced

Saco River regulars who wait until the water warms, then fish around spring holes and at the mouths of cold-inlet brooks where these browns are concentrated. Trout are also stocked each year on the lower river between West Buxton and Union Falls.

Tributaries of the Androscoggin and Saco Rivers

The Androscoggin River has a number of tributaries that provide opportunities for good trout fishing. West of Rumford, the Swift, Ellis, and Wild Rivers are waters with drastically different personalities that all contain a mixture of wild and stocked trout. The Swift is a scenic, steep-graded freestone stream, which provides an easily accessible seasonal fishery for anglers traveling up Route 17 toward the western mountains. The Ellis is a slower-moving river with deeper pools that allow more fish to hold over. Because much of this river is set back from the road and is overgrown with heavy vegetation, the best way to fish it is from a canoe. The Wild River drains the high country in the vicinity of Evans Notch and has a shallow, freestone streambed that is prone to scouring and flooding in the spring. It also has a relatively low level of biological productivity. Despite these shortcomings, many of the deeper pools found along the gravel road in the vicinity of Hastings hold decent-sized trout, and provide good places to fish throughout the summer.

East of Rumford, three other tributaries that hold trout are the Webb, Nezinscot, and the Little Androscoggin Rivers. The Webb is a fishy-looking river that flows beside Route 142 for about twelve miles from the outlet of Webb Lake until it joins the Androscoggin River at Dixfield. Fishing for small native brook trout and stocked browns is usually best in deep corner pools and at the mouths of inlet brooks in the spring. Bass become dominant here once the water warms in the summer. The Little Androscoggin and Nezinscot Rivers usually provide better trout fishing opportunities than the Webb River, primarily because they are more heavily

Dennis Welsh

When water levels are good, the Wild and several other small rivers near Bethel can provide anglers with steady action for pan-sized brookies.

stocked. Both of these rivers are divided into a number of fishable sections by dams and a patchwork of roads that crisscross them. A couple of popular stretches on the Little Androscoggin are the fast-flowing areas below the dams in Mechanic Falls and Minot, and the riffle and pool sections above the villages of Oxford and West Paris. Productive places to fish the Nezinscot River are the two miles of moving water between the Turner Mill Dam and the Route 117 bridge, and the roadside pools in the East and West Branches above Buckfield.

The largest tributary in the Saco watershed is the Ossipee River, which flows beside Route 25 for about seventeen miles. A few salmon and rainbows that migrate across the New Hampshire border are available in the upper river, but brook trout and browns make up the bulk of the catch. The stretch of river from Kezar Falls to Cornish is fished quite heavily in the spring, but warm, surface water drawn from Ossipee Lake allows bass to dominate this area in the summer.

The Little Ossipee River is a classic-looking trout stream that often provides better fishing than the main Ossipee. It is heavily stocked with brookies and browns both above and below Lake Arrowhead and has a popular catch-and-release section on the upper river. Generally, the Little Ossipee is a healthy river that is biologically productive and can produce holdover browns that measure over twenty inches. However, surveys conducted by the MDIF&W on both the Ossipee and Little Ossipee Rivers have shown that a significant loss of large trout takes place between November and April. This suggests that many stocked trout survive heavy, early season angling pressure and high summer water temperatures, only to perish during the winter. Biologist Jim Pellerin says, "This indicates that these rivers, and probably a number of others, experience a significant amount of mortality due to winterkill. Most people are familiar with the problems that elevated water temperatures pose for trout, but few realize that water temperatures below thirty-two degrees can be just as deadly. This type of winterkill typically occurs in shallow, fast-moving streams that lack a suitable amount of deep water for trout to use as a cold-weather refuge." The MDIF&W plans to conduct follow-up studies on this problem.

Sea Trout in Coastal Rivers

Sea-run brown trout and brook trout can be found in many of the small rivers and streams that flow into the Atlantic Ocean along the Maine coast. My first experience with these fish occurred on a November day more than twenty-five years ago when I traveled to the Ogunquit River with a couple of friends from a local fly-fishing club to search for sea-run browns. The day turned out to be productive, and we each took several fish from the lower river on small, white marabou streamers and various Atlantic salmon flies. After this first experience, I became a sea-run brown trout fan and explored a number of other rivers during the next few years. At that time, I found fishable populations only in the Ogunquit and Royal Rivers and had to work hard for every trout that I caught.

Today, along with the Ogunquit and Royal, sea-run browns can be caught consistently in southern Maine coastal rivers like the Mousam, York, and Spurwink. According to biologist John Boland, the major reason for this improvement is that the MDIF&W has put greater management emphasis on sea-run brown trout and has recently begun to stock larger numbers of hatchery fish in these rivers. Boland also feels that a beneficial move has been the switch from stocking spring yearlings to introducing larger fish in the fall that are better equipped to cope with ocean predators. Focusing efforts on rivers that have an extended estuary system for brown trout to feed in, rather than those that flow abruptly into the sea, has also been a key to success.

The reason I like sea-run browns so much is that the fishery peaks in the fall and winter. Long after my favorite North Woods fishing holes have begun to freeze over and all the striped bass and bluefish have headed south, sea-run browns are still available to soothe my fishing addiction. Fish average around twelve inches long but can grow to over twenty inches. In places that aren't fished heavily or where the water is flowing well, small bright-colored streamers such as the Warden's Worry and West Branch Special will draw plenty of aggressive strikes from fish when they are worked down and across the current. However, in most flatwater pools

The lower Ogunquit and several other south-coast rivers provide late-season anglers with a chance to catch sea-run brown trout along with stocked brookies and rainbows.

or in areas that receive a lot of pressure, I usually have better luck using beadhead nymphs with a small wet-fly or scud tied on as a dropper. All of these coastal rivers are currently open to spin-fishing and give up a fair number of fish to lures like Mepps Spinner, Little Cleo, and Al's Goldfish.

Most sea-run brook trout are wild fish that provide a much different angling experience than brown trout. Because they are native, they can be found in streams throughout the midcoast and down east regions. Research shows that one-third of the brook trout in these coastal streams spend part of their life in salt water. Much of this time is spent in estuaries where food is more abundant. Brook trout that have gone to sea are usually larger than those that have spent their entire life in fresh water. But even in colonial times, these Maine "salters" rarely grew larger than three pounds.

The erratic distribution and movements of sea-run brook trout make them tougher to catch than sea-run browns. They are most common in coastal streams in early spring and late fall—much of my success has come during April high water in streams that measure only a couple of rod lengths across. Typically I fish a light rod with a small spinner and worm rig that can be worked through corner pools and undercut banks. However, a couple of friends who live on the coast near Frenchman's Bay shift their efforts to larger streams as the waters drop and catch sea-run brookies on flies until the end of June.

Saltwater Fishing

When you ask people what comes to mind when they think of Maine, two common responses are lobsters and lighthouses. Indeed, Maine Department of Tourism statistics indicate that the seacoast is the primary destination for nearly two-thirds of the people who vacation here. Despite this seasonal influx of recreation-minded people, saltwater sport-fishing was not very popular until recently. This was probably due to overfishing that caused striped bass and ground fish stocks to drop to low levels. In addition, saltwater fishing in Maine had traditionally been viewed as a commercial enterprise rather than as a recreational activity.

When conservation efforts allowed striped bass populations to rebound in the 1980s, sport fishermen focused much more attention on them than they did in the past. This led to a proliferation of tackle shops and guide services that broadened the scope of angler interest to include previously underutilized species such as

sharks, tuna, mackerel, and flounder. Today, saltwater sport-fishing has grown into a multimillion dollar industry that provides many of Maine's best opportunities for quality angling.

Because of convenient access and fish that are relatively easy to catch, saltwater angling seems custom-made for newcomers to fishing. The Maine coast is particularly inviting because its myriad islands, marshes, rivers, and bays break up the ocean into a patchwork of small pieces that an angler can safely explore with a small boat or sea kayak. Of course the Maine coast also has many open expanses of blue water that can be dangerous in anything less than a twenty-five-foot powerboat. Nevertheless, if fishermen with smaller boats use common sense and keep an eye on the weather, they can usually find a safe and productive place to fish.

In a book of this size, it would be impossible to outline all of the fishing spots that can be found along Maine's thirty-five hundred miles of coastline. To keep descriptions manageable, I will group the major saltwater sport fish into three categories and discuss some of their general characteristics and the strategies to catch them.

Onshore Game Fish

Striped bass, bluefish, and mackerel are the primary targets for the majority of saltwater anglers in Maine. The best fishing occurs during the summer months when favorable water temperatures and abundant supplies of food draw large numbers of these migratory fish to Maine's coastal waters. None of these species are permanent residents, so by the time the leaves begin to change to their autumn colors, most of these fish are on their way back toward the warmer waters of the mid-Atlantic region. But life is grand on the Maine coast in the summer; for the few glorious months that these fish are here, there is no place on earth that I would rather be.

Maine's annual striped bass cycle begins in May when small fish arrive along the south coast. As the ocean waters warm, large schools of fifteen-inch to twenty-one-inch stripers gradually work their way north until they reach the mouth of the Kennebec River in early June. By late June, good numbers of "schoolies" can be found from Penobscot Bay to the Narraguagus River. Stripers become much less abundant beyond Machais. Although the fast-flowing currents of Cobscook and Passamaquoddy Bays look like ideal habitat, these waters never hold significant numbers of striped bass.

Large stripers show up in southern Maine a couple of weeks after the schoolies and travel far up most coastal rivers to feed on eels and assorted baitfish. At this time of year, schools of larger fish can be seen feeding boldly on the surface, and individual stripers can be taken using surface poppers, Rebels, Yo-Zuri Minnows, and a variety of rubber stick baits such as Sluggos. Trolling with rubber tubes tipped with bloodworms can also be effective and is a good technique to use when no fish are

Slot-sized stripers usually reach southern Maine by early June and provide steady action until the end of September.

showing on top. As the season progresses and the rivers warm, most of the baitfish and stripers drop down toward the cooler waters of the Atlantic Ocean. In August, many fishermen in search of large stripers abandon the rivers completely in favor of live-lining mackerel or fishing eels around the offshore islands. But this approach is not universally accepted—I know several guides who catch big fish on flies and surface poppers in shallow, upriver locations all summer. Regardless of where you fish, to maximize your success in the summer it's important to concentrate your efforts during the low-light periods of early morning and evening.

A tough lesson that has taken me years to learn is that most large stripers in Maine are caught along the south coast from the town of Rockland to the Piscataqua River. Because I live in the Bangor area, this has been difficult for me to accept, particularly since I have little trouble catching plenty of schoolies in the Penobscot River. Over the years, though, I have put in a lot of time hunting for a local honeyhole full of trophy stripers but never have been able to find one.

When I spoke with Maine Department of Marine Resources biologist Tom Squires about this, he chuckled and said, "The fact that most large striped bass are taken in southern Maine shouldn't be surprising. After all, Maine is on the extreme northern end of their range,

Although bluefish aren't always plentiful in Maine, they are usually large and feisty.

Cheryl Tracewski

and the only reason that these fish come here is to feed on the seasonal abundance of bait that can be found in our waters. So once a group of fish finds a place on the south coast that has an adequate water temperature and food supply, there really isn't any incentive for them to travel any further." Of course, there are exceptions to this rule; from time to time a large striper is taken around Belfast or Blue Hill. But if you are looking for a big fish, the odds are in your favor if you concentrate your efforts in southern Maine.

Mackerel are summer migrants that arrive shortly after the striped bass. But unlike stripers that come up from the south, mackerel spend the winter in the open ocean, then swarm inshore when the surface temperature approaches fifty-five degrees. Mackerel are more widely distributed than stripers and can be caught throughout the summer off almost any breakwater from Kittery to Eastport. Because they are ubiquitous, there is a tendency for some fishermen to look down on mackerel. However, many of my fondest fishing memories involve sun-splashed afternoons spent with my kids chasing schools of mackerel among the lobster traps in Belfast and Rockland Harbor. These feisty relatives of tuna can reach eighteen inches and can put up a good battle on light tackle.

Mackerel are commonly caught by trolling shiny lures like small Kastmasters or Diamond Jigs about one hundred yards offshore in twenty to forty feet of water. Many people also use multihook Christmas Tree rigs that can produce up to five fish at once when you encounter them in a large school. I enjoy fly-fishing for mackerel with bright bucktail streamers or small, yellow Woolly Worms on a sinking line. To maximize your success with flies, it's best to troll for awhile or use a fish finder to help locate a large group of fish. Once you find a school, you can break out your fly rod and catch a mackerel on nearly every cast. Often, the greatest difficulty is maintaining contact with these constantly moving groups of fish. You can solve this problem by occasionally dropping a cupful of cut bait or chum over the side of the boat.

Bluefish are the most exciting and unpredictable species of Maine's onshore game fish. Frequently, blues make only a brief, late-season appearance at a few random locations along the south coast. In some years they fail to show up at all. Maine is on the northern fringe of the bluefish's range, and we typically see a lot of them when population densities in mid-Atlantic waters are extremely high, or when large groups of baitfish draw them northward. Occasionally conditions are just right, and when that occurs these voracious predators descend on the Maine coast in schools that can cover several acres.

If you haven't watched a school of bluefish drive alewives or menhaden (pogies) to the surface, then savagely slash through them until they are gorged, the sheer ferocity with which these fish attack their prey is hard to imagine. Perhaps the best way to convey the excitement that bluefish can provide is to describe an experience that I once had on the New Meadows River.

The day began with rumors of bluefish being caught in the lower river near Cundy's Harbor. I drove to the landing, loaded two of my kids—six and eight years old at the time—into our twelve-foot boat, and set out for a couple hours of fishing. We trolled two rods with large Big Macs for about an hour without a strike. Then, just after passing the entrance to The Basin, a bluefish slammed into the lure that my daughter Kristen was trolling. The fish immediately took off on a blistering run, so I killed the motor and told my son Tyler to get his lure into the boat as fast as possible. As he was madly reeling in his Big Mac, another blue intercepted it and headed off in the opposite direction. For more than fifteen minutes, we had fish jumping, reels screaming, and bedlam raging aboard our little boat. Somehow we managed to

Party boats operate out of many different southern Maine ports and provide casual anglers with an opportunity to catch bragging-sized cod throughout the summer.

land both bluefish, which turned out to be twelve and thirteen pounders. But when the kids got a look at their gnashing teeth, they immediately jumped up on their seats and began screaming—and all hell really broke loose.

When bluefish are actively feeding, they can be caught on just about any fairly large plug, spoon, or fly that looks like a baitfish. Fresh bait like mackerel, menhaden, or alewives appeals to their olfactory as well as their visual senses and can be particularly effective. Wire leaders should be used to increase your chances of landing these toothy predators.

Because bluefish are a more mobile, open-ocean species than stripers or mackerel, frequently the biggest problem anglers face is finding them. Unreliable as it may seem, word of mouth is often the best way to determine the likelihood of encountering fish in a certain area. For example, if I am considering making a trip to John's Bay or Harpswell Sound to fish for blues, I will call a couple tackle shops or talk to some friends in the area to see how people have been doing. If they say they haven't seen a bluefish for two weeks, I'll probably stay home. On the other hand, if they say that the blues have been tearing up that section of the coast, it won't take me long to get there. Once in an area that contains fish, I often just troll and keep my eyes open for signs of surface activity, feeding birds, or clusters of other boats. Bluefish can be caught at any time of the day, but they are usually easiest to find early in the morning when the wind is calm.

Bottom Fish

What I like best about bottom-fishing is that you never know exactly what you are going to hook. Good populations of cod, pollock, dogfish, sculpins, eels, cusk, monkfish, and skates occur along the Maine coast and on many days you can catch a number of these species. Fishing for bottom dwellers is typically done using stout rods to work jigs or bait—like squid or cut mackerel—

just off the bottom in fifty to two hundred fifty feet of water. The basic approach is to position your boat over fish-holding habitat, such as offshore ledges or wrecks, then drift until you encounter fish. For the most part, this is "blind" fishing that requires prior knowledge of the area in order to be successful. Reaching most of these spots also requires a trip across several miles of open ocean. Therefore, a significant amount of the bottom-fishing that is done in Maine takes place on charter boats out of ports like Ogunquit and Boothbay Harbor.

Due to the island-studded nature of the coast, there are a number of wind-protected places where bottom fish can be taken from a small boat. Flounder are generally easiest for anglers to reach because they are usually found in fairly shallow harbors and bays, which have soft clay or mud bottoms. These tasty fish are strict bottom feeders that can be taken on a variety of fresh baits including earthworms, sea worms, cut squid, and clams. Unlike other bottom dwellers that respond to jigging, flounder bite best on a bait that doesn't move. To help keep my boat motionless, I always drop one anchor off the bow and another off the stern.

Offshore Game Fish

The primary offshore game fish in Maine are sharks and bluefin tuna. Like many other saltwater species, they are seasonal migrants to northern waters, whose fisheries peak from July through September. Sharks and tuna are strictly open-water species that are normally found between eight and twenty miles offshore. Because of the need to travel to open ocean, along with the specialized gear that is used, most people who catch one of these fish for the first time do so on a guided charter.

Once you have been shark fishing a few times and have learned the basics, it is possible to catch them on

Large Bluefin tuna become concentrated in Maine's offshore waters during late summer.

Saco Bay Outfitters

your own using spinning gear or a heavy fly rod. Safety must always be your primary concern—you should have a large boat outfitted with a dependable radio and all required safety equipment before venturing offshore. Considering the fog that frequently plagues navigation along the Maine coast, having radar and Global Positioning System on your boat is a very good idea.

Blue sharks are most common in Maine waters and generally run between six and ten feet long. Mako, porbeagle, and thresher sharks are also present, and significant numbers of each species are caught annually by sport fishermen. Since all of these sharks are strong swimmers and have a keen sense of smell, people often draw them to the boat with a chum slick, then cast a baited hook or a large chum-fly out to them. According to Captain Dave Pecci of Obsession Charters, "This technique really produces results; over the past few years, we have taken an average of six to ten sharks a day fishing in this manner."

Bluefin tuna are truly giants of the sea; most tuna caught in the Gulf of Maine average between six hundred and one thousand pounds. Early in the summer, scattered pods of bluefins roam widely, so your best chance at success is by trolling. Whole mackerel on multiple-hooked rigs called Daisy Chains are used for this type of fishing. Later in the season, bluefin tuna frequently settle into a more limited area and are most often taken by still-fishing with large chunks of bait. Because of the specialized rods, reels, line, and hooks needed to handle such enormous fish, there is little chance that the average recreational angler will ever land one. For someone who is interested in an opportunity to tangle with one of the largest sport fish in the sea, a Maine bluefin tuna fishing charter might be just what you are looking for.

Rangeley Lakes Region

Trout were plentiful and bag limits were high during the early days in the Rangeley Lakes region.

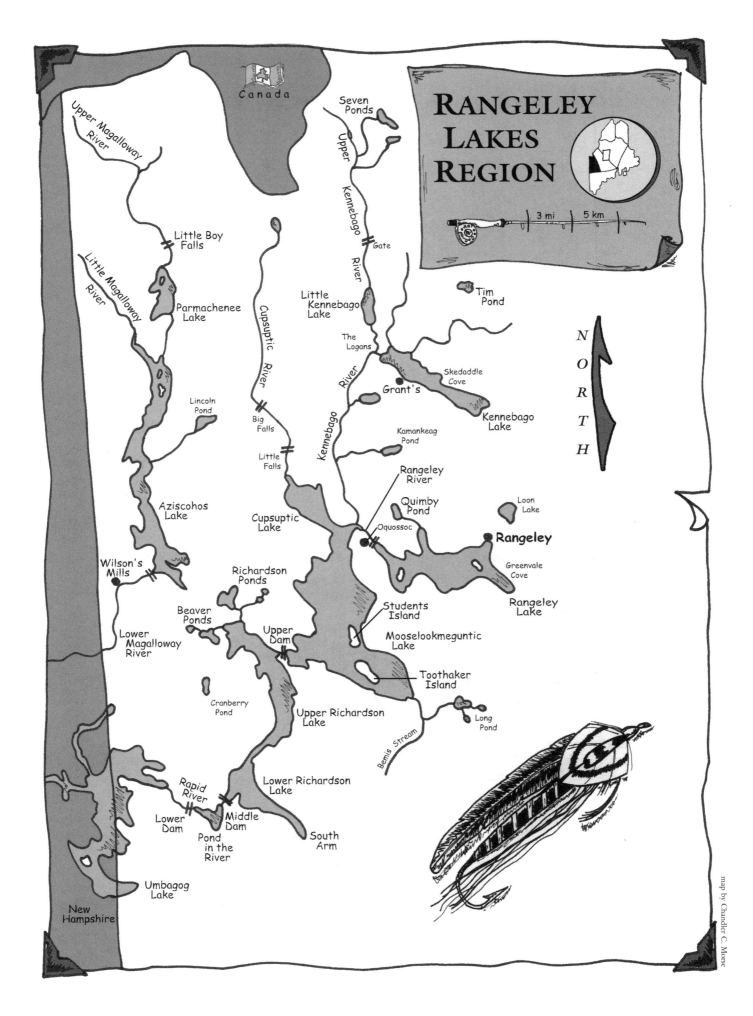

RANGELEY LAKES REGION

Canada

Upper Magalloway River

Little Magalloway River

Little Boy Falls

Parmachenee Lake

Cupsuptic River

Lincoln Pond

Big Falls

Little Falls

Seven Ponds

Upper Kennebago River

Gate

Little Kennebago Lake

The Logans

Kennebago River

Grant's

Tim Pond

Skedaddle Cove

Kennebago Lake

Kamankeag Pond

Rangeley River

Quimby Pond

Oquossoc

Loon Lake

Rangeley

Greenvale Cove

Cupsuptic Lake

Aziscohos Lake

Wilson's Mills

Richardson Ponds

Beaver Ponds

Upper Dam

Lower Magalloway River

Cranberry Pond

Students Island

Mooselookmeguntic Lake

Toothaker Island

Rangeley Lake

Upper Richardson Lake

Bemis Stream

Long Pond

Rapid River

Lower Dam

Middle Dam

Pond in the River

Lower Richardson Lake

South Arm

Umbagog Lake

New Hampshire

N O R T H

3 mi   5 km

map by Chandler C. Morse

Carrie Stevens

illustration by Sandra Nesterode-Hale

No discussion of the Rangeley area would be complete without acknowledging Carrie Stevens and the contributions that she made to Maine fly-fishing history. Carrie was the originator of the world-famous Gray Ghost and more than twenty other popular fly patterns. She lived at Upper Dam with her husband, Wallace Stevens, a well-known Maine guide.

Carrie's fly-tying career began around 1920 after the gift of some long-shanked hooks and a few other materials from a visiting angler named Shang Wheeler. In 1924 she gained national attention when a six-and-three-quarters-pound brook trout that she hooked and landed on one of her own newly created flies—the Rangeley Favorite—won second place in *Field and Stream* magazine's annual fishing contest. Shortly afterward, fishermen around the country flooded her with requests for this fly, and she suddenly found herself in the fly-tying business. The Gray Ghost evolved several years later as a slightly more elaborate version of this basic, smelt-imitating design.

The commercial trademark of all Carrie Stevens's flies were heads that featured a band of contrasting colored thread, usually red on black. Although she never had any formal instruction or watched anyone tie a fly, she was a perfectionist whose feminine touch made most of her patterns exquisite examples of the fly-tiers' art.

Beyond fly-tying, Carrie Stevens was a kind, modest person who was loved throughout the Rangeley Region. Shortly before her death, Governor Curtis proclaimed August 15, 1970, as "Carrie Stevens Day," making her the only fly-tier in Maine ever to be so recognized. A memorial that still stands was erected in her honor and unveiled at Upper Dam that August day by her good friend and longtime fishing companion Colonel Joseph D. Bates. Recently, a book celebrating her life and contribution to Rangeley's golden era was published and well received, mostly by people who had yet to be born when she died. More than anything else, the fact that the life of Carrie Stevens is still being celebrated more than thirty years after her death speaks volumes about this humble woman's impact on the world of fly-fishing.

The Rangeley Lakes region is comprised of eight large lakes and five separate river systems that combine to form the headwaters of the Androscoggin River. Such complexity can be confusing for people trying to visualize how all the components of the system fit together. But I find that it's fairly simple if you picture this region as two major drainages, the Rangeley Lakes Complex and the Magalloway River watershed, both of which eventually dump into Umbagog Lake.

The Rangeley Lakes Complex is comprised of Kennebago, Rangeley, Mooselookmeguntic, and the Richardson Lakes along with the Kennebago, Cupsuptic, Rangeley, and Rapid Rivers. Each of these waters contains healthy populations of salmon and to a lesser degree of brook trout and togue. They have produced outstanding sport-fishing for nearly one hundred fifty years. This vast area provides a variety of angling experiences that range from hiking into a remote section of the Rapid or Cupsuptic River to trolling along a shore lined with rustic camps on Rangeley or Mooselookmeguntic Lakes. This area is also of historical interest—much of Maine's fly-fishing tradition was born in local places like Upper Dam Pool and Greenvale Cove.

The Magalloway River watershed is made up of the Big and Little Magalloway Rivers and Aziscohos and Parmachenee Lakes. There is considerably less water here than in the Rangeley Lakes Complex, but when you hit it right the fishing can be just as good. This area is also deeply rooted in fly-fishing tradition and has served as the subject of several books touting the virtues of the large trout taken here in the late 1800s.

Regardless of where you choose to fish, the village of Rangeley usually serves as the major jumping-off point. Located along the northeast shore of Rangeley Lake, it offers a complete line of services including gas, groceries, several restaurants and motels, guides, a fly shop, and floatplane services. This fisherman-friendly village also has a hardtop boat launch located in the center of town.

To help maintain quality fisheries, many of the waters in the Rangeley Lakes region are managed under regulations that are more restrictive than those in other sections of Maine. For example, to guard against the overharvest of game fish, no ice-fishing is allowed in any of the area's waters.

To prevent the introduction of undesirable warm-water species, the use of live fish as bait is prohibited. And to protect the salmonid food supply, the dipping of smelts has been restricted in many places where large numbers of these baitfish had once been harvested.

The most controversial conservation measure is the gating of roads to prevent vehicular access into many of the area's most popular fishing destinations. Presently, gates block the roads leading into Upper, Middle, and Lower Dams; Kennebago, Rapid, and upper Magalloway Rivers; Parmachenee and Kennebago Lakes; and Tim Pond. All these waters are still open to public fishing, but the only way you can get to them is to walk, bicycle, or stay at one of the sporting camps that have a key to the gate.

Compared with the open access that is available in most other areas of the state, some first-time visitors to Rangeley initially view these gates as an infringement on their rights and object to them quite strongly. Eventually, though, most people realize that given the number of fishermen in the area, the gates are necessary to maintain the quality fishing that brought them to Rangeley in the first place.

History

As a young man, the first couple of times I came to Rangeley I was so anxious to get a line in the water that I hardly noticed an old sign near the south end of town that read, WELCOME TO RANGELEY—LAND OF FISHING LEGENDS. But as years passed and I began to appreciate the long and storied history of this area, the sign and everything it represented has become a lot more meaningful to me.

The village of Rangeley is named after Squire James W. Rangeley who purchased the township and arrived with his wife and four children in 1820. The unusually large brook trout that inhabited the lakes of this area were noted almost immediately in the historical record. Although the first report of sport-fishing was from Henry Stanley in 1842, the great fishing around Rangeley remained a well-kept regional secret until 1862 when New York City businessman George Page presented to his hometown newspapers a story of eight brook trout that weighed a total of fifty-two pounds. From that point on, the word about fishing in the Rangeley area spread like wildfire, and for the next forty years this region was the brook-trout capital of the world.

Traveling to Rangeley in those early years was difficult and usually involved taking a train to Phillips, then riding a stage or walking the remaining fifteen miles to the village. Anglers could fish Rangeley Lake from the comfort of a full-service hotel like the Greenvale House or continue their journey by water to more remote locations. Despite the effort required to get

A train arriving at Oquossoc Station around 1909.

The Mountain View House was one of the fine hotels that operated on Rangeley Lake during the first half of the twentieth century.

Maine State Museum

Cornelia "Fly Rod" Crosby was an early
ambassador of the Maine outdoors who wrote
articles and traveled to sportsman's shows to
promote fishing in the Rangeley Lakes region.
This studio portrait was done around 1895.

Rangeley Historical Society

Large salmon, like this eight pounder caught
by A.C. Lawrence, filled the void created when
giant brook trout disappeared from
Rangeley Lake around 1910.

Rangeley Historical Society

This 1935 photograph shows that the Rangeley region has hosted visiting anglers for many years.

into this area, during the 1860s fishing pressure rose so quickly that in 1868 a group of farsighted sportsmen banded together to form the state's first conservation organization. Headed by George Page, who first publicized the area less than a decade before, this fifty-member group was called the Oquossoc Angling Association and had a stated mission to "preserve and protect the quality of the fishing in the Rangeley Lakes region."

The real fishing boom in the region began around 1890 when a rail link to Rangeley was established and a number of hotels and lodges such as the Angler's Retreat, Bald Mountain Camps, and the Kennebago Lake House were built. Spurred on by the need to attract guests to recoup their investments, these new establishments launched widespread advertising campaigns that included everything from articles in national publications such as *The New York Times* and *Atlantic Monthly* to having the term "Vacationland" adopted as the Maine state motto. As a result of this attention, by the turn of the century Rangeley was attracting hundreds of fishermen from all the major East Coast cities. And writers, some of whom had never set foot in the region, were describing it with glowing phrases such as "a modern-day Garden of Eden for sportsmen."

The problem with promoting Rangeley's fishing so heavily was that the daily limit of brook trout was set at fifty pounds per person. As evidenced by the following quote from I. O. Woodruff, it was almost unheard of for anglers to return perfectly good fish to the water, even if they had already put far more into their creels than they could eat.

"With three flies on, the first cast hooked two beauties, and the next cast gave me one on each fly. Nothing but the toughness of my old rod, and the strength of the silk line enabled me to land the whole party. I then took off two of the flies, and would have five to ten trout throw themselves completely out of the water with each cast, even though I was standing in full sight on the bank. After hooking a fish, my guide would then land them, take them off the hook, and toss them into a little pool back of him. In two hours time, the pool was filled to overflowing with such a pile of golden beauties as Fulton Market never knew. There was not a fish under fourteen inches, and from that up to twenty-two inches for the longest."

But the true measure of angling prowess in those days was tied to the number of *large* trout an angler brought back to camp. Trophy fish were so sought after that they were almost always killed, yet rarely eaten. Their higher value was to serve as a tribute to the skills of the guides and anglers who caught them.

By the turn of the twentieth century, this over-exploitation of large brook trout had produced a sharp drop in the number of trophy fish that were logged-in at many camps. By 1910, trout over five pounds had almost disappeared. It's hard to imagine that overharvest alone could be responsible for such an abrupt decline. Indeed, many well-informed people think that the drastic winter drawdowns initiated on area lakes around this time, along with the local extinction of the blue-back trout—the principle forage fish of large brook trout—were probably more important factors. There is no denying, however, that the access facilitated by the coming of the railroads and the comfortable accommodations offered by hotels contributed significantly to the demise of these magnificent fish.

I don't want to give you the impression that good fishing in the Rangeley region was over by 1900. Landlocked salmon had been introduced into the area twenty years earlier, and by the turn of the century fish over five pounds were turning up everywhere. By this time, many of the guides and camp owners had recognized the benefit that managing the lakes for a sustainable yield of quality fish would have on their livelihood. As a result, the Rangeley region was among the first places in the country to have a Fisheries Commissioner, to require licenses for guides, and to enact sport-fishing laws that were enforced. One of the initial references to catch-and-release fishing to appear in print is in the 1897 logbook of the Rangeley area's Megantic Fish and Game Club.

"I have seen the sickening sight of nearly a bushel of trout of all sizes piled upon the shore of the landing, in a state of decay, that had been caught by vandals who did not know enough to return all except those needed for the fry-pan. Such wanton destruction of fish is unwarrantable, and no gentleman worthy of the name sportsman should ever allow it. Thus, in fishing this pond, anglers should be careful to return all trout under eight inches in length, as plenty of half and three-quarter pound trout can be taken to supply the camp with food. With proper care, the fishing here can be made better, and the trout average larger."

Rangeley Lakes Complex

The interconnected system of ponds, lakes, and streams that make up the Rangeley Lakes Complex occupies more than 75 percent of the territory in this region. The best way to summarize the fishing opportunities is to divide this complex into three separate drainages—the Kennebago River Drainage, the Mooselookmeguntic Basin, the Richardson Lakes and Rapid River—and discuss the details of each of them. I will begin with those places highest in the watershed, then work down in elevation to where the Rapid River enters Umbagog Lake.

Kennebago River Drainage

KENNEBAGO LAKE. The first white men to see Kennebago Lake were a handful of Civil War draft dodgers from Rangeley who fled northward in December 1862 to avoid entering the Union Army. They survived the winter by hunting and trapping out of a crude shelter on the north side of the lake in a wind-protected area that was subsequently named Skedaddle Cove in their honor. In the years that

Ed Grant was a backwoods fishing legend who helped build a set of sporting camps on Kennebago Lake in 1904. The camps are still in operation.

followed, Kennebago Lake was discovered by an increasing number of guides and fishermen who made the long trip to get away from the crowds that were beginning to plague them on more accessible waters. Ed Grant was the most well-known and colorful of these Kennebago pioneers. In 1904 Grant helped construct a set of sporting camps on the southwest shore of the lake that have remained in continuous operation to this day.

At five miles long and nearly one mile wide, Kennebago is the largest fly-fishing-only lake in Maine. A high rate of natural reproduction and restrictive angling regulations have produced a large population of brook trout and salmon that usually respond well to a fly. This makes Kennebago Lake a great place for novice fly fishermen. But this high density of fish, coupled with the relatively low productivity of the lake itself, produces individuals that are usually smaller

Grant's Kennebago Lake Camps around 1910.

than those at Rangeley and other area lakes. Nevertheless, Kennebago Lake fish are healthy, full-bodied specimens that are a pleasure to catch with a fly rod.

Smelts were introduced into Kennebago Lake in the 1890s and now form the base of the food chain. Like many other large lakes in Maine, early season fishing here is closely linked to the smelt runs and is done mostly with streamer flies like the Gray Ghost, Black Ghost, and Nine-Three. During May, good places to catch brook trout and salmon include the "Logans" area on the west side of the lake and near the mouth of tributaries such as Norton Brook.

Once the water begins to warm, a succession of mayfly hatches that include Hendricksons, Blue-Winged Olives, and Green Drakes occurs throughout the shallow areas of the lake. One easy way to catch fish here in June is to cast a fairly large dry-fly, like a Kennebago Wulff, in front of Big Sag or one of the lake's other brooks and wait for a trout to take it. This is a great time of year to visit Kennebago because even when fish aren't rising they often cruise just under the surface and can be taken with a Kennebago Mud-

Thick-bodied, lake-run salmon enter the Kennebago River to feed on smelts in the spring and to spawn in the fall.

dler, Hornberg, or Black-Nosed Dace fished on a sink-tip line. My standard routine is to get up early and fish the lake for an hour or so when it is calm. I usually head to the river during the middle of the day, then return to the lake and spend the evening chasing rising trout.

Prospective Kennebago Lake anglers should realize that vehicular access is available only to property owners and guests at commercial sporting camps. This long-standing history of restricted access dates back to the 1890s when the first carriage road into Blanchard Cove was built by J. Lewis York, then gated shortly thereafter. A second private road, which followed the Kennebago River from Oquossoc to Grant's Camps, was built several years later. In the twentieth century this river road went through a variety of manifestations, including a twenty-year period from 1913 until the Great Depression when it was converted to a rail line. During this entire time, access into this area has remained private.

Anglers who can't drive through the gates frequently fish on Little Kennebago Lake, which is located a couple of miles north of Kennebago Lake. This mile-long lake can be reached by paddling a canoe up its outlet for a few hundred yards from a logging-road bridge. Canoes can also be carried through the woods from a road that travels near the east shore of the lake. The seasonal calendar for hatches is similar for both of these waters, but the fish generally run larger in the main lake.

KENNEBAGO RIVER. The Kennebago River originates from a cluster of trout ponds in Seven Ponds Township and travels about twenty-five miles before flowing into Cupsuptic Lake near Oquossoc. Most discussions divide the river up into upper and lower sections and use the dams located near Kennebago Falls as the breakpoint. Because these dams block the upstream migration of fish, anglers on the lower river catch trout and salmon that come from Mooselookmeguntic and Cupsuptic Lakes, while those on the upper river catch fish of Kennebago Lake origin.

Of all the rivers in the Rangeley area, the lower Kennebago is my favorite. When conditions are right, plump brook trout that often measure more than a foot and salmon that exceed eighteen inches can be taken from a variety of pools. Yet despite its reputation, there have been days on the lower Kennebago when I fished alone for hours.

The primary reason for this solitude is that much of the river is closed to vehicular access by the same gates that prevent people from driving to Kennebago Lake. The situation on the river is different, though, because there is a two-mile stretch below the lower gate that can be easily reached from a gravel road that travels near the east bank. This road provides anglers with good access to Steep Bank Pool and several other popular places. A short run of quickwater that lies below the Route 16 bridge can also provide good, easy-to-reach fishing, especially when the water is high. Be sure to access this spot from the east bank of the river, not from the private road leading to the Oquossoc Angling Association.

The gated section of the lower Kennebago River has a well-deserved reputation as one of the best fall salmon fisheries in the state. Recently, biologist Forrest Bonney told me that each year several thousand mature salmon spawn in the river. Although this fall run can begin with the first freshets of rain in September, most

The upper Kennebago River above Little Kennebago Lake contains miles of lightly fished pocketwater.

fish remain in the lake until larger storms cool the river and significantly raise its water level. Several years ago, I was in Rangeley in early September when the remnants of Hurricane Floyd passed through the area. Shortly afterward, masses of salmon charged up the river and provided Kennebago River anglers with the best fall fishing that anyone could remember. The opposite can occur in dry years when salmon hold in deep water just off the mouth of the river until nearly the end of the season.

Because fall salmon have spawning on their minds, many people fish them with bright streamers like the Mickey Finn, Colonel Bates, or Cardinelle. I find that when the water is clear, beadhead nymphs, small wet-flies, and even dry flies—such as the Royal Wulff and Black Gnat—often work better than flashy attractors.

A June run of salmon also enters the lower Kennebago River. Although the size and number of these fish are generally smaller than those of September, June is my favorite time to visit this river. For the past three seasons, I have spent a couple days on either side of Father's Day here and caught a number of twenty-inch salmon and several nice brook trout in places such as John's, Abutment, and Powerhouse Pools. Nymphs

and dry flies like the Goddard or CDC Caddis are popular at this time of year, but I tend to catch my largest fish on streamers like the Black Ghost and the Supervisor. The number of summer-run fish in the river is very dependent on water flow and temperature, and it can vary from year to year.

The upper Kennebago River begins at the outlet of Big Island Pond and flows for about twelve miles before emptying into the Logans on the west end of Kennebago Lake. Several gates limit access to this section of the river. The lowest gate is near the bridge that crosses the river just below the outlet of Little Kennebago Lake. The short section of river from the bridge to the Logans contains several nice pools that can be reached by a fairly easy walk down the road. People with road access frequently use a canoe to float-fish this stretch.

The first time I came to the upper Kennebago was a couple of days after a heavy, fall rain, and I could hardly believe the number of fish that were in the river. On the first day, three friends and I each caught at least twenty brook trout and salmon on everything from white marabou streamers to stonefly nymphs. We probably should have quit while we were ahead—although fish continued to splash and roll throughout the week, they got progressively harder to catch. In part, this was because a number of them had already been hooked and released. However, the increasing reluctance of prespawning fish to bite also occurs in waters that receive little angling pressure and seems to be related to the amount of time that fish have been in the river. Atlantic salmon fishermen use the word "stale" to describe sluggish fish that are unresponsive to a passing fly. That term seems equally appropriate for prespawning Kennebago brook trout and salmon. Clearly, good timing is a critical factor in fall-fishing success on the Kennebago River.

The next gate on the upper Kennebago River is about four miles above Little Kennebago Lake near Crowley Brook. All motorized vehicles are prohibited beyond the gate, but foot traffic is allowed. A few ambitious anglers carry float tubes to fish the trout ponds in Seven Ponds Township, but most people stick to the easier-to-reach fishing that is available in the river. Although a number of nice pools can be found in this upper stretch, my favorite spot is at the inlet of Little Kennebago Lake. Wading is possible on a broad sandbar that extends several hundred yards into the lake. Many people also fish from canoes, which can be carried down from the nearby road. During spring and fall, trout can be taken throughout the day on baitfish-imitating streamers and on buggy-looking wet flies. In the summer, fishing is productive only during early mornings and evenings.

Rangeley Historical Society

Large brook trout, like these six and seven pounders caught by J.L. Alger in 1895, are what made Rangeley Lake famous.

RANGELEY LAKE. Of all the waters in this area, Rangeley Lake historically produced the largest brook trout. An early account by R.G. Allerton described catching thirty trout that *averaged* over six pounds. Numerous old camp records, tracings, and skin mounts indicate that until around the turn of the century trout this size were fairly common. Although genetics undoubtedly played an important role in developing such magnificent fish, quite a few biologists feel the most important factor in the production of these trophy brook trout was the forage fish that I mentioned earlier, the blueback trout—a subspecies of arctic char that colonized many Rangeley area lakes following the last ice age.

Historical documents indicate that fall spawning runs of bluebacks in places like Dodge Pond Stream and Quimby Brook were so heavy that people could practically walk across the water on their backs. The pursuit of these tasty fish as a winter food staple was intense and led to their wholesale slaughter by means of net, grapnel, and spear. By 1904, excessive overharvesting had completely eliminated bluebacks from the Rangeley Lakes region. The last of the giant brook trout also disappeared from this area around the same time.

Currently, brook trout make up only around 10 percent of the catch on Rangeley Lake, and a sixteen-inch fish is considered a good one. Conversely, the salmon fishery is flourishing: despite heavy early season pressure this lake is still one of the best places in the state to take a trophy. But these salmon are not easy to catch, and even the area's most experienced anglers find fishing to be somewhat of a hit or miss proposition.

A perfect example of this took place a couple of years ago when I journeyed to Rangeley Lake on consecutive weekends in mid-May. The first Saturday, I fished around Rangeley Lake State Park and in about five hours caught four salmon between sixteen and twenty-one inches long. I also had several more hard strikes and observed other people catching fish, including one angler who released what looked to be at least a five-pound salmon. However, on the following day and during the entire next weekend, I fished hard but managed only two hookups. In my youth, I invested a lot of time and effort analyzing situations like this to understand what made the fish behave so erratically. Lately, I've quit trying to figure them out; now I simply enjoy the action when the fish decide to cooperate.

Of all the lakes in this region, Rangeley is definitely the most user-friendly. Hardtop boat launches can be found across the street from the fly shops in both Rangeley and Oquossoc and at Rangeley Lake State Park. The first time I was out in a boat here, I was struck by the feeling that for a place with such a great reputation Rangeley Lake—at just over six thousand acres—really isn't very big. Traditional hotspots include Greenvale Cove, the gut between Doctors Island and Haines Point, and the north shore in the vicinity of Hunter Cove. But in the spring salmon can be found almost anywhere, so on days when there is heavy boat traffic I often head for an uncongested area with thirty to sixty feet of water and let my fish-finder do the rest.

Early in the season, many anglers fish sewn smelts from the surface to forty feet deep. And I do the same on days when the water is calm or when I'm being driven crazy by a fish-finder full of salmon that won't bite. Typically, though, I use streamer flies most of the time, and I am satisfied with my rate of success. Over the years, traditional tandem streamers like the Nine-Three, Rangeley Favorite, Blue Smelt, and Gray Ghost trolled at a fairly brisk speed have been productive. Lately, I've been experimenting with sparsely tied bucktail patterns and have had better results.

Restrictive angling regulations and a thriving smelt population helps maintain a healthy salmon fishery in Rangeley Lake.

RANGELEY RIVER. The Rangeley is a rather shallow, freestone river that flows for about one mile from the dam on Rangeley Lake to the inlet of Cupsuptic Lake. Holding water is limited, so fishing tends to be spotty. But when high water attracts baitfish and salmon, this little river can be surprisingly productive. Good places to fish are located directly below the dam in a small pool known as the Bathtub and in the long run below the snowmobile bridge near where the river flows into Cupsuptic Lake. Both of these areas can be easily reached from roads and thoroughly fished in a couple of hours. If there are no signs of salmon in these two pools, I generally don't bother fishing the pocketwater in the middle section of the river.

Mooselookmeguntic Basin

MOOSELOOKMEGUNTIC LAKE. Mooselookmeguntic is a moderately developed lake that supports a significant sport fishery for wild salmon and brook trout. Prior to the construction of Upper Dam in 1850, Mooselookmeguntic Lake was separated from Cupsuptic Lake by a short stretch of river. Since the completion of Upper Dam, the two lakes have been joined into one large body of water whose fisheries are similar. So for the purposes of this book, both basins will be lumped under the heading of Mooselookmeguntic Lake. At over sixteen thousand acres, "Mooselook," as it is called in local jargon, is the largest lake in the region. The busiest boat launch on the lake is located west of Oquossoc at Haines Landing. Access is also provided just off Route 16 near the mouth of the Cupsuptic River and along the South Arm Road near Toothaker Island. Traditionally, action on Mooselookmeguntic has been faster paced than on nearby Rangeley Lake, but the fish have been smaller. The recent enactment of special regulations, aided by a trend toward voluntary catch-and-release, has significantly improved the fishing here.

I usually fish for "Mooselook" salmon with streamer flies on either a sink-tip or a full sinking line. Between ice-out and the end of June, the most popular area to troll is the three-mile stretch of shoreline that runs along the Bald Mountain Road between Haines Landing and Bugle Cove. Early in the season, salmon can be caught almost anywhere, but I often fish in the Cupsuptic Basin around Birch Island. In the main lake, the rocky shoals between Stony Batter Point and Farrington Island and the shallow shorelines of the South Arm can produce good brook trout action. During May the weather can turn ugly in a hurry on Mooselookmeguntic, so be sure to bring a deep-sided boat if you plan to venture very far from the landing.

Anglers with smaller boats usually concentrate their efforts in the narrows located just west of Haines Landing. The Rangeley and Kennebago Rivers flow into the lower end of Cupsuptic Lake here and represent a natural place for game fish to search for food. A shallow bar, with deep water on both sides, extends out from the north end of Echo Cove and is worth a few passes when trolling in this area. Sewn smelts and lures like the Mooselook Wobbler and Cecil's Smelt seem to be the lures of choice for many of the people who fish the narrows—last year, my flies were badly outclassed by a friend using smelts and hardware. That said, early in the season when baitfish are present, salmon sometimes stack up in the narrows and can be caught by almost any angling method that you choose to employ.

Once the water warms, most fish drop below the thermocline and are tougher to catch. The majority of the deep water in Mooselookmeguntic is located on the east side of the lake from Haines Landing down to Students Island. In July and August, many people use downriggers or lead-core line to troll sewn bait between thirty and sixty feet down. However, longtime area guide Michael Warren told me that he catches a significant number of salmon during the dog days of summer fishing streamer flies on a sinking fly-line. His keys to success are to fish either very early morning or late evening on dull or rainy days and to troll faster than he would in the spring when the water is cold.

UPPER DAM POOL. Upper Dam Pool at the western end of Mooselookmeguntic Lake was created in 1850 by a dam built for log-driving purposes. The pool serves as the primary inlet to the Richardson Lakes and represents one of the most hallowed sites of Maine fly-fishing. In the early days, brook trout that *averaged* five pounds drew well-to-do anglers from around the East Coast to this remote spot in the Maine wilderness. Most sports traveled by railroad to Bemis Station on the south end of Mooselookmeguntic Lake, then transferred to a small steamer for the five-mile trip to the dam. A comfortable hotel was built near the north bank of the pool, and a strict fly-fishing-only protocol was maintained at all times. According to legendary Rangeley angler Colonel Joseph D. Bates, "At Upper Dam, you had to act properly and fish properly, or you just weren't in."

Long-shanked streamer hooks had not been developed, so wet flies such as the Parmachenee Belle and Atlantic salmon patterns like the Silver Doctor were used for most of this early trout fishing. In 1902 Herbie Welch reforged some bluefish hooks down to freshwater proportions and tied the first, true Rangeley-type streamers. These flies imitated the smelts that had been introduced into these waters a few years earlier and proved to be deadly on both brook trout and salmon. During the forty years that followed, Upper Dam was a hotbed for the development of streamer flies; hundreds

Upper Dam Pool represented the heart of the fly-fishing world at the beginning of the twentieth century. These nine brook trout were part of a morning's catch at Upper Dam on May 20, 1896.

of new patterns were turned out by scores of different tiers. The best known of these fly-tiers (and their creations) were Herbie Welch (Black Ghost), William Edson (Edson Tiger), Joe Stickney (Supervisor and Warden's Worry), and Carrie Stevens (Gray Ghost, Colonel Bates, and Shang's Special).

Although most of the five-pound trout disappeared long ago, fishing at Upper Dam can still be very productive for twelve-inch brookies and salmon up to twenty-two inches. The pool can be reached either by road—a one-mile walk from the gate—or by boating across Mooselookmeguntic Lake. Boaters should follow the channel markers to the public dock on the south side of the dam.

Fly-fishing methods vary greatly at Upper Dam; some anglers stand on the wooden piers and trail large marabou streamers into the roaring outflow, while others cast tiny nymphs and dry flies into one of the pool's swirling back-eddies. I like to fish here in the evenings during June and early July when the insects are active. Soft-hackle emergers, CDC Caddis patterns, Black Gnats, and small Hornbergs produce well for me at Upper Dam. I don't usually catch many monsters at this time of year, but topwater fishing for feisty, sixteen-inch salmon can be fun. Historical records indicate that the largest fish of the year were traditionally taken at Upper Dam shortly before the season closed at the end of September. Recently, the season was extended an additional month for catch-and-release fishing. Maine Department of Inland Fisheries and Wildlife reports indicate that 20 percent of the pool's total angler-use occurs in October and that more than 40 percent of its legal-size fish are caught during this month.

CUPSUPTIC RIVER. The Cupsuptic River originates in a remote pond near the Quebec border and flows south for about twenty miles before emptying into a long, shallow bay at the upper end of Mooselookmeguntic Lake. Unlike other Rangeley area watersheds, which are dominated by dam-controlled lakes, the Cupsuptic is basically a large, free-flowing mountain stream that is prone to periods of high and low water. The river supports a healthy population of resident brook trout throughout the season, but fishing for the larger lake-run trout and salmon is usually best during periods of high water. A network of ungated roads allows anglers to easily reach popular fishing spots such as Little Falls, Big Falls, and Big Canyon. Despite good access, the Cupsuptic receives less fishing pressure than most other rivers in the region.

One reason for this lighter usage might be because the Cupsuptic does not look like a classic fly-fishing river—that is, water comprised of a series of easy-to-wade, fishy-looking pools. In fact, over much of its length, it fishes more like a mountain stream than a river that can hold fish measured in pounds rather than inches. If you like to strike off on your own, the Cupsuptic River provides plenty of opportunities to park your vehicle at a convenient access point, then bushwhack upstream or downstream until you discover a small, shaded run or undercut bank where fish are holding. The pools from Big Falls up to the old Riverside Camp and the area in the vicinity of Big Canyon are good places for newcomers to get started. When the water is fairly high, small Woolly Buggers or streamers like the Black-Nosed Dace or West Branch Special are good flies to use here. Later in the summer, small wet-flies or terrestrials like grasshoppers and black ants seem to work better. Anglers with a canoe may also want to explore the deadwater that extends from the Lincoln Pond Road Bridge down to Little Falls.

In the eyes of some fishermen, the problem that all these places on the Cupsuptic River share is that during much of the year the bulk of the catch is made up of small trout and no salmon. The reason for this is that big fish need plenty of food, and this biologically unproductive river can not produce enough of it to support them. Despite the small size of most fish, the solitude and scenic rewards that this river offers has created a loyal following among the people who fish here. Maine outdoor writer Ken Allen has been traveling to the Rangeley Region for more than thirty years and is a big fan of the Cupsuptic. Frequently, he bypasses better-known area waters to fish this little river. According to Allen, "Anglers who really take the time to learn the Cupsuptic do much better with larger fish than most people realize."

In his 1940 book, *A Biological Survey of the Rangeley Lakes Region*, Gerald Cooper called the Cupsuptic River "the most important breeding stream for trout in Mooselookmeguntic [Lake]." The fall spawning period is when large fish can be reliably caught—migrating salmonids often congregate at Big Falls, an impassable barrier located about seven miles up from the lake. When water levels are good, brook trout and some salmon can also be found around Little Falls and in a variety of other lesser-known places on the lower river. Unfortunately, siltation from massive timber-harvesting operations of the 1960s has reduced the depth and overall quality of many of the smaller pools. Since then, the lack of holding water has limited the number of large

For many years, floating logs downstream during high water was the only practical way to transport them to mills. This was an environmentally destructive practice that collapsed riverbanks, scoured streambeds, and caused widespread siltation of pools.

The Maine Department of Inland Fisheries and Wildlife, the Rangeley Guides Association, and Trout Unlimited are working to repair the damage caused by early pulp drives on the Cupsuptic River.

fish that have been taken here. Recently, the MDIF&W and the Rangeley Guide's Association began a collaborative habitat-restoration project aimed at removing silt and restoring some of the Cupsuptic's degraded pools. Everyone is hopeful that these efforts will be successful and will help restore this little river to its former glory.

Richardson Lakes and Rapid River

RICHARDSON LAKES. The Richardson Lakes were originally two bodies of water connected by a short thoroughfare. When the construction of Middle Dam in the late 1800s raised the water level nearly twenty feet, the two basins were joined and have since been managed as a single seven-thousand-acre waterway. Brook trout are native to the Richardson Lakes, and seven-pound specimens were commonly caught by early anglers. Salmon were introduced in the late 1800s and soon replaced brook trout at the top of the food chain. The fishery remained stable for nearly one hundred years until an unauthorized stocking in 1975 added togue to the lakes. Landlocked alewives also became established a few years later, after dropping down from Rangeley Lake where they had been introduced to supplement smelt as a forage fish for salmonids.

Today, landlocked salmon are the primary attraction for anglers on the Richardson Lakes. In the spring, fishing can be good in the vicinity of smelt-spawning tributaries such as Mill, Mosquito, and Metallak Brooks and along the dropoffs on either side of The Narrows. In the fall, prespawning salmon will sometimes congregate near the small cove where the flow from Upper Dam enters into the lake, but normally at this time of year fish are spread out. Although boat launches at Mill Brook and South Arm Campground provide excellent access to both Upper and Lower Richardson Lakes, respectively, MDIF&W statistics show that these waters receive less fishing pressure than other lakes in the region. Bait fishing is popular—a sewn smelt or shiner trolled slowly behind a dodger or set of flashing spoons is the method of choice for many anglers. Bright spoons like the Williams Wobbler and Doctor Spoon mimic the wide-bodied profile of alewives and are used frequently in these waters. Because both lakes are quite deep, once the water warms the salmon often cruise down around the thermocline rather than near the surface. Therefore, a fish-finder and downrigger can be very helpful.

The Richardsons are the only lakes in the Rangeley region that contain togue. As I've said, these fish were introduced through an unauthorized stocking around

1975 and grew well from the start. A few years later, the MDIF&W began a regular stocking program to further develop this popular fishery. The management goal was to maintain a hatchery-fish-only population of togue whose numbers could be controlled by adjusting the stocking rate. But in the mid-1990s, wild togue began showing up in anglers' catches. Around this time, growth and catch rates of salmon began to decline. Biologists concluded that the number of forage fish in these lakes was inadequate to support the increasing number of predators, so the stocking of togue was suspended. To increase the lake's forage-fish base, several important smelt spawning brooks were closed to the dipping of smelt. The number of stocked salmon was also significantly reduced. Continued monitoring of forage fish and salmonid populations will be necessary to determine if the stocking of togue might become possible again in the future.

RAPID RIVER. The Rapid River begins at Middle Dam and flows for about four miles before entering Umbagog Lake. Despite its fine reputation, the Rapid is a remote river that has no direct road access. Traditionally, more than half of the people who fished this river were guests at Lakewood Camps and were transported by boat from the South Arm launch site. But since 1977, when the Rapid went to catch-and-release for brook trout, there has been an increasing number of fishermen who either walk or mountain bike to the river from nearby logging roads. Once at the river, most anglers use the old Carry Road that travels along the north bank to move among a dozen popular pools. People planning to fish the Rapid should realize that walking the trails and wading the river's powerful currents can be physically demanding. Each year injuries and wading accidents occur that are directly related to exhaustion. Many of these problems could be avoided if anglers invested time getting in shape before spending fourteen-hour days fishing and trekking in this remote region.

Pond-in-the-River is a natural, five-hundred-acre impoundment located less than a mile below Middle Dam and divides the Rapid River into two distinct sections. A recent survey showed that nearly 80 percent of angling activity on the river occurs in the upper stretch. One reason for this area's popularity is its proximity to Lakewood Camps, which makes it a convenient place for many people to fish. More importantly, Middle Dam provides a constant source of cold, well-oxygenated water that attracts large fish throughout the summer months.

When plenty of water is released from Middle Dam, it is easy to see how the Rapid River got its name.

Dam Pool is the uppermost pool on the river and, for the most part, is a churning froth of swirling water created by the outflow from Middle Dam. It is heavily fished, generally by anglers casting streamer flies and who station themselves on shoreline rocks or on one of the dam's wooden casting platforms. The thing I find most interesting about this pool is the subtle way its currents change at different water levels. On one day, fish will be holding behind a rock in a small pocket or in a back eddy. After a flow adjustment the following day, the fish (and frequently the back eddy itself) will be gone. Unless smelts are present in good numbers, small green-nymphs, soft-hackled wet flies, and black Woolly Buggers usually produce more fish for me here than streamer flies.

Chub Pool, located just above the Pond-in-the-River, is another very popular spot. This complicated, two-hundred-fifty-yard stretch of water is actually made up of three distinct minipools that each fish quite differently. The upper section begins at a set of rapids

Impressive numbers of eye-popping brook trout began to show up in the Rapid River shortly after catch-and-release regulations were implemented.

that spills into a long, deep run that can be fished effectively with everything from dry flies to nymphs and streamers. The middle section is made up of an enormous slick that is formed as the river bends around a small island. This area is favored by dry-fly fishermen who routinely catch very large fish on very small flies. The final spot to fish Chub Pool is right where the river flows into the Pond-in-the-River. This lower section is a great place to work a streamer on a sinking line; it is popular with both wading anglers and those who fish from small boats. I have witnessed some wild feeding blitzes at this spot, when salmon pursued baitfish with bluefish-like intensity. Over the years, I have seen a number of nice salmon and brookies taken here.

These days the biggest problem with Chub Pool is that it's getting too crowded. This became abundantly clear during my last two evening visits when, both times, I counted twenty anglers fishing the pool. The rise in fishing pressure at Chub Pool is a reflection of the booming interest in the Rapid River itself that began in the mid-1990s. To a large degree, this increase in awareness, and subsequent overutilization of the resource, can be blamed on writers and Internet users who touted the virtues of this river in a number of very public forums. Hopefully, we will heed the words of Don Henley in the Eagles classic "The Last Resort" that warns "call someplace paradise, kiss it goodbye."

Below Pond-in-the-River are nearly a dozen excellent pools accessible via fairly short trails that depart from the Carry Road on the river's north bank. The Spawning Beds Pool near the outlet of the pond and the areas just above and below the remnants of Lower Dam are all good places that are easy to reach. Farther downstream, Long, Cold Spring, Smooth Ledge, and Hedgehog are deep, classic-looking pools that generally offer more solitude than other places on the river. Because they are farther from the river's cold-water source, I tend to put more effort into them early in the year than during the dog days of summer. However, anglers who visit here regularly assure me that fish can be taken throughout the season.

Here are a couple of final points about the lower Rapid River. The small, active settlement (complete with foot-accessible fly shop) that you encounter along the Carry Road just beyond Lower Dam includes the home (Forest Lodge) where author Louise Dickinson Rich wrote *We Took to the Woods* and several other novels about early life along the Rapid River. Most of the runs and pools here are deep and powerful, so always use a wading staff and try to suppress the urge to cross the river. A few years ago on a cool, rainy evening in late May, I tried to cross near Lower Dam and ended up taking an unpleasant, wader-filled, fifty-yard swim.

Magalloway River Watershed
Aziscohos Lake

Aziscohos Lake was formed in 1910 when a dam was built across the Magalloway River near the village of Wilsons Mills. Aziscohos is a narrow, ten-mile-long impoundment with an average depth of only thirty feet.

Aziscohos Lake is known for its colorful, thick-bodied brook trout.

Brook trout are the primary attraction for most anglers at Aziscohos. Water quality and habitat are good for brookies and, lacking competition from warmwater species, trout grow at a fast rate. Restrictive regulations and the closure of many tributaries to smelting should help keep the brook trout populations here healthy. Salmon are also a popular sport fish in Aziscohos Lake, but a limited amount of coldwater habitat and seasonal water drawdowns of more than fifteen feet sometimes hurt this fishery. However, as long as forage fish populations stay strong, salmon fishing should hold up fairly well.

Good access to Aziscohos is available from a boat launch located just off Route 16 on the south end of the lake. Early in the season, people catch fish by trolling sewn smelts or baitfish-imitating streamers, like Joe's Smelt or Magog Smelt, along the east shore from Black Brook Cove to the point across from Nobb's Brook. Casting Woolly Buggers and bucktails—Little Brook Trout, Warden's Worry, and Mickey Finn are favorites—in the shallow waters near the mouths of the west-shore tributaries can also be productive. After the water warms, fish congregate in deep holes like the one on the south end of Beavers Island. These holes are excellent spots to troll with lead-core line or to still-fish below the thermocline with worms and baited jigs.

I enjoy fishing the north end of the lake in the area where the Big Magalloway River enters. In the spring, fish hold along the edges of the fast-flowing water and ambush the baitfish and nymphs that drift by. Trolling copper Mooselook Wobblers or small Daredevles through places where the current moderates can produce good action for brook trout and salmon. Casting streamer flies or Rapalas into back eddies and deep corner pools is worthwhile. Early season fish can be taken around north-end tributaries like Meadow, Big, and Twin Brooks. During fall, the boat-accessible, deep water just inside the mouth of the Big Magalloway River serves as a staging area for salmon waiting for rain to trigger their spawning run and is a good place to work a bright-colored streamer on a sinking line.

All of the better fishing places on the north end of

the lake are a long way from the public landing. To avoid a cold, bumpy boat ride, many anglers drive out on the Green Top Road, then carry a small boat or canoe down to the water from the primitive campsite near Hurricane Brook or one of the other undeveloped access points. The most convenient way to fish this area is to stay at Bosebuck Mountain Camps, which are located on the north end of the lake near the confluence of the Little and Big Magalloway Rivers and can provide clients with a boat and motor.

Parmachenee Lake

Metallak was chief of the Abnaki Indian tribe that inhabited much of the Rangeley area in the early 1800s. The chief had one beloved daughter called Parmachenee, and he picked the most beautiful lake in the region to name after her. Before the creation of Aziscohos Lake, Parmachenee was the largest lake in the Magalloway watershed and was featured in many of the early writings about this area, including several volumes of Charles A. Farrar's *Illustrated Guide to the Androscoggin Lakes.*

Throughout its history, Parmachenee Lake has been a remote and private place. Roads into the area were gated almost as soon as they were built. From the late 1800s through the 1950s, the Brown Paper Company maintained a lodge called the Parmachenee Club that was reserved for the exclusive use of their guests. The club was disbanded in the 1960s after the Brown Company sold its timberlands in this region. Today, with less than a dozen camps on the lake, things don't look too much different than when Metallak himself traveled the area.

Fishing at Parmachenee is restricted to the use of flies that can be cast or trolled. Action is often fast for foot-long brook trout and salmon that average around sixteen inches. Smelt-imitating streamers, like Grizzly King and Black Ghost, are the most popular patterns on the lake, but everything from nymphs to wet flies like the Wood Special are trolled here. Well-known guide

The upper Magalloway River has a number of classic pools that are steeped in fly-fishing history. Little Boy Falls (shown here) is a spot where President Dwight Eisenhower fished in 1955.

Carroll Ware told me that nice fish can also be caught with dry flies during the Green Drake hatch that occurs in early July.

Big Magalloway River

The Big Magalloway is a charming river that can be divided into three sections that each have a distinct personality.

UPPER BIG MAGALLOWAY RIVER. The upper Big Magalloway River arises from a series of small brooks and ponds on the Quebec border and flows for about twelve miles before dumping into Parmachenee Lake. Most of the fishing on this stretch takes place within five miles of the lake in some of the Rangeley area's most hallowed pools. Working upstream from the first vehicle turnout, you can hit Landing Pool, Cleveland Eddy, Little Boy Falls, Island Pool, Rump Pool, and the Pork Barrel in a day's fishing. Or you can slide a canoe into the river at Upper Rump and fish your way back to the bridge just above Little Boy Falls. Because all the roads in this area are gated, to fish the upper section of river you must be a property owner or a guest at Bosebuck Mountain Camps.

The upper Big Magalloway has a strong run of smelt that draws trout and salmon into the river shortly after ice-out. A rich insect fauna produces a succession of mayfly and caddis hatches that help hold fish here throughout much of the summer. Despite their reputation, I haven't found the fish in this river to be particularly finicky. Usually, a basic assortment of smelt patterns in the spring, along with some Adams, Woolly Buggers, grasshoppers, Zug-Bugs, small beadhead nymphs, and Elkhair Caddis for later in the season, are about all you need to be successful. When a hatch is occurring in a place like the flats below Upper Rump, you should have some small Comparaduns or CDC emergers. But, in general, you don't need to get too technical here. One point that Bosebuck Mountain Camps guide Ernie Spaulding emphasized when we spent an autumn day fishing together was that it is often necessary to use a sinking line to move bigger fish off the bottom in some of the deep pools and runs. As with many free-flowing rivers in Maine, angling success on the upper Big Magalloway River is often more closely tied to water flow and temperature than to fly selection. Fortunately, because of its high elevation and springfed inflows, this little river usually holds up well throughout the summer.

MIDDLE BIG MAGALLOWAY RIVER. The middle Big Magalloway is a two-mile-long section of fast-moving water that flows from the outlet of Parmachenee Lake to the head of Aziscohos Lake. One popular place to fish is on the upper reaches near the remains of the old wooden dam at the foot of Parmachenee Lake. This spot is within seventy-five yards of a spur off the main logging road and is readily accessible to anyone with a key to the gate. It contains a couple of long, fast-flowing pools below the dam that frequently hold

salmon willing to strike at a fast-stripped streamer or Dappled Stimulator. Fish also hold in the deep, boulder-laden water just above the dam. Leeches, nymphs, and assorted baitfish patterns can all be productive here, especially when fished on a sinking line from a small boat or canoe. In spring and fall, the lower end of the dead water where Black Cat Brook empties in can be particularly good.

Another popular place to fish the middle Big Magalloway is in the vicinity of where the Number-10 Bridge crosses the lower river. Since the bridge is below the locked gates, this spot gets more fishing pressure than the upper river. When the fish are in, though, it's not unusual to catch a half-dozen, legal-sized salmon in a morning's fishing. During spring's high water period it's possible to motor a small boat or canoe from Aziscohos Lake almost to the bridge. And from ice-out through early June, trolling streamer flies or smelt-imitating lures such as Rapalas and small Yo-Zuri Minnows is probably the most effective way to catch fish in this spot. As the water drops, wading anglers can fish the runs and corner pools between the bridge and

Fishing continues into the dog days of summer on the upper reaches of the Lower Magalloway because it is a tailwater river that receives cold water from the bottom of Aziscohos Lake.

the lake. Timing is a critical factor because the bigger fish usually disappear rather quickly after the water begins to warm. Although heavy rains can trigger hot fishing activity almost any time of year, it is particularly so in September when salmon stage near the head of Aziscohos Lake and wait for a rise in water level to begin their spawning run.

Upstream from Number-10 Bridge, after about a ten-minute walk anglers will encounter Long Pool. This is a fine place to fish dry flies or to use a strike indicator to dead-drift nymphs through the pool's complicated and turbulent flows. Few people travel beyond Long Pool—the river valley narrows and the trail deteriorates considerably past this point. Several years ago I decided to spend a day investigating the water upstream from Long Pool. For the most part, I found a lot of shallow, fast-flowing pocketwater that held only a few small fish. My success might have been better if I had made this trek on a day when water levels were higher and more big fish were in the river. The next time I find plenty of fish and a crowd of people around Number-10 Bridge, I plan to hike back to the solitude of this upstream area and try my luck again.

LOWER BIG MAGALLOWAY RIVER. The lower Big Magalloway River emerges from Aziscohos Dam as a cold torrent that mellows into a meandering, pastoral stream by the time it reaches the New Hampshire border about eight miles away. Easy access is provided via several good roads. Fishing pressure is heavy, however, especially in the two-mile stretch from Aziscohos Dam down to the Route 16 bridge.

A recent MDIF&W study showed that more than 75 percent of the brook trout and salmon caught in the lower Big Magalloway come from the special-regulations area on the upper stretch of river near the dam. This is a classic tailwater fishery in which the cold water drawn from the bottom of Aziscohos Lake extends the prime fishing period further into the summer than on other sections of the river. The growth rate of salmonids is also boosted by the smelts that get passed from the lake into the river through the dam.

The easiest access to these upriver pools is from the power company parking lot located just off Route 16. Most fish here have seen dozens of flies, many show evidence of being hooked, and they aren't easy to catch. Much of my success has come in early morning or late evening by using small Pheasant-Tail Nymphs or Prince Nymphs fished dead drift with a strike indicator. I have also seen people do well by casting a sinking line down from the head of a pool and slowly creeping a weighted stonefly nymph back along the bottom. Fishing space in the prime pools is limited, so when planning visits to this river try to avoid weekends.

Little Magalloway River

The Little Magalloway is a stream-sized river that originates in the mountains along the New Hampshire border and flows into the western arm of upper Aziscohos Lake. If it wasn't for the large brook trout that are occasionally taken here, this little river could easily be overlooked by anglers in search of more promising waters.

The Little Magalloway serves as the primary spawning and nursery stream for the brook trout of Aziscohos Lake. Every fall, large breeders congregate near the mouth and wait for a rise in water level before they enter the river. Because of the intimate nature of the Little Magalloway, it is impossible to point out the specific pools favored by these large fish without jeopardizing the well-being of the fishery—you will have to explore this river on your own. Mixed age-classes of brook trout can be found in the Little Magalloway River during most times of the season.

Trout Ponds

The majority of anglers who travel to the Rangeley region are initially attracted by the fishing opportunities available in the lakes and rivers. As people become better acquainted with the area, they discover the trout ponds and often end up spending a significant amount of time on them. This is particularly true of fly fishermen who come during the midsummer months when the surface temperature of the lakes is warm and the water level of the rivers is low.

One feature that endears Rangeley area trout ponds to many people is that they are usually easier to reach than similar waters in other parts of the state. Some of the better ones—Quimby, Round, Tim, and the Richardson Ponds—either have a set of sporting camps right on them or can be reached by a short drive. Other ponds, like Flatiron, Cranberry, and Sabbath Day, require varying degrees of effort to get into. Most local trout ponds lie close enough to the beaten path so that you can return to town for a hot shower and good meal after a full day of fishing.

Kennebec River Drainage

Edwards Dam blocked fish passage at Augusta for more than one hundred years. It was removed from the Kennebec River in June 1999. Striped bass, alewives, and other ocean-dwelling species quickly colonized the new stretch of flowing water that was created above the old site.

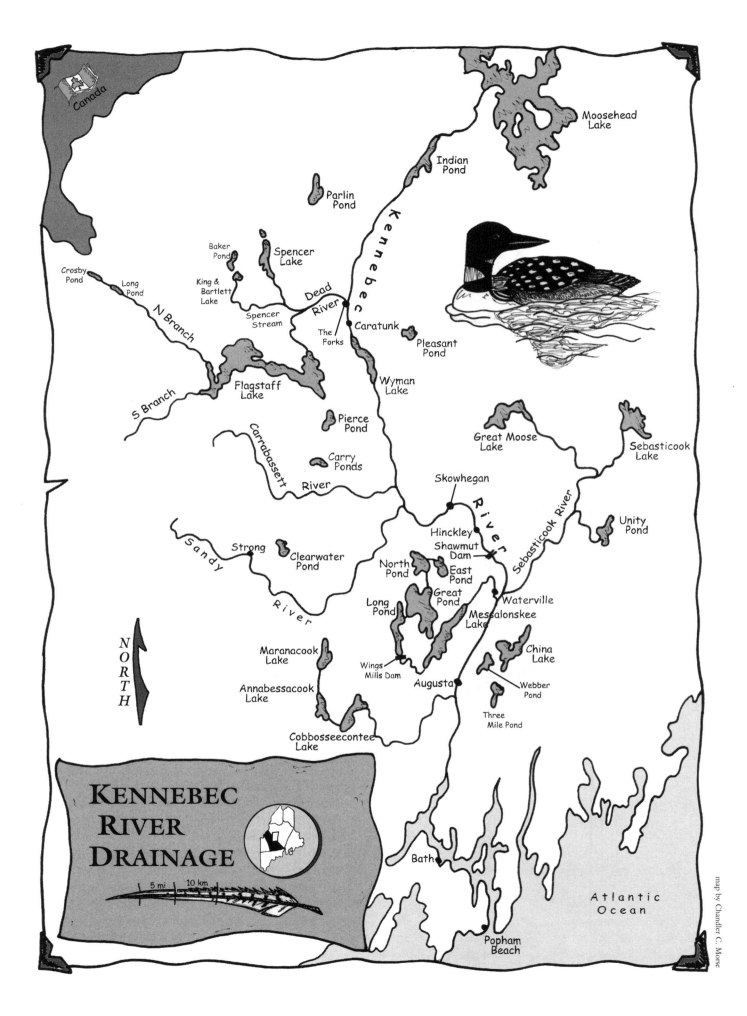

Canada

Moosehead Lake

Indian Pond

Parlin Pond

Kennebec

Baker Pond
Spencer Lake

Crosby Pond
Long Pond

King & Bartlett Lake

Dead River

Caratunk

Pleasant Pond

N Branch

Spencer Stream

The Forks

S Branch

Flagstaff Lake

Wyman Lake

Pierce Pond

Great Moose Lake

Sebasticook Lake

Carrabassett

Carry Ponds

River

Skowhegan

Unity Pond

Sandy

Strong

Clearwater Pond

River

Hinckley
Shawmut Dam

Sebasticook River

North Pond

East Pond

Waterville

Long Pond

Great Pond

Messalonskee Lake

China Lake

Maranacook Lake

Wings Mills Dam

Webber Pond

NORTH

Annabessacook Lake

Augusta

Three Mile Pond

Cobbosseecontee Lake

KENNEBEC RIVER DRAINAGE

Bath

5 mi   10 km

Atlantic Ocean

Popham Beach

map by Chandler C. Morse

Denny McNeish

illustration by Sandra Nestlerode-Hale

AS A GROUP, fisheries biologists and game wardens probably do more good and receive less credit than any other collection of people on the Maine fishing scene. In that vein, for more than thirty years Denny McNeish has been one of the most innovative and effective members of this hardworking fraternity. Denny began his career in Greenville in 1970 as an assistant to legendary fisheries biologist Roger AuClair and attributes much of his success to the knowledge he gained at that post. He then transferred down east for several years where he worked on everything from landlocked salmon in West Grand Lake to smallmouth bass in Grand Falls Flowage.

Denny arrived in the Kennebec River Region in 1980 and was one of the first people to recognize the potential that recently reclaimed industrial rivers held for sport-fishing. At that time, trout fishing on the Kennebec River between Madison and Augusta was almost unheard of. But within just a few years, Denny—in cooperation with local Trout Unlimited chapters—put a management plan into place that created the fabulous brown trout fishery that is now so popular.

Today, Denny is the Fisheries Resource Planner for the state of Maine. I recently spoke with him about some current issues and got his views on what things might look like one hundred years from now. For the most part, he would like to see the traditional image of Maine fishing preserved as long as possible. This means that stocks of native fish like brook trout and lake trout should be preserved in areas where they are still present and that activities such as ice-fishing and smelting should continue in places where their impact on coldwater fisheries will not be too significant. Denny strongly endorses the use of brown trout and splake to provide coldwater fisheries in waters that can not support other salmonids. He feels that stocking of hatchery brook trout and salmon could be increased in areas where natural reproduction is inadequate. The biggest problem facing Maine anglers now and in the future, according to Denny, is the illegal introduction of exotic species.

One hundred years from now, Denny anticipates that an increasing human population could lead to a proliferation of gates in the north woods and to privatization of many of this area's best fishing holes. While this might actually improve trout fishing in a number of places, the loss of free access would mark a major turning point in how fishing in the North Woods is managed. Downstate, however, Denny has been heartened by the success of the brown trout program on the Kennebec and feels that if fish-friendly practices such as pollution abatement and dam removal continue, the future for sport-fishing in Maine should remain bright far into the future.

Most of Maine's great rivers begin as tiny brooks that drain remote mountainsides or obscure wetlands. The Kennebec, however, pours from two large outlets on the west shore of Moosehead Lake as a full-fledged river, then rushes south for over one hundred twenty miles before flowing into the ocean at Popham Beach. Along the way it gathers water from dozens of tributaries, including other wild rivers like the Dead, Carrabassett, and Sandy.

The Kennebec is Maine's third largest river and supports the widest variety of fisheries in the state. Many fishermen think of the Kennebec in terms of brown trout because from Caratunk Falls down to tidewater this river produces bragging-sized browns. Other anglers flock to its lower reaches from May through September to fish for striped bass. Plenty of brook trout, rainbow trout, salmon, and smallmouth bass are also taken in the river.

What I find most appealing about the Kennebec River is its accessibility. Unlike many other quality fisheries in Maine, which are reached only by trips into the deep woods, much of the Kennebec River's best fishing can be accessed from paved roads and occurs close to towns such as Bath, Waterville, and Skowhegan. This drainage also provides a number of angling options in addition to the river itself. In the lower watershed, the Belgrade Lakes area provides an opportunity to catch salmon, brown trout, bass, and northern pike in a variety of settings. Farther north, the Dead River drainage is one of the best places in the state to fish for wild brook trout and rainbow trout.

The Dead River was completely filled with wood during a spring log drive in 1916.

Stratton Historical Society

History

Many of the reports from early English explorers raved about the giant white pines that grew along the banks of the lower Kennebec River. So when the European supply of tall, straight trees suitable for masts on the ships of the Royal Navy began to dwindle, King Charles II claimed the Kennebec timber for the throne of England. He did this in 1662 by issuing a proclamation that prohibited colonists from cutting pines more than twenty-four inches in diameter and seventy-two feet tall. To enforce this policy, English crews were sent through the woods to locate and mark these "mast pines" for the king. Naturally, settlers considered all the timber on their land to be their property and didn't appreciate the king's agents marking or cutting these trees. This British mast trade lasted for more than one hundred years and was one of the factors that led to the Revolutionary War.

By the time "the shot heard 'round the world" was fired in Lexington, Massachusetts, in April 1775, the American colonies were in an active state of rebellion against England. Canada at this time was also occupied by British troops. To consolidate the fighting forces of both countries, American general George Washington planned to drive the British from Montreal and Quebec City, then annex Canada as the fourteenth American colony. This plan called for Colonel Benedict Arnold to lead a detachment of eleven hundred men along an old Indian trading route up the Kennebec and Dead Rivers, then down the Chaudiere River into Quebec. But from the time the expedition left Fort Western (now Augusta) in late September 1775 until it reached Quebec City in December, more than half the men and nearly all of their supplies were claimed by the rivers and the weather. Despite being soundly defeated by the British on New Year's Eve 1775, Arnold's expedition up the Kennebec has remained noteworthy because it represented the first official naval operation (most of the expedition's men and gear were transported via rivers) in United States military history. Arnold's journal and the maps he made on this trip were used to develop an inland route to Quebec—the Canada Road—built through Jackman and the Moose River Valley in 1820.

Following the Revolutionary War, a number of towns with river-based industries sprang up along the Kennebec. Lumbering was the most visible and well-known of these industries, and every spring from 1834 until 1976 the Kennebec Log Driving Company had the sole responsibility of orchestrating the massive log drives conducted on the river. To process the bounty of wood that flowed down from the north, lumber and pulp mills were built in river towns like Madison, Skowhegan, Waterville, and Augusta. In order to transport

Maine Folklife Center

Streamlined river boats called bateaux *were used to transport men to areas where logjams needed to be broken during log drives.*

Maine Maritime Museum

The lower Kennebec River has been a shipbuilding center for many years. During the 1850s, there were ten active boatyards in the village of Bath alone. This photo shows the six-masted schooner Wyoming *as it nears completion in 1905.*

Maine State Museum

The Industrial Revolution took a heavy toll on the water quality of the Kennebec River. Pollution from lumber and textile mills, in conjunction with dams, had a particularly adverse effect on anadromous fisheries.

Maine State Museum

Ice harvesting was a big business on the lower Kennebec in the late 1800s. At its peak, more than one hundred fifty huge ice warehouses lined the river from Augusta to Woolwich.

these wood products to distant markets, steam and sailing ships were built at a number of shipyards in Bath. The North American shipbuilding industry actually began on the lower Kennebec in 1607; more ships have been constructed on the three-mile stretch of river in Bath than in any other comparable location in the world. Considering the relatively placid atmosphere on the lower Kennebec River today, it's hard to imagine the amount of activity described in the following passage written over one hundred years ago in the *Bath Daily Times*. "Yesterday, a passenger on the steamer *Henry Morrison* counted 27 schooners at Bath, 13 at Richmond, 55 at Gardiner, 16 at Hallowell and 2 at Augusta. Overall, the in-and-out traffic on the Kennebec this month has been 892 vessels."

Ice harvesting was another major industry that developed on the Kennebec River during the last half of the nineteenth century. Mogul James L. Cheeseman once described ice as, "the easiest and cheapest crop in the world to raise." During its peak in the 1890s, the ice industry employed over twenty thousand men and stored nearly two million tons of "Kennebec Diamonds" in one hundred fifty warehouses that lined the river from Augusta to Woolwich. For many years, hundreds of ships carried Kennebec River ice to cities throughout the East Coast and to places as far away as Cuba and India. However, competition from Massachusetts and upstate New York ice producers, followed by the advent of refrigeration, brought the Kennebec River ice industry to a halt soon after the turn of the twentieth century.

In its natural condition, the Kennebec River had no serious impediments to the movement of fish until migrants encountered sixteen-foot-high Caratunk Falls more than eighty miles from the ocean. As a result, the Kennebec historically supported tremendous runs of anadromous fishes such as Atlantic salmon, shad, alewives, sea smelts, and sturgeon. For hundreds of years, tribes of Abnaki Indians established seasonal fishing camps near the mouth of the river and at a number of inland locations such as Ticonic and Caratunk Falls. Because the survival of these native people depended on this annual bounty from the sea, they viewed the river and much of the land that surrounded it as sacred ground.

During the time that the Kennebec Valley was being settled, industrialization was sweeping up the East Coast; most of the white men who ventured into the valley were interested in the river as a means of transporting logs and powering saw mills. So little regard was given to the Kennebec's fisheries that in 1809 the first dam without a fishway was built in Clinton; in 1837 a larger dam was constructed in Augusta. By 1850 many of the runs of anadromous fishes that seemed inexhaustible a generation earlier were gone. Later, in addition to the effluents from textile and pulp mills, millions of gallons of raw sewage were added to the river's burden. For several months each summer, pollution caused dissolved oxygen to completely disappear from the Kennebec River between Waterville and Gardiner. Indeed, pollution levels were so bad during the first half of the twentieth century that a frustrated Director of Inland Fisheries and Wildlife described the water in the Kennebec as "more resembling that of a neglected wood yard than a river."

Fortunately, the Clean Water Act of 1972 brought pollution abatement measures to the entire watershed—today the Kennebec River is cleaner than at any time since before the Industrial Revolution. This has led to restoration of Atlantic salmon, shad, and alewives that Maine Department of Marine Fisheries biologist Tom Squires says has been, "slow, but steadily improving." According to Squires, "The biggest problem now isn't pollution, but rather the marginally useful dams that still remain on the Kennebec and its tributaries." A large step in the right direction was taken when Edwards Dam was breached in 1999. The dam had been a tidewater barrier that blocked the upstream migration of fish at Augusta for more than one hundred fifty years. The removal of several other dams is currently under consideration.

Kennebec River

The two branches of the upper Kennebec River that flow from Moosehead Lake to Indian Pond are referred to as the East and West Outlets and will be covered in the "Moosehead Lake Region" chapter. Fisheries found in the tidal portions of the lower river were discussed under Saltwater Fishing in the "Southern Maine" chapter. In this section, I'll describe the middle stretch of the Kennebec River from Harris Station Dam to Waterville.

Indian Pond to Carratunk

The sixteen miles of the upper Kennebec from Indian Pond to Caratunk is one of the wildest stretches of river in Maine and the heart of the state's white-water rafting industry. Morning and evening fishing here is best—during the midday water-release period (to accommodate rafters) anglers will often encounter unfishable high flows and dozens of boats. In the spring, salmon and brook trout, along with a few rainbows and splake (a nonreproducing hybrid of brook trout and lake trout), can be found throughout this area. As the river warms, most fish move upstream toward the cold water released from Harris Station Dam. The upper eight miles of river is called the Kennebec Gorge—access is limited to the area below the dam and to a few other places that can be reached from spurs off the Indian Pond road. Fishing pressure is generally light here, and salmon in the twelve- to sixteen-inch range are common. Larger salmon and brook trout can also be caught, especially by anglers who concentrate their efforts on the deep pools where fish congregate during low-flow periods.

The Kennebec River's east bank from The Forks to Carratunk follows U.S. Route 201 and offers many convenient places to fish. Because of the easier access, fishing isn't as good here as in the gorge. I have had the most success during the extended season in October when prespawning salmon and brook trout respond to bright flies like the Pink Lady, Mickey Finn, and Trout-Fin Muddler. The drastic changes in water level pro-duced by releases from Harris Station Dam can make this a dangerous place to wade; therefore, anglers unfa-miliar with the river should be very cautious.

Wyman Dam to Hinckley

Wyman is a massive bottom-draw dam that produces one of the best season-long tailwater fisheries in Maine. Although most fishing takes place in the upper two miles of river between the dam and the mouth of Austin Stream, I have caught trout down to the braided riffles below Gadabout Gaddis Airport. Nearby roads provide easy access, yet fishing pressure here is moder-ate. Good-sized salmon are often taken just below the dam on smelt-imitating streamers and lures like Weeping Willow and Kastmaster. Nightcrawlers and sewn minnows are also popular here during the early part of the season.

This area also supports one of the best naturally re-producing populations of rainbow trout in the state. This fishery was started with a modest number of rain-bows stocked many years ago. These fish adapted to spawning in Austin Stream and a few other local tribu-

Wyman is a massive dam whose coldwater discharges create a productive tailwater fishery near the village of Bingham.

The Kennebec is a large river with a number of good stretches to fish from a driftboat.

taries and are now completely self-sustaining. I have taken a number of sixteen-inch rainbows from this stretch of river, and I have been told by MDIF&W regional biologist Dave Howatt that they can get much bigger.

Another productive section of the Kennebec River is located between Solon Bridge and the boat launch in North Anson. Dense woods and farm fields makes road access difficult, so I generally use a canoe to explore deep holes and shaded, undercut banks along the way. The upper four miles are prime brown trout territory. (I'll never forget a twenty-inch specimen my ten-year-old daughter, Kristen, took from beneath a log.) Much of the habitat in this section of river is ideal for aquatic insects—match-the-hatch fishing can be quite good and enjoyable. As you approach North Anson, the river gets deeper and slower. Eye-popping browns are rumored to reside here, but the majority of the fish that I catch are smallmouth bass.

From North Anson to Hinckley, most of the fishing is for bass and is done by anglers who use small motorboats to fish lures and poppers along shoreline structure. However, thousands of brown trout are stocked annually in this stretch of river, and regional biologist Scott Davis says, "Nice fish are taken from

several spots around Madison and Skowhegan each year." Because summertime water temperatures and dissolved oxygen can sometimes reach critical levels, Davis adds that, "For practical purposes, this is a seasonal coldwater fishery that is fairly difficult for casual anglers to figure out. This section of river can be a real sleeper, though, for people who know how and when to fish it."

Shawmut Area

The three-mile section of the Kennebec from Shawmut Dam to Fairfield is one of the river's most productive areas. It is also one of the most heavily fished; on pleasant evenings in June it's not unusual to encounter several dozen fly fishermen within a mile of the dam. The river is one hundred yards wide and very shallow in this area, so it's fairly easy to wade around and find an unoccupied place to fish. Brown trout make up the bulk of the catch here, and a number of them in the eighteen- to twenty-two-inch range are taken each year. Anglers who fish late into the evening frequently catch large browns by using small dry-flies on light tippets. I haven't had much luck with these big fish; my excuse is that the abundance of natural food keeps them too well fed. In reality, most of these browns have been caught and released several times and are just too smart for a Shawmut-area novice like me. I know an excellent fly fisherman from nearby Benton who spends more than forty evenings a year on this stretch of river and does very well. His advice is, "When you spot a big fish, don't be in too much of a hurry. Watch his feeding pattern and make the first cast count."

Newcomers can have fun here as well because smaller browns and rainbows are almost always willing to take a well-placed Elkhair Caddis or Pheasant-Tail Nymph. Later in the season, smallmouth bass increase in numbers and provide great action for the limited number of people who target them. The dense mats of algae that often form on the rocks can be a nuisance for summer bass fishermen in the shallow upper river. This problem can be solved by using a canoe or driftboat to fish the deeper runs found farther downstream.

Waterville to Augusta

Fishing on the lower Kennebec River traditionally focused on brown trout and smallmouth bass and centered around easy-to-reach locations like Winslow's Halifax Park and the pool above the bridges in Augusta. But when Edwards Dam in Augusta was removed in 1999, its once-stagnant headpond was transformed into a number of new riffles and pools that anglers could use. Alewives and striped bass quickly colonized the ten miles of new riverine habitat created by the dam's removal and are likely to continue to benefit from this action. However, the impact of the loss of Edward's dam on the brown trout fishery is a bit more uncertain.

Some people fear that with free access from the ocean, striped bass, bluefish, and even seals will feed heavily on browns, which up until now were protected by the dam. But studies done in other states have shown that these marine predators do not typically utilize brown trout as a primary food item. One positive point of consensus is that the availability of new, high-energy foods like sea smelts and alewives should cause the brown trout that do remain in this area to grow larger. But fisheries biologist Scott Davis says that,

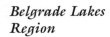

Northern pike were illegally introduced into the Belgrade Lakes region around 1980. Large pike, like this thirty-one pounder, can now be found in a number of local waters.

"Until a few more seasons have gone by, no one really knows exactly what impact the removal of the dam will have. Ultimately, the state will probably go to a fall stocking of larger browns to help cut down on predation by stripers. But until more time has passed the only thing that can be said with much certainty is that the lower Kennebec is a river in transition, whose future looks much brighter now than before the dam was removed."

Other Notable Fisheries

A number of other places in the Kennebec River drainage also provide great opportunities for sportfishing. I will begin with the Belgrade Lakes region, then discuss several other prime fishing areas while moving north through the drainage.

Belgrade Lakes Region

This region is dominated by large, moderately developed lakes and is best known for its warmwater fisheries. For many years bass were the feature fish in the area, but since northern pike were illegally introduced into the watershed they have been receiving most of the attention. The first documented report of a northern pike in the Belgrade region came from North Pond in 1981. Since then, pike have spread into East, Great, Long, and Ingham Ponds as well as into Messalonskee and Cobbosseecontee Lakes. Biologists think it's likely that northern pike will move into other waters in this region.

In a big-fish-loving state like Maine, it's not surprising that many people view the establishment of pike in the Belgrade Lakes as a positive occurrence. In fact, a recent ice-fishing survey indicated that they were the most prized game fish in the region. The problem with this newfound love affair with pike is that a few anglers are so eager to have them in their favorite lakes that they are doing the stocking themselves. Obviously, the toll that these toothy predators exact on existing fisheries can be enormous, so the MDIF&W has posted numerous signs explaining the serious consequences that individuals will face for unauthorized transport of fish from one body of water to another. Despite these warnings, the illegal introduction of pike and other highly competitive warmwater fish is still a huge problem.

In lakes where pike are already established, the MDIF&W encourages anglers to take advantage of them. And the fervor with which some people pursue pike is almost fanatical. Ice-fishing has become particularly popular—from mid-December to late March there are usually hardcore anglers in search of a monster on Great Pond and other local waters. Most serious pike fishermen set a line of traps (ice-fishing rigs) baited with six-inch shiners across a shelf or shallow bay, then spend hours waiting for a big pike to swim by. On some days only pickerel and bass cause their flags to fly. But when a fifteen-pound pike does take the bait, all of the cold hours leading up to that moment disappear before the end of the fish's first, blistering run.

Northern pike are not the only species of interest in the Belgrade Lakes, which competes each year with the down east region for the title of "Bass Capitol" of Maine. Well-known waters such as Cobbosseecontee, Messalonskee, and China Lakes along with Great and Threemile Ponds provide excellent largemouth and smallmouth bass fishing all summer. Fishing is good near dropoffs and underwater structure, but casting a popper or spinnerbait toward a rocky shoreline can also provide plenty of early morning and evening action. Anglers interested in catching large bass often concentrate on North and Webber Ponds and on Annabessacook Lake. Moving waters such as Belgrade and Cobbosseecontee Streams are overshadowed by the abundance of large lakes in the area, but these slow-flowing hideaways produce plenty of bass, especially for fly fishermen who hit them in June and early July.

The white perch is another popular warmwater species found in many local waters. Late in April they congregate near spawning brooks, and anglers sometimes carry away buckets of these tasty fish. Favored locations include the bridges on Sebasticook Lake, the breakwater along the northeast shore of China Lake,

Although hefty smallmouth bass are common throughout the Belgrade Lakes region, largemouths are hotly pursued in many of the lakes where they are found.

and both the inlet and outlet of Long Pond. Hefty white perch can also be taken near the railroad tracks along the southwest shore of Unity Pond.

The Belgrade Lakes region also supports some good coldwater fisheries. Salmon fishing on Long Pond used to be so good that outdoor writer Ken Allen once called it "one of the best places in the state to catch a salmon over five pounds." Since the introduction of pike, the salmon fishery here has taken a downturn. Early in the season, though, the inlet from Great Pond, the outlet below Wings Mills Dam, Castle Island, and the shoreline adjacent to the deep hole southeast of the boat launch are still popular places for anglers to gather. Echo Lake and Parker Pond are other local waters that offer good salmon fishing.

Brown trout form the heart of the coldwater fishery in this area. Waters like Cobbosseecontee and China Lakes and McGrath and Great Ponds regularly produce brown trout over sixteen inches long. Regional biologist Bill Woodward is pleased with the area's brown trout stocking program and says "Despite heavy angling pressure and competition from northern pike, a number of browns over five pounds are taken each year." He attributes this to the fact that "Browns eat a wider range of foods and are harder to catch than salmon and brook trout. Coupled with their longer life span, this leads to the production of some really large fish." In the spring and fall, many brown trout move from the lakes into flowing waters such as Cobbosseecontee Stream. The pool below the dam at the outlet of Cobbosseecontee Lake and the riffles below Collins Mill Road often provide good fly-fishing.

Sandy and Carrabassett Rivers

The Sandy and Carrabassett are medium-sized rivers that are free-flowing for most of their length. Steep gradients in many places cause the rivers' beds to be scoured by spring floods; thus, productivity and fishing potential are not as high as they might be. Both rivers are readily accessible from a number of roadside locations and have attractive pools that are easy to wade and to fish. The lower Sandy River is regularly stocked with brown trout, and each spring many pan-sized fish are taken from Strong down to New Sharon. I have a friend from Farmington who fishes the Sandy regularly and catches large holdover fish. During midsummer, bass become more active and comprise the bulk of the catch on the lower river.

According to regional biologist Forest Bonney, "Brook trout are available in the upper river all summer for anglers who take the time to investigate the deep, shaded pools found above Phillips." He also says, "Even though this area really isn't known for its lakes, good fishing for wild but rather slow-growing togue is available in Clearwater Lake and Embden Pond, and nice brook trout can be found in Kimball and McIntire Ponds." The Carrabassett River is stocked

Despite elevated water temperatures during midsummer, a number of holdover brown trout are caught in the Sandy River each year.

annually with several thousand brook trout and rainbows as far up as Kingfield and is primarily a seasonal fishery that provides good sport for anglers traveling along Routes 16 and 27.

Wyman Lake Area

Wyman Lake is a narrow, eleven-mile-long impoundment that was created when the Wyman Dam was built in 1930. For many years, it was known for large smelts and small salmon, and it didn't draw much attention from serious fishermen. Splake were introduced into Wyman Lake in 1999 and are providing a better fishery for both open-water anglers and ice fishermen. Each year, a limited number of nice rainbow trout and togue are taken here.

Pierce Pond is located about fifteen miles northwest of Bingham and is the Wyman Lake area's most

During June and July, reliable hatches of mayflies and caddis at Pierce Pond give fly casters a chance to catch bragging-sized brook trout and salmon.

popular fishery. On early season days when the wind is howling, this scenic, sixteen-hundred-acre body of water can fish more like a big lake than a trout pond. But on calm June evenings when mayflies are hatching in the shallows, Pierce Pond can be a fly-fisherman's dream.

Maine Department of Inland Fisheries and Wildlife statistics show that in the last thirty-five years, Pierce Pond has produced more brook trout over four pounds than any other similar-sized body of water in the state. This includes an eight-pound, five-ounce wall-hanger that held the state record from 1958 to 1979. Despite a steady increase in fishing pressure, the enactment of special regulations and conservation land trust measures appear to be maintaining the quality of this fishery.

Because Pierce Pond provides the opportunity to catch big trout in a relatively easy-to-reach location, a number of its regulars are hard-core, been-everywhere-done-everything fishermen who have settled on this pond as their home water. Early in the season, many of them will troll Rapalas or smelt-imitating streamers along the shorelines of the Lower Basin. But when the water warms and insects become active, most anglers anchor their boats and cast nymphs and small Woolly Buggers around rocky points and dropoffs until surface activity begins. I like to fish the area around Caribou Narrows because the trout and salmon respond well to dry flies even when nothing is hatching. The best thing about this pond is that with a small boat and motor you can prospect from one end to the other until you find a spot that produces for you. Outlying ponds such as Kilgore, Grass, and Horseshoe also offer good fishing and can be reached by trails that leave from Upper Pierce Pond.

The Carry Ponds are located a few miles south of Pierce and are where Benedict Arnold left the Kennebec River during his 1775 march to Quebec. East and West Carry Ponds have the best coldwater habitat and can provide good fishing for brook trout. Smelts were illegally introduced into East Carry recently, and biologists are still evaluating the impact that they will have on the fishery. The roads into these ponds have been gated for a number of years.

Dead River Drainage

The Dead River has a large watershed that covers over twelve hundred square miles of Franklin and Somerset Counties. The North and South Branches rise in the mountains west of Eustis and are separated from the larger mainstem of the Dead River by eighteen-thousand-acre Flagstaff Lake. Fishing opportunities vary in each of these waters; thus I will be discuss them separately.

NORTH AND SOUTH BRANCHES OF THE DEAD RIVER. The North Branch of the Dead River begins at the dam on Lower Pond and flows for over ten miles before emptying into Flagstaff Lake. Route 27 follows the river most of the way and provides easy access to many inviting riffles and pools. Brook trout that average around ten inches make up the bulk of the catch on this fly-fishing-only water, but larger fish are caught regularly. Many of these are native brookies produced in one of the river's cold tributaries and that benefit from the forage they get from the adjoining lakes. Some stocked brook trout and a few salmon are also caught here.

In the spring, fish can be taken throughout the North Branch. Weighted nymphs or Conehead Muddlers and Woolly Buggers are good flies to use when the water is cold. Hornbergs and small baitfish patterns fished on a sinking line can also be effective at this time of year. Later in the season, trout look for cool water and often congregate at the mouths of inlets like Nash Brook. The stretch below the dam and around Greenbush Pond can also be productive. Some good hatches of mayflies and caddis take place on the North Branch during June and July. Alder Stream is a fishable tributary that is known for its Hendricksons.

The South Branch is a smooth-flowing, alder-lined river that begins at Saddleback Lake near Rangeley and travels for over twenty-five miles before entering Flagstaff Lake at Stratton. Route 16 provides good access to its middle section, where anglers fish for a mix of native and stocked pan-sized brookies. I caught my first trout on a fly in the upper South Branch many years ago, and it is still my favorite section to fish. You can drive a short distance on a dirt road from Route 16 to near where Cold Stream enters, then wade upstream or downstream from there. The fish aren't very sophisticated and will smother most buggy-looking flies that come floating by. Terresterials like ants, grasshoppers, and the Madam-X produce well here. Be sure to bring bug dope—if there isn't a breeze, black flies can be thick. When the water is up, the South Branch also offers a number of good floats for people who like to fish from a canoe. Casting worms and small spinner-rigs are particularly popular among boat anglers who fish the lower river near Flagstaff Lake.

MAINSTEM DEAD RIVER. The mainstem of the Dead River begins at the outlet of Flagstaff Lake and flows for twenty miles before entering the Kennebec River at The Forks. Grand Falls is located about six miles below the dam at the outlet of Flagstaff Lake and separates the river into two distinct sections. The fairly deep and smooth-flowing upper section is often referred to as Grand Falls Flowage and is best known for rainbow trout over twenty inches long. This is a local, naturally reproducing, population that probably began from an illegal stocking years ago. The density of rainbows isn't high, but they grow well on the smelts that wash into the river from Flagstaff Lake. Most fishing occurs within one mile of the dam where anglers can wade the riffles in the vicinity of the Big Eddy. A boat is needed to fish the lower part of this flowage. Yo-Zuri Minnows and Rapalas account for many of the larger fish that are taken in the spring. Smelt-imitating streamers like the Winnipisaukee Smelt and Thunder Creek are also popular here. Because Flagstaff is a shallow lake the water in the river gets warm and inhibits salmonid activity in the summer. Occasional heavy water-releases (to accommodate rafters who float the lower river) can produce a spurt of good fishing around the dam. Along with rainbows, brook trout and a few salmon are also available in Grand Falls Flowage.

Below Grand Falls, the lower mainstem Dead River provides anglers with nearly fifteen miles of riffles and pools. Access is limited to a handful of places where a road extends down to the water, so if you are looking for solitude you can find it on the middle section of the lower Dead River. Areas that are easier to reach—Grand Falls, Spencer Rips, and Poplar Hill Falls—receive much more pressure. Most fishing on the lower river is for wild brook trout and salmon with an occasional rainbow trout, brown trout, or splake (from Wyman Lake) mixed in. Generally, fish don't get as large here as on the upper river, but there are exceptions.

Because the lower Dead River runs warm in the summer, salmonids are often found near the mouths of cool inlets like Spencer and Enchanted Streams. Fish also congregate around spring seeps located on the bottom of some of the larger pools. Although spin-fishing is legal here, many anglers float nymphs, small streamers, or wet flies through good-looking pools and riffles. Recently, I spent a day with guide Victor Smith, who likes to fish dry flies, and he said that his clients catch fish here on everything from Grasshoppers to Elkhair Caddis. The lower Dead is a white-water river that provides about a dozen high-water days each season for rafters and kayakers to enjoy. During these high-flow periods, the river is unfishable and should be avoided. Release dates are published well in advance on most rafting and whitewater Web sites.

DEAD RIVER DRAINAGE LAKES. Flagstaff is a man-made lake created in 1950 when Central Maine Power Company built Long Falls Dam and backed up twenty miles of the Dead River. The project was unusual because it flooded several small towns and created a large lake with an average depth of less than fifteen feet. This impoundment was built for water storage purposes, and in late summer it is often drawn down to the original river channel. With broad stretches of shallow water open to the sun, temperatures can reach seventy-five degrees for weeks at a time.

Flagstaff Lake provides plenty of good habitat for warmwater species and is best known for the monster pickerel it produces. This lake also has a surprisingly strong smelt run in the spring, which in turn produces good fishing for brook trout and salmon. The best places to fish for salmonids are around the fifty-foot-deep hole above Long Falls Dam and the area between Eustis and Stratton where the Dead River's North and South Branches dump in. The quickwater near the bridge and the area around the old Eustis Dam are particularly popular spots. Some surplus brook trout and salmon are occasionally stocked in Flagstaff Lake, but most salmonids here are wild.

Chain of Ponds is a group of deep lakes that form the headwaters of the North Branch of the Dead River. Historically, this basin contained five separate lakes connected by short streams, but when a dam was built at the outlet of Lower Pond, it raised water levels enough to connect the lakes. All of these are deep, oligotrophic lakes with good spawning and nursery habitat for brook trout, salmon, and togue. Some fish are occasionally stocked here to offset the fishing pressure that results from the easy access provided by Route 27. Since Chain of Ponds is one of the few coldwater fisheries in the western mountains that is open to ice-fishing, they get hit particularly hard in the winter. This was clearly illustrated on my last trip to Long Pond on a windy, sub-zero day in January when there were a half-dozen other parties set up within sight.

DEAD RIVER DRAINAGE PONDS. I first developed an interest in the ponds in the Dead River drainage after reading the following passage about Hathan Bog in an 1887 fish-and-game club logbook. "The record for

Stratton Historical Society

Flagstaff was a village of five hundred people located in the Dead River Valley near Bigelow Mountain. The entire town was flooded when the Central Maine Power Company built Long Falls Dam in 1950. This photo shows the water beginning to rise on Main Street.

trout fishing came last September when on our way to a fine pool around 4:30 in the evening, I offered club attorney Mr. Charles Hanks a wager that I could easily catch seventy-five trout before we returned, if they were in the biting humor. The bet was eagerly taken by the barrister, but after my first cast induced two or three trout to rise, and my second seemed to set the waters boiling, terror was plainly depicted on his face. The guide kept a tally and held a watch, and called 'time' at 5:54, just as two half-pounders were landed. This made seventy-six trout caught in sixty-nine minutes!" Of course, fishing here today isn't anything like that, but people who put in the effort can still catch nice trout.

Jim is my favorite pond in the area, probably because I caught an eighteen-inch brook trout the first time I fished here. It was a beautiful

Randy Ury

A June evening spent with a friend on a remote trout pond in the upper Kennebec drainage is as good as it gets for a Maine fly fisherman.

late-September evening, and I took that fish on a small, brown Woolly Bugger less than fifteen minutes after putting my canoe in the water. Subsequent trips to this easy-to-reach pond have always produced trout, but never anything that matched my first brookie. The road is gated just beyond Jim Pond, but for those willing to walk a couple of miles, Little Jim and Everett Ponds are open to the public and can produce some nice fish. Much of the land beyond the gate is owned by the King and Bartlett Club, which manages more than a dozen trout ponds for the exclusive use of their guests. Although I haven't fished there, I've been told that the fly-fishing during the Green Drake hatch can be outstanding. Trout fishing opportunities west of Route 27 are available at Round Mountain, Arnold, and Blanchard ponds.

Moosehead Lake Region

Bangor and Aroostook Railroad

Small steamers were used to transport anglers and their guides to far corners of Moosehead Lake.

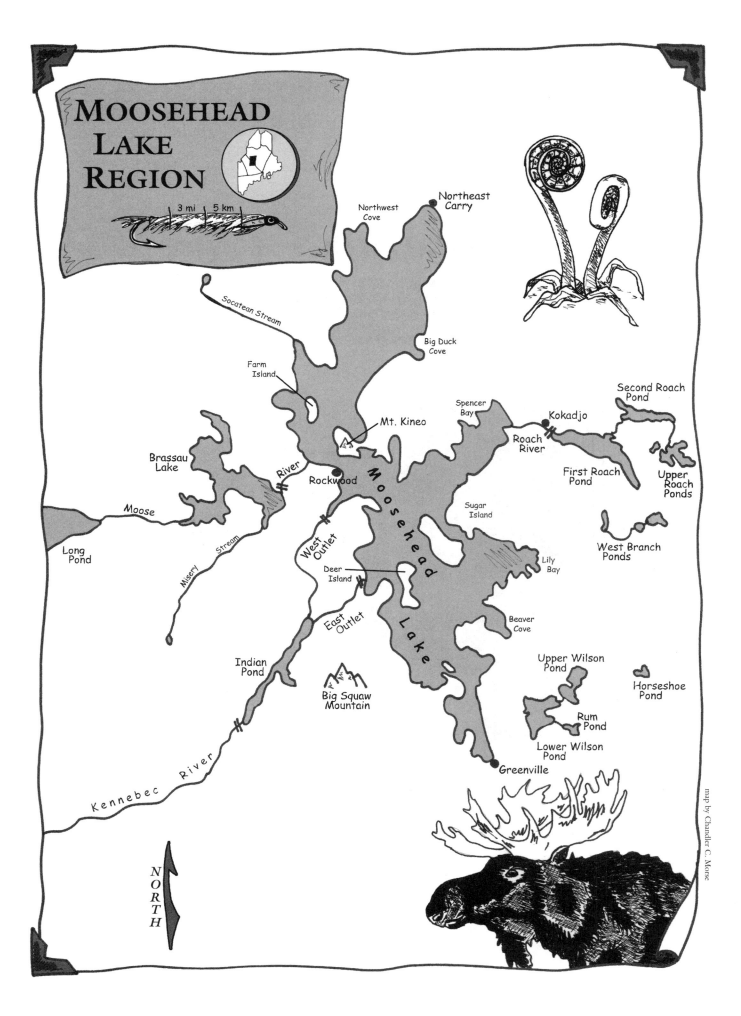

MOOSEHEAD LAKE REGION

3 mi 5 km

Socatean Stream

Northwest Cove

Northeast Carry

Big Duck Cove

Farm Island

Mt. Kineo

Spencer Bay

Kokadjo

Second Roach Pond

Brassau Lake

River

Rockwood

Moosehead Lake

Roach River

First Roach Pond

Upper Roach Ponds

Moose

Sugar Island

West Branch Ponds

Long Pond

Misery Stream

West Outlet

Deer Island

Lily Bay

Beaver Cove

East Outlet

Indian Pond

Big Squaw Mountain

Upper Wilson Pond

Horseshoe Pond

Rum Pond

Lower Wilson Pond

Kennebec River

Greenville

NORTH

map by Chandler C. Morse

Dan Legere

illustration by Sandra Nestlerode-Hale

TO ANGLERS THROUGHOUT New England, Dan Legere is the definitive authority on fishing in Piscataquis County, and his Maine Guide Fly Shop is what lies at the heart of the Moosehead Lake region. For many people (myself included), no trip to the Greenville area is complete without stopping at the shop to pick up a few flies, to find out where the fish have been biting, or to catch up on the local news from Dan and his lovely wife, Penny.

These days, Dan Legere and the Moosehead Lake region are so synonymous with each other that many people forget he once worked as a commercial fly-tier in Southern Maine and as a trolling guide at Rideout's Lodge on East Grand Lake. But Dan was—and still is—a river fisherman at heart, and he ultimately wanted to settle in an area that would provide a clientele more inclined toward this activity. He admits that from a business perspective, initially he wasn't sure if there was enough fishing activity around Greenville to support a full-service fly shop. But he says, "After spending a couple of weekends in the spring of 1981 sitting at the top of Indian Hill and counting the number of trucks coming into town that were either towing boats or had canoes on their roof, I knew I would do all right."

Since then, Dan has walked, paddled, or flown over nearly every square foot of water within fifty miles of his shop and remains as enthusiastic about the local fishing today as when he moved into the region. Despite being located only a few hundred yards from the state's largest lake, Dan spends most of his time either floating nearby rivers in his driftboat or doing float-tube trips into local ponds. He says he likes to promote such alternatives because "they take some of the pressure off the big lake and show people that there is much more to this region than just Moosehead."

Dan is an active conservationist who plays an important role in protecting the future of the region. He told me that, "Right now, development pressure up here is strong, and the State of Maine needs to do more to protect its natural resources." Dan added that, "Conservation easements, where large landowners can continue to harvest timber, are the best way to protect Maine's wild and undeveloped backcountry. With large tracts of remote land changing hands at an alarming rate, now is a critical time to put easements in place. This is the best way to guard against development and protect the traditional usage we have taken for granted for many years."

The Moosehead region contains the largest lake in the state, three major rivers, and more than a dozen trophy-trout ponds. Greenville is at the southern tip of Moosehead Lake and is the largest town in the area. It offers a complete line of conveniences that include restaurants and motels, floatplane services, and one of the best fly shops in the state. Another important jumping-off point is about halfway up the lake's western shore in the village of Rockwood. Located at the mouth of the Moose River, Rockwood is home to a number of sporting camps that have catered to the needs of fishermen for generations. Several general stores, a nice boat launch, and a shuttle-boat service to Mount Kineo are available here.

History

Long before destinations like Alaska and New Zealand became viable options for avid anglers, wealthy "sports" throughout the Northeast ventured to Maine to fish Moosehead Lake. The first hotel was constructed in Greenville around 1850, and a spur from the Bangor and Aroostook Railroad arrived in 1884. A number of steamboats were built during this era, primarily to haul logs across the lake. But it wasn't long until regular passenger service was established on steamboats traveling between Greenville and Rockwood. To serve the needs of visiting anglers, sporting camps soon sprang up along the route. Unlike the do-it-yourself style of housekeeping camps that are popular in the region today, many early establishments were elaborate, full-service resorts that catered to anglers and their families.

The Mount Kineo House was the most famous of all the Moosehead Lake sporting camps, but it began in 1845 as a one-room log tavern. By the turn of the century, it had grown into a sprawling five-story hotel that could accommodate over five hundred guests. Located on a scenic point across the lake from Rockwood, this wilderness hotel had electric lights, hot running water, and two elevators. It also offered recreational amenities such as croquet and tennis courts, a bowling alley, a baseball diamond, a nine-hole golf course, and an

The Fitzpatrick party, in front of the Mount Kineo House, with one day's catch from Moosehead Lake in June 1898.

orchestra that performed two concerts daily.

There were three reasons why the Mount Kineo House went to such extremes to provide for the needs of its guests: (1) Moosehead Lake attracted some of the richest and most influential men of the time; (2) visiting anglers were almost always accompanied by their families who needed to be entertained while the sports were fishing; and (3) because of the effort required to reach this remote area, the length of a typical stay was much longer than it is today. By the late 1920s, however, the proliferation of automobile travel allowed an increasing number of people to drive to Greenville on their own or to make day trips to the lake. This expansion of private travel opportunity led to the elimination of rail service to the area in 1933 and significantly reduced the need for many of the services provided by a full-service hotel. The demolition of the Mount Kineo House in 1939 marked the end of the golden era on Moosehead Lake.

The Moosehead Lake region lies in the headwaters of the Kennebec River watershed. Historically, Moosehead Lake was isolated from sea-run fish by Caratunk Falls (located near the present-day town of Solon) and by the falls at the outlet of Indian Pond. Consequently, brook trout and togue were the only game fish that occurred naturally in the lake. Fish culture and hatcheries become popular around 1885, which led to the introduction of salmon and smelt into the lake around that time. These species didn't become fully established in Moosehead Lake until nearly twenty-five years later.

There are numerous early reports of outstanding fishing on Moosehead Lake. One of my favorites was written in 1894 by W. H. Gannett of Augusta and appeared in the *Maine Sportsman* magazine. "From a day's fishing on Moosehead with wife and daughter, caught 21 trout weighing $52\frac{3}{4}$ pounds. Of these, 13 were squaretails weighing $34\frac{3}{4}$ pounds. One of mine weighed $5\frac{1}{4}$ pounds, the largest taken from the lake this season. Mrs. Gannett caught a $4\frac{1}{4}$ pounder." At that time the legal weight limit was fifty pounds of trout per person per day, and when conditions were right it

Mooosehead Marine Museum

Well-appointed steamers were used to shuttle Moosehead visitors from the train depot in Greenville to hotels farther up the lake.

wasn't unusual for an angler to reach it. Increased fishing pressure caused this limit to be reduced several times during the next ten years. In 1908, the weight limit was set at fifteen pounds per person and remained at that level until around 1940. Fishing was good on Moosehead Lake throughout this period, and area guides stated that there were few days when the fifteen-pound limit was not reached. They also noted that it was unusual to catch fish less than the legal length and that their sports released many good-sized fish, particularly salmon and togue.

In the early days, most fishing was done from canoes. Sports typically trolled rods baited with minnows or streamer flies while their guides slowly paddled them along the shore. Steamboats were often used to shuttle parties to various bays and islands around the lake. Given the number of guests that could be accommodated by the area's hotels and sporting camps, former Moosehead area biologist Roger AuClair stated that at times "there could have been up to one thousand anglers fishing the lake from ice-out through June." As a result of this intensive spring fishery, AuClair said that "it was probable that more than fifty thousand pounds of brook trout and lake trout were harvested from Moosehead Lake annually in the late 1800s." This is comparable to the harvest of salmonids that occurs on the lake today.

Fishing on Moosehead Lake began to decline in the late 1930s when improved roads and widespread use of automobiles made traveling to Greenville easier. This brought more fishermen to the lake and in 1942 necessitated a reduction in the weight limit to seven and a half pounds. World War II provided Moosehead with a brief respite from angling pressure, but when fishermen with outboard motors and improved tackle returned in force during the late 1940s, catch rates soon dropped to around two fish a day. Since that time, fishing on the lake has been cyclical; typically, several years of good fishing and large fish alternate with periods of reduced abundance. That doesn't mean that fishing in Moosehead Lake today is poor, but the days

Maine State Museum

In the early days of fishing on Moosehead Lake, many large brook trout were caught by sports using metal or bamboo rods to trail flies behind a canoe paddled along the shoreline.

are gone when you could catch fifty pounds of trout by trailing a fly from a canoe being paddled around the shoreline.

Moosehead Lake

Moosehead Lake is the largest naturally occurring body of freshwater located entirely within the boundaries of one of the lower forty-eight states. The lake sprawls over seventy-five thousand acres, and traversing it from south to north requires nearly a forty-mile boat ride from Greenville to Northeast Carry. Because of its size, the most manageable way to discuss fishing in Moosehead Lake is to outline the opportunities that are available within a reasonable distance of its major access points. Well-maintained boat launches can be reached via paved roads at Greenville Junction (south shore), Lily Bay State Park (east shore), and Rockwood (west shore). The less developed north end of the lake can be accessed from

more primitive boat launches at Northeast Carry and the Seboomook Campground.

Popular fishing locations on the south end of the lake include Harford's Point, Bolton Cove, Burnt Jacket Point, and the gut between Black Sand and Moose Islands. The string of small islands running from Cove Point up toward Sandy Bay provide good fishing in the spring when salmon are cruising near the surface. Productive areas on the east side of the lake—Black Point, Beaver Cove, Sugar Island, and the narrows at the entrance into Spencer Bay—are best reached from Lily Bay State Park. The east shore of Deer Island is another good spring fishing spot that is fairly close to the state park.

Moosehead Lake's most popular fishing hole is nearly within sight of the boat launch in Rockwood and lies between Mount Kineo and the mouth of the Moose River. When smelts are running in the river, salmon and togue sometimes congregate here in tremendous numbers: there are times when so many fish show on my fish finder that it seems impossible not to hook any of them. Other hotspots, including Hardscrabble Point and Farm Island and the Toe of the Boot, can also be found on the west side of the lake.

In addition to these well-known locations, Moosehead Lake has dozens of other places that offer good fishing. Experienced guides say that you're likely to find fish if you investigate any inlet that is dumping a decent volume of water into the lake. Three such places in proximity to Rockwood are Baker Brook and Tomhegan and Socatean Streams. By using DeLorme's *Map and Guide to Moosehead Lake* as a guide, you can find many more fishable spots.

Specialized tactics aren't required to catch any of the three major sport fish when you are spring trolling in Moosehead Lake. But you can greatly increase your chances of catching a given species by following some simple guidelines. If you want to catch brook trout, fish close to shore. When water temperatures are below sixty degrees, most brookies feed on baitfish and insects that are found in less than ten feet of water. Areas with large boulders or other structure are often best, but depending on wind conditions and time of day brook trout can be found almost anywhere. According to veteran guide Dan Legere, "You want to troll the edge of the drop-off where you can see bottom on one side of the boat but not on the other. If you're fishing for spring brookies and don't need a new propeller at the end of a week, you aren't fishing where they live."

Salmon can also be caught in close, especially along shorelines that quickly drop off into deep water. Because salmon are more commonly taken a bit farther offshore, I often troll in a zigzag pattern that starts close to shore and extends out about two hundred yards. If this method doesn't produce action, trolling across the mouth of a large bay or in the gut between the shore and an island may help you locate fish. Frequently, fish will hold well below the surface in these locations, so it's helpful to have a fish finder and downrigger. Most togue are also caught offshore and down in the water column.

This five-and-a-half-pound fish was landed by Ziggy Tracewski in 1980 and still holds the family record for the largest landlocked salmon caught on a fly.

The methods used to catch fish in Moosehead Lake are as varied as the people who fish here. Live smelts and fresh, sewn bait are popular when smelts are running in the early spring. Plugs such as Rapalas and Yo-Zuri Minnows and spoons like Mooselook Wobblers, Harry Lures, and Sutton Spoons can be effective throughout the season. However, streamer flies are the choice of most serious anglers on the lake and, over the years, nearly one hundred patterns have been created. Most are tied tandem-style and are designed to imitate a smelt.

The Pink Lady, Gray Ghost, Black Ghost, Magog Smelt, and Joe's Smelt are among the most popular flies used on the lake. But getting seasoned Moosehead anglers to agree on the best pattern is nearly impossible. Dan Legere once told me, "Considering how fast conditions change on the lake, there really isn't one fly that will work all the time. I approach each day as an experiment and present fish with a series of different patterns until I find one that works. Along with boat speed and location, the most important element in successful trolling is to vary the form, flash, and color of your flies." This advice has served me well for nearly twenty years and led me to the realization that successful angling in Moosehead Lake is determined more by the fish than by the fisherman.

Other Area Lakes

In addition to Moosehead itself, there are four other lakes in the region that are popular with anglers. Although three of these bodies of water are referred to locally as "ponds," in terms of size and type of fisheries they are legitimate lakes of substantial acreage.

Brassua Lake

At just under nine thousand acres, Brassua Lake is the largest of the four other Moosehead region lakes. It was created by a dam built on the Moose River several miles west of Rockwood and serves as an important water storage facility for Moosehead Lake. In the springtime, Brassua can provide good fishing for colorful brook trout around inlets such as Misery Stream, Fletcher Stream, and Johnson Brook. The ledges around Black Point and the area in Little Brassua Lake where the upper Moose River flows in can also be productive. Salmon are stocked here, but they tend to run smaller than those in Moosehead Lake. Among the locals, this lake is probably best known for its winter smelt fishing. The primary boat launch on Brassua is located a couple of miles past the dam on Route 15. The lake is subject to a nearly thirty-foot drawdown in summer, and access can be difficult during these low-water periods.

Wilson Ponds

The Wilson Ponds are less than ten minutes from downtown Greenville and provide anglers with an attractive alternative when the wind is blowing hard on Moosehead. This twenty-five-hundred-acre body of water is made up of two similar-sized basins connected by a shallow thoroughfare that can be navigated with a small boat or canoe. Access is from a well-maintained boat launch located near the outlet. Although the ponds have a moderate amount of shoreline development, the scenic mountainous backdrop makes this a very pleasant place to spend a day.

Before the illegal introduction of white perch in the mid-1980s, brook trout like this one were taken regularly from upper Wilson Pond.

Lower Wilson is a deep, crystal-clear lake that offers good salmon and togue fishing to springtime anglers who troll sewn smelts or streamer flies around the mouth of the narrows. My most memorable catch here, however, was an eel that my friend David Saucier and I landed one evening during a family campout when our children were young. I'll never forget how excited all five kids were as the unseen fish pulled hard on the end of the line, then how fast they ran away when we slid three feet of snakelike fish onto the shore.

Upper Wilson Pond was once a native brook trout fishery that had a reputation for producing good numbers of thick-bodied fish. Trout fishing has declined significantly though since white perch became established in the mid-1980s.

Indian Pond

Indian Pond is a thirty-eight-hundred-acre flow-through impoundment on the Kennebec River that was created when Harris Dam was built in 1953. Nice boat launches are available on the north and south ends of the lake. Togue are often found near the deep hole a mile or so up from Harris Dam. The north end of Indian Pond is fed by the waters of Moosehead Lake's East and West Outlets and provides a great spring fishery for brook trout and salmon. These fish are also frequently taken around the mouth of Indian Stream. Smallmouth bass were illegally introduced around 1990, and they have since caused problems for the salmonids. Bass have become so prevalent that I recently picked up a brochure in Greenville that touted Indian Pond as "the best smallmouth bass fishery in the region." Indeed, quite a few people now visit Indian Pond specifically to fish for bass. Although that might sound like great news to a casual angler, illegal introductions of warmwater fish into coldwater habitats is a critical problem occurring at an alarming rate throughout the state. Many biologists rate this as the single, most serious threat to Maine's traditional fishing heritage.

Roach Ponds

There are seven interconnected Roach ponds that begin at the village of Kokadjo and stretch east for nearly fifteen miles. First and Second Roach are the largest and have roads, boat launches, and a fair amount of development along their south shores. Healthy populations of salmon, brook trout, and togue are present in these waters, and trolling with streamer flies or sewn bait are the most popular methods of fishing. On First Roach Pond, inlet brooks and a sand bar located about three-fourths of the way up the lake are good places to search for fish in the spring. The short stretch of river that connects First and Second Roach can be productive for fly fishermen.

The best access to Third Roach Pond is from a gravel road that passes within one hundred yards of its north shore. This pond contains brook trout and a few salmon. In addition, it provides anglers with a good chance of seeing moose feeding in the shallows along the shoreline. Fourth Roach has been stocked with splake several times during the past decade and reports indicate that they are thriving. The upper

Roach drainage consists of several small, remote trout ponds that can be reached only on foot.

Moosehead Region Rivers

Three of Maine's finest rivers are associated with Moosehead Lake. These rivers are fairly short, dam-regulated, and accessible from paved roads. The Moose River is the lake's primary inlet and flows into it near the west-shore village of Rockwood. The upper Kennebec River serves as the lake's outlet and is located a few miles south of Rockwood on the west shore. It is divided into two branches referred to as the East and West Outlets. The Roach River, another important Moosehead tributary, enters the east side of the lake about ten miles north of Lily Bay State Park.

The seasonal angling calendar in these rivers is quite similar because the majority of their large fish are seasonal migrants from Moosehead Lake. Early in the year, most fishing is done with streamer flies and is closely linked to runs of spawning smelts. As the waters begin to drop and warm, there is a fairly intense spell of insect activity when fish seem eager to develop a close relationship with a dry fly or dead-drifted nymph. After a midsummer period when fish migrate back to the cool depths of the lake, the action picks up again in the fall when they return to the rivers to spawn.

Lower Moose River

The dam at the outlet of Brassua Lake blocks the upstream movement of fish from Moosehead Lake and serves as a logical place to separate the Moose River into lower and upper stretches. I'll discuss the upper Moose River in the Jackman Area section later in this chapter.

The lower Moose River flows about four miles before dumping into Moosehead Lake near the village of Rockwood. But this short stretch gets a lot of attention from anglers because of its large seasonal runs of smelts and salmonids. Powerhouse Pool is located along the south bank of the river directly in the outflow of the Brassau Dam. It is the most productive pool on the river—I've seen people catch fish here with everything from surf-casting rods to bamboo poles. One

All three Moosehead region rivers provide fly fishermen with excellent opportunities to catch salmon in the spring and fall.

reason why this pool is so good is that there is no fish ladder in the dam, so fish attempting to move up river often accumulate in large numbers. Another thing that holds fish is the cold water and steady supply of smelts that are killed as they get drawn through Brassau Dam's turbines.

Most fish are caught by anglers who stand on the large rocks along the south shore. Early in the season, smelt-imitating streamers are the flies of choice. But from June through late summer, nymphs and dry flies account for a surprisingly large number of salmon and brook trout. Because of easy access and limited casting space, it's not unusual for this pool to become crowded.

The Pasture is a smooth-flowing pool located several hundred yards below the dam's spillway on the north bank of the river. Historically, it was a favorite holding spot for large fish—many years ago I caught three salmon over twenty inches in a couple of hours. When a new powerhouse was added to the dam in 1992, the river's flow was altered and fishing in this pool dropped off a bit.

Three other named pools exist within a mile of the dam. But when water levels are good, fish can be taken almost anywhere from The Fingers to below the Cribworks. This section of river is classic freestone pocket-water whose fish-holding ability benefits greatly from cold water drawn off the bottom of Brassau Lake. Healthy populations of stoneflies, mayflies, and sculpins occur here, so fishing a Marabou Muddler with a nymph as a dropper can be productive. Trails exist on both sides of the river, but I prefer the south shore because of ease of fishing the runs between pools.

The gradient of the river flattens out beyond the Cribworks, and from here down to Moosehead Lake most fishing is done from small boats and canoes. Scott, Gilbert, and Rockpile are popular pools that can be fished by either trolling or casting. Smelt-imitating streamers like the Governor Aiken or Nine-Three are all you need to catch early season fish. Although the water is usually swift and cold, I find that offerings fished quickly near the surface of these pools usually produce more strikes than those presented in a typical (deep and slow) early season fashion. Once insects become active, many fish and fish-ermen shift their attention to the hatches. Standard dry flies like the Hendrickson, Adams, and Elkhair Caddis will all work. Small nymphs like Zug-Bugs and Prince Nymphs along with soft-hackle flies and Hornbergs are worth a try when nothing is showing on the surface.

The lower two miles of the Moose River are mainly fished by people who troll up from the lake. Most anglers launch boats at the public landing in Rockwood and travel to just beyond the Moose River Bridge. When the water is high, it's not unusual to see twenty boats in this fairly limited area. Despite the congestion and the occasional tangled line, everyone does quite well. Many people fish with tandem streamers on a sink-tip line, but Rapalas, Flash Kings, and almost anything else that imitates a smelt works when the fish are in.

Biologists are fearful that recent, illegal introductions of white perch and smallmouth bass will cause brook trout like these to become a thing of the past on Moosehead area rivers.

Upper Kennebec River

The upper Kennebec River is divided into two branches that serve as Moosehead Lake's princi-ple outlets. The West Outlet is the smaller of the two and flows for about eight miles before reaching Indian Pond. Brook trout stocked at the pool below the West Outlet Dam and in Long Pond provide popular put-and-take fisheries. A few good salmon are caught each spring by anglers trolling in the deadwaters or casting around some of the rips. Bass fishing is the big-ger attraction on the West Outlet; once the water warms, fishing around some of the islands and submerged rockpiles by the mouth can be fast-paced.

The East Outlet is only about four miles long, but it has a larger volume of water and a better flow than the West Outlet, and it generally holds more salmon and trout. This river contains multiple

The pool below the East Outlet dam is enormous and can comfortably accommodate a dozen fly casters.

sets of brawling rapids, so other than anglers on guided drift-boat trips or boaters near the outlet's mouth, almost all the fishing here is done by wading. Twelve hundred cubic feet per second (cfs) is an ideal water level for wading the East Outlet. At around two thousand cfs, the bowling-ball-sized rocks found on much of the streambed can get slick and dangerous. Flows over three thousand cfs makes the river unwadeable. Traditionally, a big problem for anglers has been that the flow fluctuated drastically on almost a daily basis. Recently, the power company has made an effort to operate the dam so that more constant flows are maintained. If you are traveling to the Moosehead Lake region specifically to fish the East Outlet, it's wise to call the water-flow hotline (800-557-3569) to get current and projected flow rates.

The upper section of the East Outlet has easy access from Route 15, and fishing is often good in the pool right below the dam. This pool is nearly one hundred yards across and consists of two huge back eddies that wash against the face of the dam. Fishing from the deck of the dam is legal, and anglers commonly use it or the riprap boulders along the north side of the pool. Gauge Pool is just above the railroad bridge located one-quarter mile downstream. This pool is fairly small and can be tough to wade, but it often produces fish for anglers who can get a good drift in its tricky currents. Many people also fish the pocketwater between the Route 15 bridge and the dam.

Because of heavy fishing pressure, the key to success on this stretch of river is being different. Small, dark-colored flies—particularly soft-hackles and nymphs with peacock herl bodies—work well here. I have also had good luck with small Muddlers and western-style dry flies like the Renegade and various Wulffs. At certain times of year, there can be large numbers of fish in this short section of river. Because you see other anglers fishing here doesn't mean you should pass up this area. But remember that the fish have seen a lot of flies—especially streamers—and it might take extra effort to catch them.

Below the Route 15 bridge, a gravel road follows the north bank of the river downstream for more than a mile. Several vehicle turnouts and short trails lead to riffles and runs that provide a more private fishing experience than you are likely to get on the upper river. Beach Pool is a beautiful one-hundred-fifty-yard-long glide found close to where the road breaks away from the river. This deep, smooth-flowing pool is most productive at its head and tail, especially when fish are rising in the evening. It also

provides access to several other lightly fished spots that can be reached by walking downstream.

Swimmer's Hole is the name given to the last one-quarter-mile run of moving water on the East Outlet before the river gets backed up by Indian Pond. The easiest way to access this spot is to drive the Burnham Pond Road to the boat launch on Indian Pond, then use a canoe or small boat to motor back up to the pool. You can also reach this area by walking down a rough trail from Beach Pool. The river is swift and wide here; therefore, though wading is possible in some places, anglers often use a small boat to fish the various lies that can be found from the ledges down to where the current ends.

Early in the season, trolling with hardware and tandem streamers is the most popular way to fish the lower section of this long pool. The East Outlet is a fly-fishing-only river, however, which means that no trolling is allowed above the red markers set about halfway down each shoreline. Many early season fly fishermen use bright streamers like the Barnes Special or Pink Lady along with Hornbergs and various floating-smelt patterns to fish right along the edge of the fast water. Once insects become active in June, pods of salmon will sometimes position themselves in the tail-outs of the deeper lies and pick off helpless emergers and duns as they float by. This can produce great dry-fly fishing for people who happen to perfectly time their visit. Crayfish and large, black stonefly nymphs are good patterns to try here when no fish are showing.

Roach River

The Roach River is twenty miles northeast of Greenville and can be reached by a paved road that leads to the village of Kokadjo. Unlike the two big rivers—lower Moose and upper Kennebec—on the west side of Moosehead Lake, the Roach is more of a narrow stream that often has a dense border of trees extending down to the water's edge. All fishing is done by wading, and the best results usually come from a dozen or so of the river's well-known pools.

You will find four good pools in the upper mile of river. Dam Pool is deep and well-oxygenated and is located almost directly under the bridge at Kokadjo. First Roach Dam forces fish coming from Moosehead Lake to stack up, so despite almost constant angling pressure many fish are caught here. Dump, Corner, and Warden's are three other excellent pools that can be reached by a one-half-mile trail along the north bank of the river. The trail begins near a store on private property,

"Fish on" at the Warden's Pool.

Lazy Tom and several other small Roach River pools can accommodate only one or two fishermen at a time.

and permission should be sought before using it. Vehicles can be parked in the public lot near the dam. Because of easy access and availability of good fish, these three pools are heavily fished. However, similar to Dam Pool, in spite of the pressure large brook trout and salmon are taken during the spring and fall.

The upper trail deteriorates a short distance beyond Warden's Pool. To reach the middle and lower pools, I usually drive the gravel road that runs along the north side of the river, then park at various vehicle turnouts. Good midriver pools include Flatlander, Highlander, Corner, Spring, and Slaughter. These pools are connected by a riverside trail that, when I'm wearing waders, takes me nearly an hour to cover. Individual pools can also be accessed from several different trails that lead down from the gravel road. Lower pools include Ledge, Flat Rock, and Moose Hole and are separated from the midriver pools by a long stretch of "bony" pocketwater. Lake Pool is formed where the Roach River dumps into Moosehead Lake and is most easily reached by boat.

Spring fishing on the Roach River is usually good a week or so after ice-out on Moosehead Lake. At this time of year, spawning smelts draw salmon and brook trout into the river where many of them stay until the water warms in July. During wet springs, high water can sometimes make the river difficult to fish. For best results, look for flows under four hundred cubic feet per second. Early in the season, bucktail and marabou streamers like the Black Ghost and Thunder Creek are popular flies, though Hornbergs and Muddlers account for quite a few fish. Once the smelts have left the river, nymphs, wet flies, and dry flies become most effective. I've had good luck with a variety of simple, impressionistic soft-hackle and wet-fly patterns fished with a dry line through the tailouts of pools. Fish get wary as the season progresses; thus, more sophisticated emergers and Comparaduns are often required for consistent success.

Because the Roach River is an important spawning tributary for a large number of Moosehead Lake's salmon and brook trout, fall is an excellent time to fish here. Depending on rainfall and the amount of water

Dan Legere

Special regulations were instituted in 1996 to ensure that brook trout like these are always present in Moosehead area ponds.

released from the dam, fish sometimes begin their upstream migration as early as the last week in August. By mid-September, it's almost certain that trout and salmon will be found in nearly every pool. Over the years, I've had somewhat of a love-hate relationship with the Roach River in the fall. On good days, this river's small pools and intimate surroundings offer a sense of peacefulness not normally found in many places. On other days, crowds of people can make finding a place to fish a frustrating experience.

The Roach is the only major river in Maine that is fly-fishing only and completely catch-and-release. Because of its remoteness and importance as a spawning ground for Moosehead Lake salmonids, the State recently purchased a one-thousand-foot-wide corridor along the river to ensure public access and freedom from development. To maintain the wilderness character of the area and to limit angling pressure, the current plan is to leave access road and trails in an unimproved condition. Although it might be a bit difficult to reach a favorite pool on Roach River, it is usually worth the effort.

Moosehead Region Trout Ponds

Several dozen good trout ponds are located within twenty miles of Moosehead Lake. Close to Greenville, four waters that are heavily stocked and readily accessible are Gravel Pit, Shadow, Sawyer, and Prong Ponds. Less accessible ponds found east of Moosehead Lake between Route 11 and the Golden Road are discussed below. I describe ponds located west of Moosehead in the Jackman Area section of this chapter.

Katahdin Iron Works Road

There are numerous trout ponds along the road from Greenville to Katahdin Iron Works. Years ago, ponds such as Rum, Secret, Salmon, Indian, and Brown were known for producing large brook trout. But the road was improved in the late 1960s, and increased angling pressure soon wiped out these big fish. Fishing in these ponds has become dramatically better since 1996 when trophy management regulations were enacted.

Spring often comes late to mountain ponds in the Moosehead area, so check your neoprenes for leaks before embarking on early season float-tube trips.

The Little Lyfords and Horseshoe are other area ponds that are perfect for novice fly fishermen because they contain plenty of smaller trout that rise readily and are usually easy to catch. Small Hornbergs, Devil Bugs, Adams, and grasshoppers are all good flies to use here. Mountain Brook and several other small fly-fishing-only ponds can be found nearby. Anglers who want to get farther off the beaten path can follow the Appalachian Trail one and one-half miles to East Chairback Pond or continue another three miles to West Chairback.

Jo-Mary Area

Another group of productive trout ponds is located east of Kokadjo in the Jo-Mary area. Big Lyford and the West Branch Ponds are easily accessible, fly-fishing-only waters that produce a lot of pan-sized native brookies. Yoke, Alligator, and the Boardways are ponds that can yield bigger fish. Early in the season, most trout are taken on small streamers and bucktails like the Edson Tiger and Black-Nosed Dace. These are very good dry-fly ponds, so I generally wait until the second week in June before venturing up here. Jo-Mary area ponds often have a heavy Green Drake hatch because

their silty bottoms provide ideal habitat for burrowing mayflies. But midsummer fishing here can be tough—some area ponds are shallow and warm quickly.

Jackman Area
Moose River

The Moose River begins its journey to Moosehead Lake as a series of small brooks that flow from the rugged mountains on Maine's western border with Quebec. It is divided into three sections by Jackman area lakes and Brassua Dam. The upper river is over twenty miles long and is unusual because a lengthy section of it can be accessed at different ends of the same pond. Referred to as the "Moose River Bow," this remote stretch of river is one of Maine's most popular wilderness canoe trips. Below Jackman, the middle river contains two productive sections of moving water that are interrupted by Long Pond. The lower river begins at Brassua Dam and was described earlier.

Above the "Bow," the upper Moose River ranges from meandering deadwater on its lower end to a small freestone stream on its upper reaches. Miles of native-brook-trout water can be accessed by driving the

Spencer Lake Road to Skinner, then walking the railroad tracks that follow the river. An old MDIF&W survey indicated that most fish in this area were less than ten inches long, but Regional Biologist Scott Roy said that "bigger trout could be found in places where beavers dammed the river and in some of the area's local ponds."

The Moose River Bow trip is a forty-mile canoe excursion that begins and ends at Attean Pond. It starts with a long paddle across two lakes separated by a one-and-a-half-mile portage. Once on the river, the first ten miles are through swampy lowlands that aren't particularly good brook trout habitat. The fishing changes abruptly at Holeb Falls where nice rips usually produce pan-sized brookies. Several other sets of rips in the last ten miles of the trip also hold fish. The best chance for larger trout—along with salmon and splake—is in the Attean Falls area, which is only a couple of miles up from the lake. Fishing is usually best shortly after ice-out, and many people motor up to this area when the water is high. Early season tactics range from fly-casting to trolling smelts, but most of the fish I have seen taken here have been caught with bait.

The middle section of the Moose River begins at the outlet of Wood Pond; moving water here provides people with an opportunity to catch salmon from the U.S. Route 201 bridge in downtown Jackman. The majority of anglers fish this mostly flat section of river from small boats or canoes, especially around inlets and near where it dumps into Long Pond. I usually fish the middle section of the Moose River below Demo Bridge or in the Mackamp area. Both of these stretches have large, wadeable pools and riffles that can produce both trout and salmon. Fall is a prime time to visit because lower water levels make wading easier. Railroad tracks near the south bank can be used to walk upstream or downstream.

Jackman Area Lakes

There are seven waters—locally referred to as both lakes and ponds—that provide good fishing for Jackman area anglers. Big Wood Pond is located right in town and contains good populations of splake and salmon as well as some brook trout. Popular fishing spots are around the mouths of Wood Stream and the Moose River and off the south side of Hog Island. Anglers also fish for smelts, cusk, and yellow perch, especially in the winter. Little Wood Pond is located a few miles west of Big Wood, but it is much less developed. The rough access road and primitive boat launch also hold down the fishing pressure. Stocked splake and wild salmon are the primary targets—fish up to twenty inches are not uncommon. Trolling with streamers or sewn smelt work well in this lake, particularly along the shorelines of the west basin. Easy snowmobile access has led to a substantial increase in the number of ice fishermen that come here. Several years ago on a warm, sunny day in March, I counted ten parties set up on this relatively small lake. And they all seemed to be catching fish.

Attean Pond is popular at ice-out because it is the only local water that is closed to ice-fishing. Early season anglers concentrate their efforts in the southeast corner of the pond near where the Moose River dumps in. Salmon are the primary target, but good-sized brook trout and splake are also caught here. Later in the season, most of these fish move into the deep, narrow basin on the west side of the pond. Much of the water in the rest of the pond is less than twenty feet deep and not worth fishing during summer. On the plus side, dozens of scenic islands provide beautiful sheltered spots in which to kayak or swim.

Holeb is another fairly shallow pond that produces brook trout and splake. When the water is cool, numerous rock piles, points, and islands provide countless places for fish to hold, and searching is often required to locate them. Anglers often troll to start the day, then switch to casting small spoons or flies around productive areas. Worm and spinner rigs are also popular. It's a long drive on a gravel road to the boat launch, so access can be a problem during mud season. Recently, Holeb Pond has experienced an increasing amount of ice-fishing pressure.

Three other good fishing spots in the Jackman area are Parlin Pond, Long Pond, and Spencer Lake. Parlin Pond is located along U.S. Route 201 and has a boat launch on its south end. Brook trout are the main attraction in Parlin Pond, but wild salmon are also present. Although this pond is fly-fishing only, it has a special regulation that allows trolling, which is popular early in the season with flies like the Black Ghost, Hornberg, and Wood Special. Once the hatches begin, dry-fly fishing can be good on calm evenings. Trout here are chunky, but they don't seem to get much over twelve inches.

Long Pond is an eight-mile-long flow-through waterway on the Moose River east of Jackman. It offers good fishing for brook trout around inlets such as Parlin Stream and in areas with some current, like the Upper and Lower Narrows. Spencer Lake is a deep, five-mile-long body of water south of Jackman that has

Despite fairly heavy angling pressure, Jackman area lakes can produce good results during the open-water and ice-fishing seasons.

the best togue fishery in the area. Fat, hard-fighting salmon are also a prime attraction. Trolling along the shore with hardware or sewn bait and a few colors of lead-core line is a proven method for catching early season fish. Streamers are good later in the season, especially when trolled during early morning or late evening. The land surrounding Spencer Lake went into private ownership in 2000, and questions remain concerning public access. Anglers should check locally before attempting to launch a boat here. Ice-fishing is popular on both Long Pond and Spencer Lake.

Jackman Area Trout Ponds

There are dozens of small ponds in the Jackman area that can produce memorable trout fishing. A local sporting camp operator once told me that his clients are sometimes overwhelmed, even frustrated, by the choices of places to fish. I find the best way to solve this "problem" is to divide the area's trout ponds into categories based on access, hatches, and potential for big fish.

For example, I frequently stay at a camp in Jack-man with a group of friends who like to fish for a few hours before breakfast. Local ponds with good access—Rancourt, Smith, and Daymond for example—contain a lot of pan-sized trout that provide a perfect opportunity to enjoy easy early morning fishing. Around noon, we usually pair off and select more remote ponds in which to fish for the remainder of the day. A couple of early season favorites are found in the Benjamin Valley and can be reached by walking a gated road that runs behind Sally Mountain. A number of ponds, such as Enchanted, Rock, and Snake, can be found south of Jackman off U.S. Route 201.

Over the years, I have enjoyed many memorable evenings fly-fishing in ponds throughout the Jackman area. I've also had trips when an eagerly awaited hatch did not materialize. With time, I've come to appreciate that these wild-trout ponds are enchanting places even when the fish don't cooperate. Sometimes, when the sun drops behind the trees and the sky turns a brilliant orange, it seems as if catching fish is a bonus that an ordinary person like me might not deserve.

Schoolie striper, Harraseeket River.

Blue Flag, Iris versicolor.

Crooked River, near Edes Falls.

PLATE 1

St. George River, Thomaston.

Storm over Aziscohos Lake.

PLATE 2

Randy Ury

Kennebago Lake.

John's Pond Pool, Kennebago River.

PLATE 3

Spring Pool, Roach River.

Rangeley boats at Tim Pond.

PLATE 4

Cheryl Tracewski

September morning on Great Pond, Rome.

PLATE 5

Covered bridge over Presumpscot River, Windham.

Low tide at Blue Hill Falls.

PLATE 6

Flagup.

Female Hendrickson, Ephemerella subvaria.

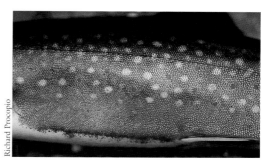

Male brook trout in spawning colors.

Moose River, Rockwood.

PLATE 7

Streamers

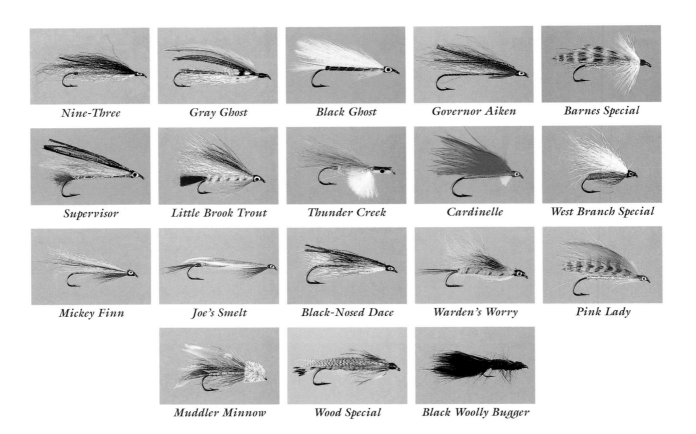

photographs by Richard Procopio

Nine-Three   Gray Ghost   Black Ghost   Governor Aiken   Barnes Special

Supervisor   Little Brook Trout   Thunder Creek   Cardinelle   West Branch Special

Mickey Finn   Joe's Smelt   Black-Nosed Dace   Warden's Worry   Pink Lady

Muddler Minnow   Wood Special   Black Woolly Bugger

Wet Flies

Hornberg (Wet)   CDC Caddis   Sparkle Caddis Emerger   Soft Hackle Emerger   Hendrickson Wet Fly

PLATE 8

Dry Flies

photographs by Richard Procopio

Green Drake · Stimulator · Kennebago Wulff · Grasshopper · Black Ant

Devil Bug · Black Gnat · Goddard Caddis · Elk Hair Caddis · West Branch Caddis

Hornberg (Dry) · Red Quill · Dark Hendrickson · March Brown · Adams

Nymphs

Hare's Ear · Brassie · Stone Fly Nymph · Zug Bug · Tellico Nymph

Bead Head Prince Nymph · Caddis Larva · Bead Head Pheasant Tail Nymph

PLATE 9

Down east traffic jam, Stonington.

PLATE 10

Dale Wheaton

East Grand Lake salmon.

Cheryl Tracewski

Magic hour on a North Woods pond.

Penobscot River, near site of old Bangor Salmon Pool.

PLATE 11

Floatplane on Millinocket Lake, T8 R9.

Sunrise over Daicey Pond, Baxter State Park.

PLATE 12

Old Town Canoe Company

Baxter Park at first light.

PLATE 13

Cheryl Tracewski

Father and son, Penobscot River.

Garrett Conover

Shore lunch.

Garrett Conover

North Woods campsite.

PLATE 14

St. John River, near Fort Kent.

St. Francis Lake, T8 R16.

Allagash Falls, T15 R11.

Fiddlehead along
Kenduskeag Stream.

PLATE 15

Rising trout in down east beaver flowage.

Red River Camps, Deboullie Reserve.

PLATE 16

Down East

The Passamaquoddy Indians began to guide sport fishermen in the Grand Lakes region around 1830. Well-known guide Athean Lewey is shown here with his birch-bark canoe in 1879.

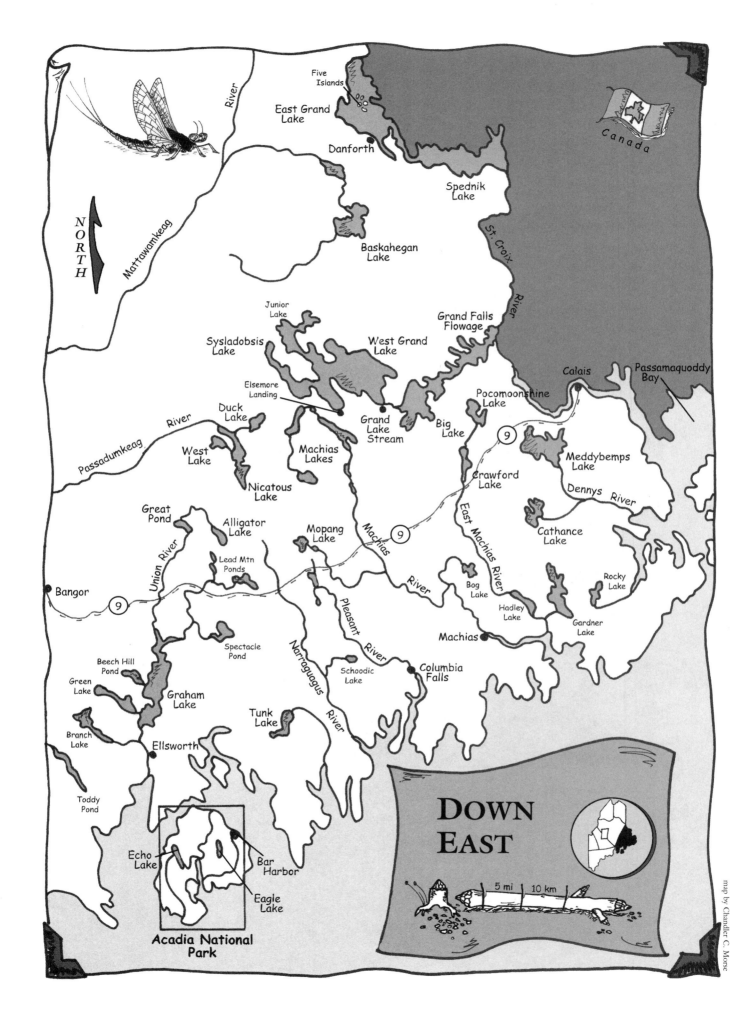

NORTH

River

Mattawamkeag

Five Islands

East Grand Lake

Danforth

Canada

Spednik Lake

Baskahegan Lake

St. Croix River

Junior Lake

Sysladobsis Lake

West Grand Lake

Grand Falls Flowage

Calais

Passamaquoddy Bay

Elsemore Landing

Duck Lake

Grand Lake Stream

Pocomoonshine Lake

Passadumkeag River

West Lake

Machias Lakes

Big Lake

9

Meddybemps Lake

Crawford Lake

Dennys River

Nicatous Lake

Great Pond

Alligator Lake

Mopang Lake

Machias

9

East Machias River

Cathance Lake

Rocky Lake

Union River

Bangor

9

Lead Mtn Ponds

River

Bog Lake

Hadley Lake

Gardner Lake

Spectacle Pond

Narraguagus River

Pleasant River

Machias

Beech Hill Pond

Schoodic Lake

Columbia Falls

Green Lake

Graham Lake

Branch Lake

Ellsworth

Tunk Lake

River

Toddy Pond

Echo Lake

Bar Harbor

Eagle Lake

Acadia National Park

DOWN EAST

5 mi   10 km

map by Chandler C. Morse

Dale Wheaton

illustration by Sandra Nestlerode-Hale

DALE WHEATON grew up in the village of Grand Lake Stream and began guiding when he was fifteen years old. He claims that he was not particularly qualified, but his father, Woodie Wheaton, who guided down east for more than sixty years, needed a warm body to tend sports staying at the family's lodge in Forest City. As a result of spending every summer of his adult life in the stern of a Grand Laker, Dale developed a deep love and respect for both the woods and waters of Washington County and for the profession of guiding.

You don't need to know Dale Wheaton long to understand that he is a no-nonsense guy whose primary allegiance is to down east Maine. He says, "Good guiding is always a fine balance between providing people with enough information so that they can be successful, while holding back enough to protect the resource." And he willingly admits that "if I err, I usually do so on the side of the resource even if it costs me money." Dale thinks that teaching clients about conservation is a critical part of a guide's job, and he says that if you educate people about the issues, they will usually make the right decision. For example, he explains that it can take twenty years for a down east smallmouth to reach four pounds and that such a fish was probably caught and released a number of times during its life. Then, if a client is fortunate enough to catch a big smallmouth that day, they often choose to release it.

Dale is strongly committed to the profession of guiding and is passionate about passing the traditions on to the next generation of Maine guides. Each year when he organizes the dozen or so guides that work out of his lodge in Forest City, he does so with an eye to the past and insists on performance that even the most discerning of the classic, old-time guides would be proud of. His philosophy is that "it really doesn't take much more effort to do things the right way than the wrong way." He expects his guides to handle everything just right, and he wants them to make it appear effortless.

Preparing a shore-lunch is a perfect example. This down east tradition is the centerpiece around which most fishing trips are built. And Dale doesn't think that rain, wind, wet wood, or bugs should prevent it from being prepared perfectly. "After all," he says, "for many people this will be the only time in their lives that they will have a shore-lunch prepared for them by a Maine guide, so we damn well better be sure it comes out right."

When you ask people to look at a map of Maine and point out the "down east" region, they usually indicate a spot along the coast between Bar Harbor and Machais. The problem with down east is that if you ask twelve people where it is, you're likely to get a dozen different answers. The reason for the confusion is that, although almost everyone associates the words down east with the Maine coast, people can't agree on where the region begins or ends.

For my purposes in this book, I will take a broad view of the down east region and include all of Hancock and Washington Counties. At just over five thousand square miles, this region is larger than Delaware, Rhode Island, and the District of Columbia combined, yet it contains less than 2 percent of their population.

For fishermen, the most appealing aspect of the down east region is the variety of angling opportunities that it offers. Grand Lake Stream is a classic fly-fishing-only water that provides a challenging opportunity to pursue large fish in an intimate setting. Each spring, big lakes such as East Grand, West Grand, Junior, Tunk, and Green attract legions of trollers who battle with salmon and togue cruising near the surface. This region is best known for numerous warmwater lakes like Big, Meddybemps, Third Machais, and Pocomoonshine that support a world-class smallmouth bass fishery that Boston Red Sox Hall-of-Fame left fielder Ted Williams once described as, "the best damn fishing this side of heaven." Brown trout and splake were recently introduced to down east waters, and Flanders, Walker, Patrick, and Mopang Lakes are now producing fish up to twenty inches long. My favorite down east activity is pursuing native brook trout in the small streams, beaver ponds, and deadwaters that can be found in the region. I often return from these adventures bug-bitten and exhausted—and I rarely catch a fish over twelve inches—but the opportunity to discover a honeyhole full of wild brookies is something that I find exciting about this area.

History

The majority of the down east region is less than four hundred feet above sea level. During the last ice age, the tremendous weight of the one-mile-thick sheet of ice that covered Maine caused the elevation in this area to be significantly lower than it is today. Therefore, when

One of the first photographs taken in down east Maine shows the tents of Indian guides set up on the lower end of Grand Lake Stream on June 8, 1864.

the glaciers retreated about twelve thousand years ago, most of down east Maine was covered by the Atlantic Ocean. With the weight of the ice gone, the land slowly uplifted and transformed the bulk of the remaining water into the vast network of lakes, bogs, and streams that now characterizes this area.

When the ocean receded, Atlantic salmon were trapped in the St. Croix and Union River watersheds. These fish adapted well to fresh water and evolved into the landlocked salmon that we catch today. The down east region is the ancestral home of Maine landlocked salmon—three of the state's five original populations developed in Green, West Grand, and East Grand Lakes. Historically, brook trout were the most widely distributed coldwater species and dominated nearly every watershed in the region. Togue and whitefish are also native and thrived in many of the area's deep oligotrophic lakes. In warmwater habitats, white perch were at the top of most food chains—smallmouth bass and pickerel were not introduced until around 1900. Biologists believe that a lack of competition from these two voracious predators allowed brook trout to colonize more marginal habitats than they occupy today.

Accounts of sport-fishing in the down east region were published as early as 1830, and by 1850 Grand Lake Stream was a well-known angling destination. Most sports traveled to Calais by steamer, then hired a Passamaquoddy Indian guide to transport them by canoe up the St. Croix River to Gould's Landing. Despite the effort required to get to Grand Lake Stream, in her book on the history of the area Minnie Atkinson wrote, "Throughout the 1850s and 1860s, sometimes as many as 50 tents would dot the woods along the sides of the stream during the spring season." She also noted that "all of the salmon fishing was done in Grand Lake Stream itself, or in the moving water located just above the dam. And outings where sports would catch upwards of 20 fish that averaged two pounds or better were not unusual."

The region changed dramatically in 1870 when the Shaw Brothers of Boston built a tannery along the east bank of Grand Lake Stream. Within a year, hundreds of workers had descended on the area to build a sawmill, dig a canal, and erect several dozen buildings needed to serve the tannery and its employees. The site was chosen because it was surrounded by forests that

The first fish hatchery in the United States was established at Grand Lake Stream in 1877. Fisheries Commissioner Charles Atkins (far right) is shown here inspecting rearing boxes.

In 1920, this steamboat was used to shuttle anglers and their canoes to far corners of West Grand Lake.

could provide a steady supply of hemlock bark, which was a critical element in the leather-tanning process. Business boomed, and within five years thousands of hides were shipped annually to Grand Lake Stream from places as far away as California, Argentina, and India. Supporting the world's largest tannery had a serious impact on the environment throughout the down east region. During the peak of the tannery's operation, Grand Lake Stream was little more than an open sewer filled with hair, skin, sawdust, and chemicals.

Despite all of this pollution, the fish survived. When the tannery was ravaged by fire and halted operations in 1887, Minnie Atkinson wrote that "the people in the village turned their attention from the humble job of providing sole leather for the world, to the pleasanter task of catering to its pleasures and its health." Most of the men in Grand Lake Stream quickly shifted from laborers to guides, and a half-dozen sporting camps were built to accommodate visiting anglers. Two of the finest camps, the White House (ca. 1888) and Ouananiche Lodge (ca. 1893), are still in operation today under the names of Weatherby's Resort and the Colonial Sportsman's Lodge.

Early in the post-tannery era, craftsmen living in Grand Lake Stream developed and refined the Grand Lake canoe, which became the defining feature of this area. The first Grand Lakers evolved from the birchbark canoes used by Passamaquoddys and other local tribes and were wood and canvas double-enders built to be paddled. Steamships like the *H.L. Drake* ferried rafts of canoes to distant parts of the West Grand chain of lakes where guides would use them to paddle anglers along the shoreline. Shortly after Ole Evinrude produced his first outboard around the turn of the century, the idea soon followed of building a square-stern Grand Laker that could accommodate a motor.

Billy Galley and Nye Whiting are credited with building the first square-stern Grand Lake canoe in 1904. From most accounts, their canoe was narrow, sat low in the water, and was quite unstable. This made it nearly worthless as a fishing boat on the West Grand chain of lakes. During the next twenty years, a number of local guides—including Joe Sprague, Arthur Wheaton, and Herb "Beaver" Bacon—improved this design and created their own models of square-stern canoes. All of these canoes were around nineteen feet long and had a very narrow stern: Outboard motors from this era had no water pumps and could not be operated at trolling speed; therefore, canoes had to be small enough for guides to paddle while their sports fished. The trend to make Grand Lakers longer, broader, and flatter began in the 1940s after improvements to outboards facilitated motorized trolling. Today, many canoe designs called Grand Lakers are more boat-like than the originals because most people no longer have the need, or desire, to paddle them.

Coldwater Lakes

The down east region has nearly fifty coldwater lakes that offer good fishing for salmon, togue, whitefish, splake, brook trout, and brown trout. I will provide detailed descriptions only for the area's two most popular destinations, West Grand Lake and East Grand Lake. All other salmonid fisheries are categorized and described geographically by their position relative to Route 9 (north or south of Route 9) that runs from Bangor to Calais.

West Grand Lake

West Grand Lake is a sprawling fourteen-thousand-acre body of water divided into a number of smaller sections by several prominent coves, points, and large islands.

The village of Grand Lake Stream is located at the outlet and has the best boat launch on the lake. The village also provides a full line of lodging and guide services. The remainder of the lake's one hundred fifty miles of wooded shoreline is accessible only by water and is almost completely wild.

Maine Department of Inland Fisheries and Wildlife surveys indicate that salmon are the principle target for most of the people who fish West Grand Lake and that nearly 75 percent of the fifteen thousand angler-days of use takes place between ice-out and the last week of June. Despite this heavy fishing pressure, salmon average around two pounds and are caught in West Grand at a higher rate than in other local waters. This fine fishing is due to the lake's thriving smelt population and the catch-and-release ethic promoted by local sporting camps and guides.

Good areas to troll that are fairly close to the boat launch include Munson Island, Big Mayberry Cove, Kitchen Point, and Dyer Point. Many people fish the rugged northeast shore in the vicinity of Bear Trap Landing, Pineo Point, Mark's Island, Hardwood Island, and Whitney Cove. During spring, I catch a lot of fish along the southwest shore around Norway Point, Birch Island, and Coffin Point. Beyond the Narrows, West Grand is connected to a number of other large lakes such as Junior, Pocumpus, Sysladobsis, and Scraggly.

A shore-lunch prepared over an open fire is a traditional feature of a guided fishing trip in the down east area.

Although salmon on West Grand Lake average around two and one-half pounds, a few eye-popping fish like this are taken every year.

To avoid the long boat ride from Grand Lake Stream, many people who fish these outlying lakes trailer their boats to one of the smaller launches located at Elsemore Landing, Sysladobsis Dam, or Bottle Lake.

A variety of trolling methods are used on the West Grand chain of lakes. Just after ice-out, sewn smelts fished behind a flashing spoon or dodger account for a sizable number of nice salmon. Rapalas, Yo-Zuri Minnows, Mooselook Wobblers, and other assorted hardware can also be effective, especially when fished close to the boat in the outboard motor's prop wash. Using a fly rod to troll a streamer fly close to the shoreline rocks is my favorite way to fish here. The use of "fly-bait" is a local modification of traditional streamer fishing that has proved effective. As the name implies, fly-bait involves attaching a small piece of bait to your fly. Typically, a small shiner is added to a single-hooked streamer. Originally developed by Grand Lake Stream guides to give their sports an edge over the competition, this combination is still deadly today, especially when fished slowly on a sinking line in areas where fish show up on the fish finder but are reluctant to strike. West Grand also yields good togue to anglers who use lead-core line and downriggers to work large spoons with sewn bait along the bottom.

East Grand Lake

East Grand is a sixteen-thousand-acre lake whose east shore lies in Canada. Hardtop boat launches accessible from the U.S. side are located on the south shore at Greenland Cove and Butterfield Landing. A small, unimproved boat launch is also available on the north shore at the Boundary Road Bridge near the Custom Station. Although much of East Grand is undeveloped, there are camps along the lake's large southern cove (locally referred to as "The Arm"), Greenland Cove, Dark Cove, and on the northwest shoreline. The town of Danforth is located near the southwest end of the lake and offers gas, groceries, and a couple of small restaurants. Anglers staying at area sporting camps typically obtain their meals and other essentials such as bait, tackle and guides at these establishments.

Traditionally, East Grand has been a salmon lake that produces many football-shaped specimens in the four-pound range. From ice-out through June, popular places to troll include Little River Cove, Hayes Point, Five-Islands, and the southwest shore between the mouth of Greenland Cove and Meetinghouse Point. In the spring, everything from hardware to smelts sewn behind a dodger can produce fish, but if I had to choose one method it would be a tandem Joe's Smelt trolled briskly with a sinking line and fifteen-foot leader. Salmon are also taken during the summer months, mainly by locals or guides, who use lead-core line or downriggers to get their offerings below the thermocline. Large togue are present in the deep sections of East Grand Lake and are usually caught by people specifically fishing for them with heavy gear.

Lakes South of Route 9

There are numerous down east lakes located within twenty miles of the coast that also support healthy populations of salmonids. Green, Branch, Phillips, Beech Hill, and Brewer Lakes are all close to U.S. Route 1A and have hundreds of camps on them. Despite heavy open-water and ice-fishing pressure, good numbers of well-proportioned salmon are taken here regularly. In large part, this is due to a sound fisheries management plan that includes a reduction in the number of salmon that are stocked and a ban on the dipping of smelts from the spawning brooks. Togue fishing is also surprisingly good in these popular lakes. I know several people who, throughout summer, use lead-core line to catch fish that average three pounds. Beech Hill is known for producing large togue, and many fish over fifteen pounds—including the longtime state record of thirty-one pounds—have been caught here. Green is my favorite local lake, and when the smelts are running in April I usually fish at the mouth of Great Brook or near the sandbar on the east end of the lake.

Good salmon fishing is available at Tunk, Schoodic, Cathance, and Nash's Lake. Because the boat launch at Tunk Lake is located directly on Route 182, it is the most well-known and heavily fished of these waters. Tunk is managed as a trophy fishery and has a one-fish limit. Action can be slow, but large salmon and togue

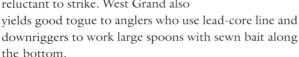

Each year, large salmon are taken through the ice at East Grand Lake.

Cheryl Tracewski

Smelts often begin their spawning runs before ice-out is complete on many lakes. Ambitious anglers who carry a small boat to fish around the mouths of inlet brooks can be rewarded with good fishing.

are caught by anglers who patiently troll the shorelines or fish near the deep hole at the south end of the lake. Cathance is another good lake that is easily accessible at the boat launch off Route 191. Fishing can be erratic here, but during years when the smelt population is healthy and the fish are growing well, this small lake produces a surprising number of hefty salmon in the four-pound class.

The down east region also has a number of lakes where the management strategy has shifted from salmon to brown trout and splake. According to regional biologist Ron Brokaw, "Back in the 1980s, we experimented with stocking brown trout and splake in several lakes that provided a marginal coldwater habitat for salmon and found that they often thrived in places where salmon struggled. Since then, this program

The Maine Department of Inland Fisheries and Wildlife has worked hard to provide coldwater fishing opportunities in many marginal habitats. Biologist Tim Obrey holds a five-pound splake taken during a fall, trap-net survey.

has expanded quite a bit and now produces some of the most popular fisheries in our area." Many of the best brown trout fisheries are found in the Eastbrook area and include Spectacle, Molasses, Georges, and Flanders Ponds. Nice browns are also taken at Bog, Rocky, Patrick, and Pennamaquan Lakes. The best splake fishery in the region is probably at Beddington Lake, followed by Pleasant River Lake and Peaked Mountain and Toddy Ponds. None of these places are pure salmonid fisheries, so anglers should expect to catch pickerel, bass, and perch along with brown trout and splake.

Lakes North of Route 9

Good salmon fishing can be found north of Route 9 in West, Alligator, Duck, and Nicatous Lakes. These are all lightly developed waters within ten miles of each other. They are on paper company land and can be reached by gravel roads. Because these lakes are close to Bangor, all of them are fished fairly heavily during both the open-water and ice-fishing seasons. As you might imagine, anyone who writes a statewide guidebook on fishing is apt to be more fond of, and familiar with, some areas than others. That said, these lakes are among my personal favorites, primarily because they are close to my home. In addition, I have seen a number of hefty salmon taken from them. In order to sustain quality fisheries in waters with heavy angling pressure, special regulations must be included in a management plan. So for the past ten years, Alligator has been one of the few lakes in the state to have a one-fish, sixteen- to twenty-inch, no-kill slot limit designed to allow salmon to reach their full potential. Judging from the positive comments I have heard during the last decade, the state's management program seems to be working. Encouraged by this success, some local anglers believe even more restrictive regulations—including a "no-power" law both summer and winter—should be instituted here.

Fine salmon fishing can also be found on Big, Lewey, Crawford, Pocomoonshine, and Spednick Lakes. But regional biologist Rick Jordan warned, "For the most part, these are all warmer water lakes that have large populations of bass and can be prone to cyclic fluctuations in the populations of smelts and the quality of the salmon fishing." Jordan also noted that brown trout and splake are doing well in waters such as Upper Lead Mountain Pond, Great Pond, and Mopang Lake that in the past provided only marginal habitat for salmon. Because this region has quite a few lakes and ponds like these, he thinks that the stocking of brown trout and splake is likely to increase in the future.

Grand Lake Stream

Grand Lake Stream is a three-mile ribbon of gin-clear water that flows from the dam at the outlet of West Grand Lake. This well-known fly-fishing-only stream has

An ice shack on a down east lake is a good place to introduce kids to fishing.

provided fine salmon fishing for generations of down-easters. Because of its small size, Grand Lake Stream isn't capable of sustaining a resident population of large salmon—all of the big fish caught here have spent the majority of their lives feeding on baitfish in the neighboring lakes. Like salmon taken in many popular Maine rivers, fish here are seasonal migrants caught when they move into the stream to feed on smelts and aquatic insects in the spring, and when they arrive again to spawn in the fall. What makes Grand Lake Stream special is the size of the watershed from which it draws fish and the sheer numbers of salmon that congregate in some of its pools.

The fishing season for most Maine waters opens on April 1, and the big pool below the dam on West Grand Lake is one of the most reliable places in the state to catch an opening-day salmon. During winter, many of the fish that spawn in the fall work their way upstream toward the fish ladder at the base of the dam. Thus, in early April this deep pool can be jammed with hungry salmon willing to strike at a passing fly. Traditional streamers like the Gray Ghost and Black Ghost are usually all you need to catch fish here, but nymphs and wet flies can also be deadly. Don't expect football-fat salmon—as a result of their spawning ordeal, most are still thin and lack the fight they will have in a couple of months. Nevertheless, after a long winter of tying flies and studying maps, this is a great spot to get the feel of a fish on your line.

My favorite time to fish Grand Lake Stream is the period from around Mother's Day through mid-June. A reliable hatch of Hendrickson's is followed by a variety of caddisflies; impressive numbers of salmon can often be taken on small, dead-drifted nymphs and dry flies. The quality of spring fishing here is influenced by how much water was released from the dam earlier in the season. In dry years—that is, when the outflow from West Grand Lake is low in March and April—fewer salmon enter the river than in years when the gates are wide open. Thus, even though a dynamite hatch is coming off, there might not be many fish around to take advan-

Big Falls is a popular angling location on Grand Lake Stream.

tage of it. Conversely, in years when early high-water attracts salmon, you can usually do well even when no fish are rising.

Because Grand Lake Stream is rather small, there are times when some of the pools become crowded and the salmon get spooky. Most of the fishing pressure is concentrated in obvious places like Dam Pool, Hatchery Pool, and the picnic area at Little Falls and can be avoided by staying away from these popular spots. Since the stream is only a few miles long, when the fish are in they are likely to be found almost anywhere. On those days when a lot of anglers are working the stream, I often fish the smaller pockets and riffles that can be reached from the footpath that follows along the east side of the river.

Baitfish-imitating streamers like the Gray Ghost and Nine-Three account for many of the salmon taken during the first month or so of the season. After that, more fish are caught on nymphs such as the Hare's Ear, Tellico, Sparkle Caddis, and Brown Stonefly. Dry flies and emergers also produce well when insects are active; evenings in June are particularly good for small flies on

light tippets. In the fall, anglers often switch back to streamers and favor bright patterns like the Golden Demon, Montreal Whore, and Pink Lady. I find that nymphs also work well at this time of year.

Down East Smallmouth Bass

Most of Maine's freshwater angling traditions developed around venturing to remote bodies of water to fly-fish for brook trout and salmon. As a result, for years the state's fabulous smallmouth bass fishing was largely ignored. Bass were considered a prized game fish in most other areas of the country, however, and well-known outdoor writers like Al McClane and Joe Brooks, traveled down east to fish for smallmouths and to collect story material. I still remember an *Outdoor Life* article from the 1960s that listed the top one hundred smallmouth bass lakes in the country. The piece has stuck in my memory for so long because the first five choices were within a twenty-mile radius of Grand Lake Stream. Local guides and sporting camp owners eventually came to appreciate this fantastic resource and began to promote the reliable, season-long action that these hard-fighting bronzebacks provided. As a result, the reputation of down east bass fishing has grown tremendously, and today a trip to this area is on the wish list of anglers throughout the country.

Because there are dozens of waters in this region that provide excellent bass fishing, biologist Ron Brokaw suggests that anglers choose their lake based on the number and size of fish that they hope to catch. On the eastern end of the down east region, lakes like Meddybemps, Cathance, and Baskahegan offer a chance to land large numbers of bass up to fourteen inches long. On the region's west side, Graham, Phillips, Eskutasis, and Madagascal Lakes also provide fast action for mostly small fish. Anglers interested in larger bass that average around two pounds will find good fishing in Crawford, Pocomoonshine, Gardner, Hadley, Wabash, and Big

Boston Red Sox, Hall-of-Fame, left fielder Ted Williams was a big fan of down east smallmouths.

Bangor and Aroostook Railroad

Lakes. Third and Fourth Machais, Silver Pug, Wabassus, Webb, and Abrams Lakes are managed as trophy waters and can produce smallmouths that weigh over four pounds.

Although better known for their coldwater fisheries, East and West Grand Lakes and adjoining waters like Scraggly, Sysladobsis, Junior, and Spednick Lakes provide exciting smallmouth bass fishing. *North American Fishermen* magazine called East Grand, "the best bronzeback lake in the U.S." And members of the Grand Lake Stream Sporting Camp and Guides Association told me that smallmouth bass now generate more income for the community than salmon, trout, and togue fishing combined. Top-notch flowing-water bass fishing is also available in the St. Croix River between Vanceboro and Calais and on the lower end of Baskahegan Stream.

My favorite time to fish these waters is during the

Dale Wheaton

Casting surface poppers to the shoreline is a productive way to catch spawning down east smallmouths.

smallmouth's spawning period in June. Males defend nests in shallow water and will attack almost anything that moves into their territory. At this time of year, Sluggos, Rapalas, assorted jigs, and crankbaits will all produce aggressive strikes. Because these ornery smallmouths are willing to hit floating Deerhair or Cork-bodied Popping Bugs, many anglers also fly-fish when the wind is calm. Later in the summer, bass move into deeper water and hold along the edges of drop-offs and other shoreline structure. Favorable water temperatures allow them to feed heavily on minnows, crayfish, leeches, and aquatic insects, so catch rates remain good throughout this period. Historical records from Wheaton's Lodge show that more trophy bass are landed in August than any other month.

The increase in bass-fishing pressure that many down east lakes have experienced has caused concern about their long-term ability to sustain quality fishing. Therefore, special regulations that increase size restrictions and reduce bag limits have been applied to the area's most vulnerable waters. The problem is that bass grow slowly in Maine and are generally easier to catch than salmonids. If anglers kill even a few large bass each time they go out, the older age-classes will soon disappear from the population. This vulnerability to fishing pressure is illustrated by a report from West Grand guides Dave Tobey and Ken Whittaker. During one afternoon's fishing, their two clients caught twenty-eight bass: twenty-seven of these fish had been previously captured and marked in a MDIF&W study. Records show that fisheries personnel fished this remote two-mile section of shore-

Most down east beaver flowages and dead waters hold native brook trout.

line five times and applied tags to the seventy bass they caught. This means that in one afternoon, Tobey and Whittaker's two sports were able to catch nearly 40 percent of the marked bass present in the area.

Down East Brook Trout

The down east region is one of the few places in Maine whose bass lakes are better known than its trout ponds. Indeed, the majority of waters here are more suitable for warmwater fish than for salmonids, and most guides and sporting camps seriously promote bass fishing. Of course, that does not mean trout fishing isn't available in this area. Each spring, anglers catch brookies on the west side of the region in places such as Loon, Crystal, Long, Tilden, Hopkins, Simmons, and Youngs Ponds. Typically, most action is with fish around ten inches that were stocked the previous fall, but holdovers exceeding two pounds are always possible. Regional biologist Nels Cramer recently told me that he has begun to stock a couple of longer-lived strains of trout in this area, and he expects this to have a favorable impact on the percentage of larger fish that are produced. Stocked ponds such as Shattuck, Goulding, Vining, the Monroes, and Orie Lake support popular brook trout fisheries in the eastern half of the region.

My favorite way to pursue down east brookies is to spend a day on one of the area's small streams or deadwaters. Coolwater tributaries that flow into larger rivers like the Machais, Pleasant, Narraguagus, and Union are good places to explore. But any small stream can hold trout, so if you're driving a rural road that crosses a large culvert don't hesitate to get out and investigate the

Solitude can be found by down east anglers who take the time to explore the miles of remote waterways in this region.

Cheryl Tracewski

Schools of mackerel swarm along the rock-bound coast of Mount Desert Island in the summer and provide a great opportunity for shore-anglers of all ages to catch fish.

stream. It may lead to some surprisingly good fishing for native brook trout, especially if you can find a beaver dam or two along the way.

Another enjoyable way to fish slightly larger streams is to spend a day float-fishing from a canoe. Good spots close to Route 9 include New, Old, and Mopang Streams and the Crooked River. All of these waters are narrow and might require you to drag your canoe over a beaver dam or deadfall. During May and June, brightly colored trout will rise to the mayflies and caddis that hatch from these tanin-stained flows. Although a twelve-inch fish is considered a monster, each spring I try to spend a couple of days immersed in the solitude and beauty that these down east streams offer.

Acadia National Park

The majority of Acadia National Park is located on a glacier-carved slab of rock called Mount Desert Island that juts ten miles into the Atlantic Ocean. Prior to the mid-nineteenth century, this island was inhabited by a small number of people who earned a living from fishing, lumbering, farming, and shipbuilding. Around 1860, a number of wealthy artists, journalists, and sports-

men began to spend summers here and to extol to the world the virtues of this beautiful place. As a result, by the turn of the twentieth century, Bar Harbor contained more than thirty inns and hotels and had a national reputation as a summer resort.

That reputation encouraged prominent families like the Rockefellers, Morgans, Astors, and Vanderbilts to build spectacular summer "cottages" on the island. It was largely a desire to preserve the beauty and tranquility of this area that in 1916 led these people to finance the creation of the first national park east of the Mississippi. Acadia National Park originally covered roughly five thousand acres and was centered around Cadillac Mountain and the Beehive on the northeast end of the island. But over the years, the park has grown to over forty thousand acres and now includes much of the Schoodic Peninsula and Isle Au Haut. Along with one hundred twenty miles of hiking trails, Acadia also contains fifty-five miles of crushed-stone carriage paths constructed by John D. Rockefeller Jr. between 1915 and 1933. Originally built as tracks on which Rockefeller's family and friends could ride horses, today these paths are enjoyed by cyclists, hikers, cross-country skiers and fishermen.

Brook trout are the most sought after species in Acadia National Park. Witch Hole, Halfmoon, and the Breakneck Ponds are well-stocked and easily accessible from the carriage paths out of Bar Harbor. Regional biologist Greg Burr grew up on Mount Desert Island and told me that despite the pressure from summer visitors, these ponds produce plenty of twelve-inch trout and a surprising number of larger fish. Upper and Lower Hadlock are two productive ponds found along Route 3 near Northeast Harbor. Over the years, I have taken a number of chunky brookies and browns from the Hadlocks.

Stocked salmon and naturally reproducing populations of togue are present in Eagle Lake, Echo Lake, and Jordon Pond. Because of their fondness for cold water, most of these fish have left the shallows by the time the shorebound summer anglers arrive. As a result, most salmon and togue are taken by locals who either fish for them through the ice or use lead-core line to work deep water during the summer months.

The best opportunity for summer visitors to get into fast action is provided by the large schools of mackerel that inhabit the waters around Mount Desert Island from June through September. These fish range from ten-inch "tinkers" to horse mackerel that weigh nearly three pounds. Mackerel are voracious eaters that will attack almost any small metal spoon or lure cast in their direction. They are also fond of cut bait and small, white marabou streamers and provide great sport on light tackle. Mackerel are ideally suited for visitors to Acadia National Park because they can be caught from shore. The municipal piers in Northeast, Southwest, and Bar Harbors are convenient places to fish. Other possibilities include the ledges on the north side of Somes Sound that are accessible off Sargent Drive and the Schoodic Peninsula's rockbound coast out of Winter Harbor. To maximize success, you should keep in mind that mackerel are schooling fish most often within casting range of shore around high tide.

Penobscot River Drainage

The lower Penobscot has a number of pools that are best fished from a canoe.

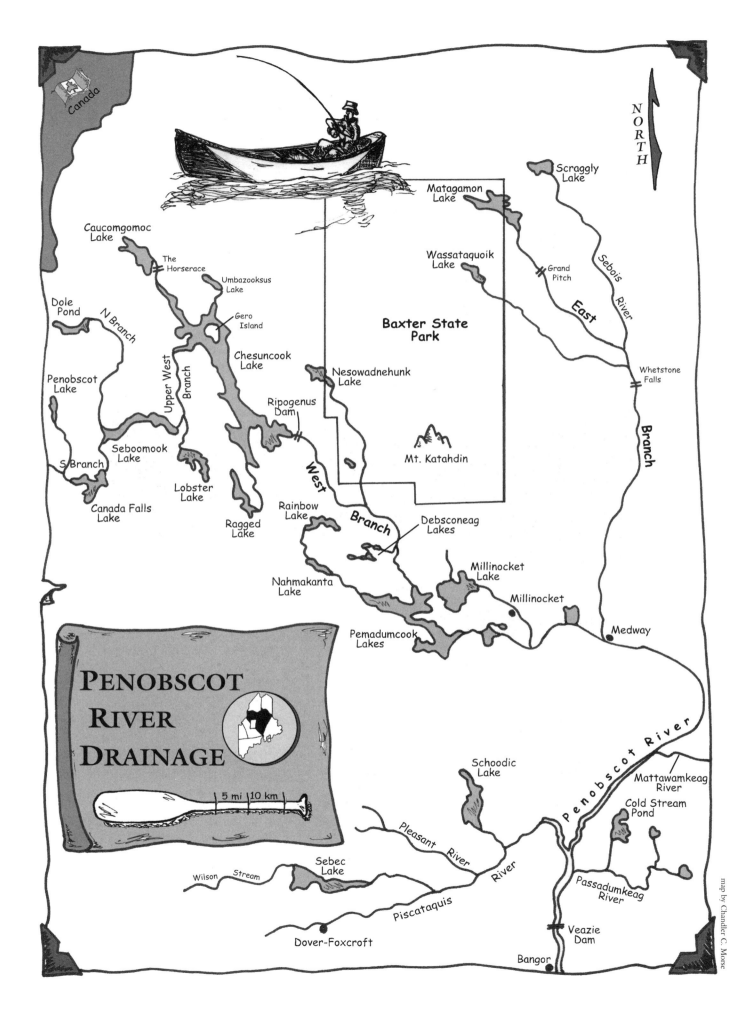

Canada

NORTH

Scraggly
Lake

Caucomgomoc
Lake

Matagamon
Lake

The Horserace

Wassataquoik
Lake

Grand
Pitch

Sebois
River

Umbazooksus
Lake

East

Dole
Pond

N Branch

Gero
Island

Chesuncook
Lake

Baxter State
Park

Whetstone
Falls

Penobscot
Lake

Upper West Branch

Ripogenus
Dam

Nesowadnehunk
Lake

Branch

Seboomook
Lake

S Branch

Lobster
Lake

West

Mt. Katahdin

Canada Falls
Lake

Ragged
Lake

Rainbow
Lake

Branch

Debsconeag
Lakes

Millinocket
Lake

Nahmakanta
Lake

Millinocket

Medway

Pemadumcook
Lakes

PENOBSCOT
RIVER
DRAINAGE

5 mi 10 km

Schoodic
Lake

Penobscot River

Mattawamkeag
River

Cold Stream
Pond

Pleasant River

River

Passadumkeag
River

Wilson   Stream

Sebec
Lake

Piscataquis

Veazie
Dam

Dover-Foxcroft

Bangor

map by Chandler C. Morse

Wiggie Robinson

illustration by Sandra Nesterode-Hale

WIGGIE ROBINSON is a fascinating person who probably knows more about the Penobscot region than anyone else alive in the early years of the twenty-first century. He has guided locally since 1951, and he has written a regular column called "Katahdin Country" for over twenty-five years. Wiggie has held a number of statewide positions in the Department of Inland Fisheries and Wildlife, including chairman of the Advisory Council. He has been an examiner on the Guide Certification Board and a cohost of a popular radio show called *Maine Outdoors*. Wiggie is also involved on the national scene and has received a number of awards, including the 1999 Outdoor Writers Association of America Jackie Pfeiffer Memorial Award for generosity and kindness.

Wiggie is undoubtedly the most well-known and respected guide in the Penobscot Valley. He is an accomplished naturalist who has frequently been referred to as a "walking encyclopedia" of the Maine outdoors. Over the years, he has been the subject of several television shows and has had a number of book chapters and magazine articles written about him. People sometimes wonder how a person who was the seventh of twelve children in a Millinocket working family, and who spent over thirty years in the paper mills before retiring in 1980, got to be so popular. The fact is, Wiggie himself often wonders about this.

To me the answer is simple; the man has charisma, which the dictionary defines as "magnetic charm or personal magic." After spending a short time with Wiggie, it's easy to see why people are drawn to him. He has boundless enthusiasm and a captivating way of describing his various exploits afield. He is also a curious person who often asks more questions than he answers and shows a genuine interest in everyone he meets. Probably the most important reason for Wiggie's long-standing popularity stems from this reputation as a straight shooter who is not afraid to stick with his views, even when they might run contrary to prevailing opinions.

Wiggie turned eighty years old in May 2002, yet on the day I visited, he had already been planting pole beans in his garden for three hours before I showed up. After eating lunch and spending a few hours on his front porch talking, we headed off to fish the evening hatch. Wiggie took me to one of his many secret ponds, and I was fortunate enough to catch a fat, fifteen-inch brook trout on a dry fly. Any other time, that beautiful fish would have been the highlight of my day. However, having an opportunity to spend time fishing with Wiggie was a pleasure that even the largest trout in the pond couldn't top.

From its headwaters in the vast timberlands of north-central Maine, the Penobscot River flows nearly two hundred miles before reaching tidewater in Bangor. Along its course, the river collects more than a half-dozen major tributaries and passes through some of the most rugged territory in the state. Because of its length, the Penobscot is a river of contrasts, both in its character—which ranges from brawling whitewater to dam-impounded lakes—and in the opportunities it provides for fishermen.

The West and East Branches of the Penobscot River join at Medway. The West branch is a large river that produces some very big fish. Landlocked salmon are most common, but brook trout are also available, especially in the waters below Seboomook Dam. The East Branch is a much smaller river with an abundance of scenic pitches and waterfalls. Good fishing for brook trout and salmon exists from Matagamon to Grand Falls. Smallmouth bass increase in numbers as you move downriver toward Medway. Road access to many prime fishing spots on both the West and East branches is good, but aside from the town of Millinocket and a few small stores at Abol Bridge, Northeast Carry, and Matagamon no services are available. The lower Penobscot River—often referred to as the mainstem—is about seventy miles long and flows from Medway to Bangor through a moderately populated valley. Access to the water is good, and full services are available in several towns. The river is wide, fairly flat, and has numerous islands that provide some of the best smallmouth bass fishing in New England.

The Penobscot River has a huge watershed that covers an area roughly the size of Vermont. It includes more than a dozen large lakes that provide water storage for the river system and the habitat base for important fisheries. Chesuncook is the drainage's largest lake and stretches nearly twenty miles from Ripogenus Dam to Chesuncook Village. Matagamon, Lobster, Nesowadnehunk, Caucomgomoc, Scraggly, and the Pemadumcook Chain are other lakes in the drainage that warrant the attention of anglers. The Penobscot River watershed also has dozens of productive trout ponds, which are primarily located in the Nahmakanta Reserve, Baxter State Park, and the Penobscot Lake area.

History

The Penobscot has been a working river for nearly two hundred years. The first lumbering venture began in 1828 near the present-day town of East Millinocket,

A log boom on the Penobscot River near Howland, Maine, around 1910.

and within twenty-five years more than a dozen log-driving companies had set up operations along the river. Small dams to control the flow of water were constructed on most tributaries, and booms to sort and store logs were built on many lakes and slow-moving sections of the river. By the 1870s, more than two hundred fifty sawmills were operating on the lower Penobscot and its tributaries. For about fifteen years following the end of the Civil War, Bangor was the lumber capital of the world.

By 1900 much of the area's prime white pine and spruce had been harvested. Sawmills were soon replaced by pulpmills, and workers from companies like Great Northern Paper created several large milltowns from Millinocket to Bucksport. Papermaking needed a year-round supply of water to transport logs and generate electricity, and the process placed a different set of demands on the river than those imposed by the lumber industry. To accommodate these needs, Great Northern Paper constructed a number of large dams, many of which remain in operation. These dams had a significant impact on the landscape and transformed the Penobscot from a river that responded dramatically to snowmelt and rainfall into one with a much more constant flow.

For more than a century, almost all of the area's logs were transported to the mills by water. Because of its central location and its physical features, Chesuncook Lake (in the Abnaki language Chesuncook means "place where many streams empty") served as an important hub for log-driving operations. The first permanent settlement was established on the northwest end of the lake in 1849. This outpost became known as Chesuncook village, and by 1885 it contained more than six hundred people and thirty dwellings. It also served as the base for the tugboats and steamers that hauled massive rafts of logs to the sluiceway at the foot of the lake. Shortly after World War II, road construction took place throughout this region, and log drivers were slowly replaced by truck drivers. The last log drive on the Penobscot occurred in 1971. Since then, the paper companies have built hundreds of miles of roads that have significantly changed the character of this area.

Fisheries on the Penobscot have also changed dramatically over the years. Prior to the construction of dams, shad and alewives could be captured nearly one

Around 1900, this ship on the lower Penobscot River was being loaded with lumber.

Horses played an important role in logging in the Penobscot region until the 1950s.

Horace Chapman presents the presidential salmon to Herbert Hoover in 1931.

hundred fifty miles from the sea and represented the most important fisheries on the river. Numerous historical accounts, like the following by Patrick Ford, attest to the abundance of these fishes. Ford wrote, "One seine haul on the lower river in May 1827 took 7000 shad and 100 barrels of alewives. And on a recent trip to the Pleasant River [near Brownville], alewives were observed crowding up to spawn in such abundance that they filled the river from shore to shore."

Prior to industrialization, an annual run of around sixty thousand Atlantic salmon also ascended the Penobscot. Most of these migrants were fish over ten pounds, and they traveled upstream as far as Ripogenus Falls. The dramatic impact that the construction of dams had on adult salmon is well documented. The introduction of pickerel and smallmouth bass into the river—lumber camp operators introduced them as a food fish in the mid-1800s—proved equally devastating to juvenile salmon. This is reflected by an 1867 Fisheries Commission report that states, "These [pickerel and bass] are the most ruthless destroyers among all fresh water fishes and their advent in salmon waters is a great misfortune." Commercial harvest records show that following these human interventions, the annual catch of Atlantic salmon dropped from over twenty thousand fish prior to 1865, to less than fifty salmon in 1947, the last year that commercial fishing was legal.

Sport-fishing on the Penobscot River is closely tied to the Atlantic salmon and began in June 1886 when lumber baron Fred W. Ayer landed a twenty-four-pound fish below the Bangor Waterworks Dam. Keen interest in Atlantic salmon fishing quickly developed, and by the turn of the twentieth century the Bangor Salmon Pool had become a renowned angling destination. This tidewater pool was productive because the dam impeded the upstream migration of salmon. Predictably, this dense concentration of fish attracted a large number of anglers. To alleviate crowding, a rule was passed that allowed only members of the prestigious Penobscot Salmon Club to fish in this pool. Soon, a rivalry to catch the first salmon of the season developed between some of the area's most well-to-do citizens. For a number of years, this first fish was sent to a prominent national figure such as Andrew Carnegie or auctioned to a local restaurant.

In 1912, Bangor-area boatbuilder Karl Anderson caught the season's first salmon and decided it would be "fitting and proper" to have it shipped directly to President William Howard Taft in Washington. This began a "presidential salmon" tradition that lasted more than fifty seasons and put a fresh Penobscot River salmon on the plates of ten different presidents. Bangor-area suasage-maker Adolph Fischer holds the record for catching the most (six) presidential salmon. During his twelve years in the White House, Franklin D. Roosevelt received the most fish. This grand tradition was discontinued in 1995 when the Bangor Dam was removed from the river.

Penobscot River

The Penobscot River offers top-quality fishing for landlocked salmon, brook trout, and smallmouth bass. Each of these species occupies a different habitat, so anglers must decide which fish they want to pursue before visiting a section of river. Probably the best way to get a handle on the Penobscot River as an angling destination is to visualize it as four separate bodies of water—headwaters, West Branch, East Branch, and mainstem—each of which has its own physical characteristics and fisheries.

Headwaters Penobscot River

The headwaters of the Penobscot River consist of the North Branch, which arises from Dole Brook and several other small tributaries near Big Bog, and the South Branch, which drains a series of small deadwaters along Maine's mountainous western border near Jackman. Both of these remote streams flow for about twenty miles before joining in a broad bay at the head of Seboomook Lake. Road access to these waters is good, and nice campsites are located along both branches. During the early 1900s, the Great Northern Paper Company built Pittston Farm, an outpost along the lower South Branch that provided food, lodging, and supplies to its employees. This site was recently restored and now features an inn, restaurant, and campground that are popular with anglers traveling in this remote region.

The North and South Branches offer good brook trout fishing, but typically these rivers hold significant numbers of trout only from mid-May until the end of June. During this prime period, pan-sized trout can be taken from a number of pools within easy walking distance of roadside access points. Due to the influence of Canada Falls Lake—a large, man-made water storage area on the South Branch—fish tend to run larger in this river. Most fishermen focus their attention on the three miles of swift water below the outlet of Canada Falls Lake, but over the years I have heard reports of good fish being taken above the lake. Despite its remoteness, many anglers visit this area in the spring, and

Lightweight kayaks are popular with anglers who fish remote ponds.

at certain times (like Memorial Day weekend) it can get crowded.

A number of the ponds in this area also provide excellent fly-fishing opportunities for brook trout. Duncan, Welman, and Wounded Deer Ponds in Prentiss Township, Dingley and Grenier Ponds in T4 R5, and Alder Pond in Alder Brook Township are some of the best. Pond fishing is generally at its peak during June and September, but good trout can be caught throughout the season during low-light periods or around springholes. Because it is often difficult to locate the roads and trails leading into the best waters, anglers exploring this country for the first time should consider hiring a guide or staying at one of the sporting camps that serves this area.

West Branch Penobscot River

The West Branch of the Penobscot River travels more than fifty miles in a wide arc that reaches from just beyond the north shore of Moosehead Lake to the south slopes of Mount Katahdin. In many of its best-known sections the river can be easily reached from the Golden Road. The West Branch also contains inaccessible stretches that see little angling pressure. Land-locked salmon that weigh over five pounds are present in both accessible and inaccessible areas. Because the West Branch is a large river that is divided in half by Chesuncook Lake, I will describe its upper and lower sections separately.

UPPER WEST BRANCH (SEBOOMOOK LAKE TO CHESUNCOOK LAKE). The upper West Branch begins at Seboomook Dam and flows about twenty-five miles to Chesuncook Lake. This section of the river is best known for its fall landlocked salmon fishery: soon after Labor Day fish from Chesuncook and Lobster Lakes move into the river to spawn. Fly-fishing with bright marabou streamers such as the Cardinelle or Barnes Special can be very exciting at this time of year, especially when fast, erratic retrieves are used with a floating line. Road access along the upper West Branch is poor, and roadside fishing opportunities are limited to a handful of pools within a few miles of Seboomook Dam. Many people fish this section of river from motorized canoes or small boats that they launch at the Lobster Stream or Hannibal's Crossing Bridges. This area is well-suited for an overnight trip—riverside campsites can be found from Moosehorn Stream to below Big Island. If your timing is right, the fishing in many of this area's classic pools can be outstanding. On several occasions I have caught a half-dozen three-pound salmon during an evening's fishing. However, you can also get skunked if your timing is bad and you arrive before significant numbers of fish have moved into the river.

Fishing can also be good on the upper West Branch in the spring, but because of limited access and high water few people take advantage of it. Just after ice-out, salmon follow spawning smelts into the river, and shortly thereafter brook trout show up. Early in the season, many anglers use a fly rod rigged with a sinking line to troll a Gray Ghost or Mooselook Wobbler back and forth across the strong currents. Because I prefer to anchor in specific pools and cast though, I usually wait until spring runoff has subsided before venturing here. When water temperatures are favorable, fish feed throughout the day on a variety of natural organisms; thus, along with smelt-imitating streamers, fly fishermen should bring an assortment of weighted nymphs, Muddler Minnows, crayfish, and Woolly Buggers. Mayfly and caddis hatches are common in June, so a good selection of dry flies and emergers is also useful. Surface-feeding fish can be quite elusive in the large, slick pools of the upper West Branch. Sometimes they can be so tough to catch that the late proprietor of Chesuncook Lake House, Bert McBurnie, once said "I have seen schools of two-pound trout feeding on nymphs in the spring that would make a saint curse trying to get them to take a fly."

Large, smelt-imitating streamers, like this Black Ghost, can be very effective for spring salmon.

LOWER WEST BRANCH (RIPOGENUS DAM TO MEDWAY). One of the best-known landlocked salmon fisheries in Maine is the scenic six-mile stretch of the lower West Branch that runs from Ripogenus Dam to Nesowadnehunk Deadwater. This area contains a number of famous pools like Big Eddy, Little Eddy, and Steepbank Pool that support a tremendous amount of angling activity. Studies done by biologists from Great Northern Paper Company and the MDIF&W show that more than 60 percent of the sport-fishing effort that occurs on the entire river takes place in this relatively short stretch. However, the Golden Road provides excellent access along the south bank, so despite the large number of anglers who fish here, it's fairly easy to find a pool of your own if you avoid the most popular locations.

Most anglers who frequent this area say that it's the opportunity to catch large fish in moving water that draws them. Indeed, creel-census data show this stretch of river to be one of the best places in Maine to catch a salmon over four pounds. The reason salmon do so well here is linked to several of the river's physical and biological characteristics that combine to create an ideal environment. It begins with the West Branch itself, which is much larger and deeper than most other landlocked-salmon rivers in the state. A steady supply of cold, well-oxygenated water discharged from the bottom of Ripogenus Dam allows salmon to remain active year-round. It is the tremendous food supply, though, that causes fish to grow so quickly. Stoneflies, mayflies, and caddisflies occur in tremendous numbers and are crucial for the development of juvenile salmon. But according to Ed Spear, a biologist from Great Northern Paper Company who has worked on the river for over twenty-five years, "The thing that really sets this section of the West Branch apart and allows fish to grow so large, is the smelts that are available to them." One study done during 1981 and 1982, estimated that more than twenty-eight thousand pounds of these baitfish are passed through the turbines at Ripogenus Dam's McKay Station each year. Another study, conducted in 1986, indicated that more than twenty thousand pounds of smelts were discharged into the river between March and December.

As anglers might expect, smelt-imitating flies such as the Gray Ghost, Supervisor, and Joe's Smelt are quite popular on the river. Because many of the smelts that pass through the turbines are injured or killed, I find quill flies and other floating patterns to be extremely effective. Spin fishermen do well with Rapalas and baitfish-imitating spoons such as Swedish Pimples and Flash Kings.

With all the baitfish that are available to salmon, many anglers are surprised to learn that insects play a major role in their diet. But according to Kendall

Warner, a fisheries biologist who has worked on the Penobscot since the late 1960s, "When a significant hatch is occurring, large fish often become extremely selective and gorge themselves exclusively on that particular insect species." This is a well-known fact among West Branch regulars, and once insects become active around the end of May, flies like the Hendrickson, West Branch Caddis, and Pheasant-Tail Nymph probably account for more large salmon than any other patterns used on the river.

Below Nesowadnehunk Deadwater, the river flows for ten miles before reaching Ambajejus Lake. Despite containing a bit more flatwater than the section below Ripogenus Dam, this area supports significant populations of landlocked salmon and brook trout. Popular fishing locations include Nesowadnehunk and Pockwockamus and Debsconeag Falls, Wheelbarrow and Hopkins Pitches, and the mouths of Nesowadnehunk and Katahdin Streams. Since this section of river is farther removed from the icy tailwaters of Ripogenus Dam, by early July it has usually warmed enough to force salmon—and anglers who pursue them—to move upstream. Therefore, despite good access and decent fish populations, angling pressure and the rod-catch are usually much lower in this part of the river.

From the outlet of Elbow Lake to Medway, the lowermost ten miles of the West Branch supports five dams and two large papermills. Water quality here isn't bad, though, and a few salmon can be taken in the quickwater below the dams. Angling pressure is usually light along this section of the river.

SEASONAL CALENDAR OF THE WEST BRANCH. The West Branch of the Penobscot is one of the few rivers in Maine where you have an honest chance to catch a trophy landlocked salmon on any day of the fishing season. Location and feeding habits vary dramatically during this six-month period, so it is important for

anglers to be attuned to the salmon's seasonal patterns of movement and activity.

One of the most popular early season fishing destinations in northern Maine is Nesowadnehunk Deadwater. I have been at the "Deadwater" on opening day and watched as several dozen boats were dragged over snowbanks so anglers could get to the water and troll in a blizzard. The near-fanatical attractiveness of this spot focuses on the large landlocked salmon that spawn in the West Branch during the fall, then migrate here to spend the winter. Each year, a number of trophy fish are caught in April. Trolling with smelt-imitating lures or streamer flies is the method of choice for most anglers, and places where the river narrows and the current picks up—like Salmon Point or the head and tail of the deadwater—seem to produce the most fish.

Fishable numbers of early season salmon can be found in many other places in the lower West Branch. From April through late May, I fish most long, flat pools from Big Eddy down to the "Boomhouse" at the mouth of Ambajejus Lake. At this time of year I usually fish streamer flies and Rapalas using a very effective "troll up and drift back" technique that was shown to me by longtime Medway resident and Maine Guide Kevin Borello. Since the pools that are far-removed from Ripogenus Dam provide a narrow window for opportunity and are at their best at this time of year, I concentrate my early season efforts here.

Insects usually become active around Memorial Day, and Hendrickson's provide the first reliable hatch of the season. Dry-fly fishing usually remains good until at least the middle of July. Caddisflies are the most prevalent insects on the water throughout the majority of the season. Traditional imitations like the Elkhair Caddis can be effective in assorted sizes and colors, but emergers and pupae or local patterns like the West Branch Caddis often do better. Pheasant-Tail Nymphs, small Hare's Ear Nymphs, or impressionistic wet flies

Nesowadnehunk Falls is one of the many scenic spots available to fly fishermen working the West Branch of the Penobscot River.

Dennis Welsh

106

tied with soft, webby feathers are sometimes more effective than flies fished on the surface. Bigger fish in popular pools have seen lots of flies and can get fairly selective, so light tippets and good presentations are required to consistently fool them.

Hatches become sporadic in August, and long hot spells greatly reduce aquatic activity during most of the day. However, salmonids are attracted to the cold water discharged from the bottom of Ripogenus Dam, and the upriver pools from Big Eddy to McKay Station are often jammed with salmon. Fishing is usually best from just before sunset until around 10:00 PM. At this time of year, fishing small flies (Nos. 16 to 22) at the tail-outs of large pools is often the best method for catching quality fish.

The best September fishing on the West Branch also takes place in proximity to Ripogenus Dam. However, salmon are more dispersed when water temperatures drop and the spawning urge kicks in, so pools as far down as The Horserace provide good action. Because fall is the most difficult time of year for me to consistently catch fish in the West Branch, I alternate

between bright, attractor-type streamers—to draw territorial strikes from aggressive prespawning salmon—and standard nymphs and dry flies.

East Branch Penobscot River

The East Branch of the Penobscot River begins at the outlet of Matagamon Lake and travels for about forty miles before joining the West Branch near the village of Medway. The river flows through some of Maine's most scenic country with views of rugged waterfalls and the mountains of Baxter State Park. Access is along the west bank on unimproved dirt roads that begin at Matagamon Campground on the north end of the East Branch and at Whetstone Falls Bridge in the south. Although these roads veer from the river in many locations, they are rarely more than a few hundred yards from the water and often have small turnouts with well-beaten paths to the best pools.

Anglers should be wary of fishing this river in a canoe. I have read several accounts indicating that the East Branch is good for a combination canoeing and fishing trip. Although I am a fairly experienced

The upper East Branch of the Penobscot River has a number of scenic falls and pitches where brook trout can be taken.

whitewater canoeist, I would not run this river in a canoe loaded with valuable fishing gear. If you want to canoe the East Branch, wear a lifejacket and helmet. If you want to fish it, walk in from the dirt roads.

The East Branch regularly produces native brook trout between twelve and fifteen inches. Productive locations include Stair Falls, Haskell Deadwater, Grand Pitch, Spencer Rips, and the areas where major tributaries such as Lunksoos Stream and the Sebois River flow into the East Branch. Healthy populations of aquatic insects are nurtured in this river's extensive riffles, and I have had good results fishing small nymphs such as Tellicos, Zug-Bugs, Sparkle Caddis, and Brassies with a strike indicator and a floating line. March Browns, Hendricksons, Quill Gordons, and impressionistic patterns like Renegades, Irresistibles, and various Wulffs are also popular. Throughout the season, though, I find Elkhair Caddis in assorted sizes and colors hard to beat here. Slicks at the tails of large pools, just where the current begins to increase in velocity, are particularly good places to fish nymphs and dry flies. Later in the summer, many fish migrate to the river's deeper areas or congregate around cool springs and inlet brooks. Fall fishing is somewhat dependent on rainfall and water releases from the dam, but generally brook trout become active during the last few weeks in September.

Although a good-sized landlocked salmon is occasionally taken on the East Branch, fish under fourteen inches make up most of the catch. According to fisheries biologist Mike Smith, the main reason for this preponderance of short salmon is their slow growth rate due to the lack of smelts in the river. This point has been demonstrated by several studies that showed the size of three- to seven-year-old salmon in the smelt-rich West Branch to be significantly larger than similar-aged fish in the East Branch. Because of this slow growth rate and a general dissatisfaction with the quality of the salmon fishery, the MDIF&W discontinued stocking salmon in the East Branch during the mid-1990s and now manages the river primarily for native brook trout.

Mainstem Penobscot River

The mainstem of the Penobscot River begins at the confluence of the East and West Branches in the village of Medway. On its seventy-mile journey to tidewater in Bangor, the river widens and braids among scenic islands and offers excellent smallmouth bass fishing. On an average summer day, an angler can usually land more than a dozen bass between one and three pounds without much trouble.

Smallmouths can be caught in the mainstem of the Penobscot River from mid-April through October. However, because of cold water temperatures and heavy spring runoff, fishing doesn't peak until the bass move onto their spawning beds in June. At this time of year, Deerhair and Cork-Bodied Popping Bugs cast tight to the bank and chugged through the shallows can draw smashing surface strikes from bass defending territories. After spawning, these river smallmouths move into slightly deeper water and establish feeding lanes along the edges of weedbeds or around islands. Soft rubber baits, like Sluggo and Banjo Minnow, fished with an erratic retrieve seem almost irresistible to these bass when their metabolism is high and they are in the feeding mode.

The lower Penobscot River is a topnotch smallmouth bass fishery where anglers of all ages can enjoy a day on the water.

Although the mainstem of the Penobscot can be successfully fished from the bank in a few places—Winn Rips and the dams in Mattaseunk and West Enfield— the best way to experience the fishing and natural beauty of this river is to float it in a small boat or canoe. Paved roads run along both banks and lead to more than fifteen launch sites that offer anglers a variety of float trips ranging from a few hours to overnight. Generally, most of the faster water is located above Lincoln, but small sets of rips can be encountered throughout, so floaters should keep an eye on the water at all times. Despite its proximity to Bangor and several small towns, the mainstem of the Penobscot

The pool below Lowe's Covered Bridge on the Piscataquis River near Guilford is stocked with trout in the spring and is a popular spot for anglers to stop and make a few casts while traveling along Route 15.

is a remarkably uncrowded and peaceful place that provides opportunities to see wildlife such as otters, bald eagles, and deer without traveling too far from home.

Mainstem Tributaries. The Piscataquis, Passadumkeag, and Mattawamkeag are three large rivers that flow into the mainstem of the Penobscot below Medway. From Abbot Village to Dover-Foxcroft the Piscataquis River is heavily stocked with brookies and brown trout and provides a convenient roadside fishery for locals as well as for people traveling on Route 15 to Moosehead Lake. Fishing is best in the spring and fall, but trout can be taken near springs and around the mouths of cold brooks all summer. A good population of small native brook trout is present in the upper section of river above Blanchard.

A few early season salmon are usually caught in the upper Passadumkeag watershed around Grand Falls and in Nicatous Stream. Brook trout fishing can be good in the upper deadwaters and in tributaries such as Lord

Brook. The lower Mattawamkeag River is best known for its smallmouth bass fishing, but each year a few brook trout are taken near Gordon Falls and in tributaries like Gordon Brook and Mattagodus Stream.

Atlantic Salmon and the Penobscot River

Atlantic salmon fishing on the Penobscot River has gone through a dramatic series of ups-and-downs over the past century. One hundred years ago the salmon fishing was first-class; indeed, each spring well-to-do anglers traveled long distances to fish the Bangor Pool. During the first half of the twentieth century, dam construction and industrial pollution had a devastating effect on the Penobscot—by the late 1950s Atlantic salmon were nearly extinct in the river. After the passage of the 1972 Clean Water Act water quality improved dramatically, and during the late 1970s both Atlantic salmon and fishermen returned to the river *en masse*. Interest in salmon fishing on the Penobscot boomed throughout the 1980s and early 1990s. Then a succession of years with disappointing returns forced the Maine Atlantic Salmon Commission to close salmon fishing (in 1999) on the Penobscot River.

From 1993 to 1999, disappointing returns of Atlantic salmon occurred in rivers throughout Maine and the Canadian Maritime Provinces. This suggests that nothing inherent to the Penobscot is causing the problem. In fact, the river itself is in better shape now than it has been for nearly one hundred years. Many biologists think the decline of Atlantic salmon is related to problems with their food supply or to a change in open-ocean currents.

Because the number of Atlantic salmon pools on the Penobscot River is limited, a rotation system is used to provide everyone with an opportunity to fish.

Atlantic salmon stocks became so low in all Maine rivers that in November 2000 the U.S. Fish and Wildlife Service and the National Marine Fisheries Service

placed Maine's wild Atlantic salmon on the federal endangered species list. According to U.S. Fish and Wildlife Service director Jamie Rappaport Clark, "Less than 10 percent of the fish needed for the long-term survival of wild Atlantic salmon are returning to Maine rivers. Without the protection and recovery programs afforded by the Endangered Species Act, chances are this population will die out completely." As of January 2004, Maine Atlantic salmon were still listed as endangered; thus, salmon fishing in the Penobscot—and all other Maine Rivers—remains closed. But progress is being made: a number of scientists at the Craig Brook National Fish Hatchery in Orland and the University of Maine are cautiously optimistic that in the near future the Penob-

Opening-day catch of Atlantic salmon at the Bangor Salmon Pool in 1933.

scot River may reopen for catch-and-release Atlantic salmon fishing. In anticipation of that day, I have included the following information on Atlantic salmon.

The majority of Atlantic salmon fishing on the Penobscot occurs within a ten-minute drive from downtown Bangor along a two-mile stretch of river located directly below the Veazie Dam.

This easy access combined with the river's proximity to multitudes of Atlantic-salmon-starved anglers from the entire East Coast makes this stretch of the Penobscot an attractive destination for fly fishermen. Two additional factors contribute to this area's popularity: Atlantic salmon fishing in the Penobscot is considerably less expensive than in most Canadian rivers, and all of the river's pools are public. Fishing on this section of the Penobscot is governed by a fairly strict rotation system that allows each angler a prescribed amount of time in a pool; thus, crowding isn't as big a problem as you might expect.

The rotation system dictates that upon arrival at the river, you place your rod in a streamside rack behind the rods of anglers who were there before you. When someone completes a rotation, the first person in line starts fishing at the head of the pool, and all rods in the rack are shifted down one position. Most pools accommodate from two to six people, and protocol dictates that anglers take one step downstream after each cast. Of course, when a salmon swirls directly behind your fly without getting hooked—and you are reluctant to take that required step—most of your fellow fishermen won't mind if you pause for an extra cast or two. Some people, however, habitually move at a snail's pace. I once heard longtime *Bangor Daily News* outdoor columnist Bud Leavitt tell a particularly deliberate angler, "When guys sitting on the bench begin to throw rocks at you [which occurs now and then], it's time to start moving a little faster."

Two of the most popular Atlantic salmon fishing locations on the Penobscot River are Wringer and Eddington Pools. The Wringer is located on the west shore just upstream from the Pipeline Pool and is usually most productive in moderate to low water. The majority of salmon are taken from the ledge on the Wringer's upper end and from the fast-moving water near the tailout. Eddington Pool is found on the river's east shore directly below Veazie Dam and holds fish throughout its one-hundred-fifty-yard length. Both of these pools can be fished effectively with a floating line by wading or from a small boat or canoe. That said, anglers quickly learn that the techniques and the assort-

ment of flies used to catch Atlantic salmon are as varied as the people who favor them.

One of the most successful Atlantic salmon fishermen on the Penobscot during the 1980s and 1990s was Claude Westfall, a retired professor from the University of Maine. During those years, I spent many days watching him hook one fish after another from his Grand Lake canoe, while no one else on the river was catching anything. A few years ago while describing his philosophy on Atlantic salmon fishing in an interview for a book on the restoration of the Penobscot, Westfall said, "When I first started salmon fishing, like most people, I carried all kinds of different flies. But over the years, there are six fly patterns that I originated for the Penobscot: the Wringer, CZ Special, Foxfire, Pink Onyx, Penobscot Devil, and the Green and Mean. Now I fish with these flies exclusively, because I have been successful, and because like most fishermen, I enjoy taking salmon on flies I have tied myself. People kid me because when I open a fly box, all that might be in it are Wringers in different sizes. But I believe in sticking to a few good patterns that I have confidence in."

Would-be salmon fishermen should note the importance that such an accomplished angler as Claude places in the nontechnical, intangible aspects of fishing—aspects such as confidence and attitude. In that same book-related interview, he responded to another question about his success by saying, "When people ask why some individuals are successful Atlantic salmon fishermen and others aren't, I tell them about my three C's. (1) Covering the water. You watch some [unsuccessful] people go through a pool and they cast one length of line without really changing the line speed or presenting the fly in a different manner. (2) Consistency. You cannot fish for barely an hour and expect to always hook a salmon. You have to stick with it and not give up. (3) Confidence. This is the most important factor of all. I do not know any individual who is engaged in any kind of activity or work who will do well if they do not have confidence in their performance. When I cast a fly, I always expect to catch a salmon."

Lakes in the Penobscot River Drainage

The Penobscot watershed contains more than fifteen large lakes that offer good fishing for landlocked salmon, togue, and brook trout. I will provide in-depth descriptions for the watershed's three most popular lakes: Lobster, Chesuncook, and Matagamon. I will discuss the remaining lakes collectively under three general headings: pristine lakes, developed lakes, and water storage impoundments.

Lobster Lake

Lobster is a remote, crescent-shaped lake that is managed as a trophy landlocked salmon and togue fishery. Located in an isolated basin several miles south of Hannibal's Crossing, the lake is most commonly reached either by boating up Lobster Stream from a secluded launch site near the West Branch of the Penobscot River or by flying in from Greenville. Beautiful campsites with sand beaches and great views of the surrounding mountains provide a fitting complement to the fishing and make the effort to get here worthwhile.

Maine Department of Inland Fisheries and Wildlife statistics indicate that fishing on Lobster Lake can be fairly slow, but when fish are caught, they are often large. A Maine Department of Conservation ranger, Barry Welch, who has lived on the lake for many years has confirmed the presence of trophy salmon and tells me tales of oversized fish nearly every time I see him.

The lake's trophy potential is reflected in its management plan, which includes a no-stocking regulation and a one-fish limit. Currently, the minimum length limit is twenty-three inches for togue and twenty inches for salmon. To prevent the introduction of undesirable species, live fish can't be used as bait in Lobster Lake.

Chesuncook Lake

Chesuncook is comprised of three separate lake basins that were joined when water levels rose after the construction of Ripogenus Dam. Some people still refer to Ripogenus Lake (nearest the dam) and Caribou Lake (along the Golden Road) separately, but for ease of discussion, I will group them with Chesuncook itself. This impoundment is nearly twenty miles long and is the third largest body of water in the state. Despite its size, there are only a few places where the lake is visible from the road. Shoreline development is light, and the only improved boat launch can be reached by following a sign to the U.S. Forest Service Ranger Station located on the Golden Road about three miles beyond Ripo-

Fish from Chesuncook Lake move into the lower end of Ragged Stream when the water is high during spring and fall.

genus Dam. Primitive boat launches can be found near Ragged Stream and on the northeastern end of the lake at Umbazooksus Stream.

Landlocked salmon are the primary target for the majority of anglers who fish Chesuncook. Most salmon are taken from ice-out until late June by fishermen trolling streamer flies or sewn smelts near points and around drop-offs. For many years an abundant supply of smelt allowed fish to grow well and made Chesuncook one of the better lakes in Maine to catch a salmon over twenty inches. When former MDIF&W commissioner Bucky Owen was looking for a site to establish a blue-ribbon landlocked salmon fishery, Chesuncook was one of his top choices. Unfortunately, local opposition forestalled the implementation of his program, which in large part called for catch-and-release fishing. In recent years, the smelt population in the lake has declined, and this has significantly reduced the growth rate of the salmon.

Togue are another important component of the Chesuncook sport fishery. Many people focus their trolling efforts in the deep waters off Togue Ledge or north of Caribou Point. But I have taken togue in the spring while trolling Rapalas on the surface for salmon and in the fall while casting flies at Ragged Stream. Togue can also be caught on bait or while jigging during ice-fishing season. Historically, the togue population in Chesuncook has suffered tremendous losses from early winter drawdowns of the lake, which leave their eggs high and dry. Recently, the paper companies and the MDIF&W have engaged in a cooperative effort to manage water levels in a way that is more sensitive to the biological needs of these spawning fish. Occasional stocking and migration of juveniles from Lobster Lake adds to the togue fishery.

Brook trout are present in Chesuncook, but their numbers are depressed by habitat degradation in their spawning streams and by competition with white perch. However, reasonable numbers of trout are still caught each year, especially in the spring and fall around inlets such as Mud, Ripogenus, and Frost Brooks.

Matagamon Lake

Matagamon Lake is located along the northeast corner of Baxter State Park and is a large body of water comprised of two basins that were joined after the construction of a dam. Although almost all of Matagamon Lake's shoreline is undeveloped, rental cabins and a commercial campground are located at the south end of the lake near the boat launch. Native and stocked brook trout, landlocked salmon, and togue support popular spring and fall fisheries. Most people troll along the shoreline and islands of the deep lower basin. Anglers who know their way among the feeder streams and drop-offs in the upper lake find this area productive. The northwest cove where Webster Stream enters the lake is a particular hotspot in late May and early June. Many longtime Matagamon anglers feel that the salmonid fishery has suffered significantly from competition with warmwater species—perch, chubs, and suckers—which proliferate in the shallows created after water levels were raised by construction of the dam.

Pristine Lakes

The Penobscot watershed has seven other large lakes that are almost totally undeveloped. Scraggly, Harrington, and Caucomgomoc Lakes are the most accessible and can be reached by fairly good gravel roads that lead directly to their boat launches. Harrington Lake is the deepest of the three and is located just off the Telos Road about five miles north of Ripogenus Dam. Years ago, I took nice salmon from the pool at the foot of the dam, but after it was decommissioned and breached in 2000, water levels in both the lake and outlet stream have dropped. Trolling is the method of choice employed by most anglers on Harrington Lake. Scraggly is a gorgeous lake located entirely on Maine Public Reserve Land in northern Penobscot County. Fishing for salmon and brook trout tends to run either hot or cold on Scraggly, but during good years when fish are biting, the eastern basin in the vicinity of Owl's Head is usually the place to get them. Caucomgomoc Lake has traditionally produced some large, hard-fighting salmon, but recently most of the fish caught here have been under eighteen inches. This remote lake can be reached by traveling fifteen miles north of Hannibal's Crossing on the Ragmuff Road. Trolling the northwestern shore near Hubbard and Black Points is a reliable way to take salmon on Caucomgomoc Lake. During the spring and fall, the upper two-mile section of Caucomgomoc's outlet stream offers opportunities for fly fishermen to catch salmon in moving water—when water levels are ideal, fishing in Caucomgomoc Stream can be exciting. A few primitive campsites are available at the dam.

Rainbow, Nahmakanta, and the Debsconeag chain of lakes are other waters located in a remote, mountainous region southeast of Ripogenus Dam. Rainbow is the largest lake and is most commonly reached via the Appalachian Trail or by flying in from Millinocket

Caucomgomoc Stream has a number of inviting pools that hold salmon.

or Greenville. Despite the effort required to get here, Rainbow Lake is a popular destination for brook trout fishermen. Action can be fast for pan-sized fish, but trout over sixteen inches are much harder to come by. Although trolling is the method of choice for most anglers who have access to a boat, a good many trout are caught on flies and hardware cast from ledges and points, especially along the south side of the lake. Small outlying ponds—Doughnut, Bear, and the Beans, along with the Rainbow Deadwaters at the outlet of the lake—are also popular with fly fishermen.

Nahmakanta is a deep four-mile-long lake that can be accessed via floatplane or at a small, hand-carry boat launch near the outlet. Rustic sporting camps are located on the north end of the lake and many people who travel to Nahmakanta stay here. Salmon and togue are the principle targets for most anglers and are caught by trolling smelt-imitating streamer flies and lures along the lake's rocky shorelines. Healthy populations of brook trout that rise to a fly are also present. According to former camp owner Paul Nevell, "There are times in June that can be mighty exciting for fly fishermen who

are in the right place at the right time." A number of outlying but productive trout waters such as Gould and Crescent Ponds can be reached by way of trails that begin at the camps on the north end of the lake.

The Debsconeag chain of lakes consists of eight interconnected lakes and ponds that empty into the West Branch of the Penobscot River at Debsconeag Deadwater. First Debsconeag Lake is about a half-mile from the river and is best reached by boating up the outlet from the Omaha Beach access point of the Golden Road. This long, narrow lake is the most heavily fished of these waters and contains togue, brook trout, and some salmon that migrate in from the river. Second through Fifth Debsconeag are also large lakes that support brook trout and togue fisheries. Fourth Debsconeag has a set of sporting camps on its northeast shore and is the only lake in the chain that is readily accessible by road. Sixth, Seventh, and Eighth Debsconeags are small ponds that can produce some nice trout.

Penobscot Lake lies within two miles of the Quebec border and can be reached by a rough road that leads to a campsite and small boat launch. This lake is the only body of water in the Penobscot basin that contains blueback trout, an ancient relative of the arctic char that was considered extinct in Maine until the 1940s when these fish were discovered in a handful of places. Penobscot Lake contains a healthy population of brook trout, and the last time I fished there, I caught more than a dozen plump brookies on a Wood Special and small Black Ghost that I cast and trolled along the shoreline.

Developed Lakes

Sebec, Cold Stream, and Schoodic Lakes have over two hundred dwellings on their shores and are subject to significant amounts of recreational boating traffic. But good water quality, healthy populations of smelt, and regular stocking make these lakes consistent producers of quality salmon and togue. Creel-census data from the lakes indicate that due to increased fishing pressure it usually takes longer to catch a legal-sized fish here than in many of the more remote waters farther north. But over the years, I have taken bragging-sized fish from all of these lakes

Sebec Lake is of particular interest because it produces some very large togue and salmon. Fishing is usually best in the west basin around the narrows and in the area where Wilson Stream enters the lake. The Packard family has been operating sporting camps at the head of the lake since 1894. In response to a question about how the current fishing compares to the good old days, current owner Jerry Packard said, "I guess it must be pretty good because during certain weeks in the spring, we won't have any openings until somebody dies." During the summer months, Sebec Lake has a thriving smallmouth bass fishery along its rocky shorelines and in its coves.

Water Storage Impoundments

The Pemadumcook Chain is a sprawling thirty-thousand-acre waterway made up of six separate basins that were joined after a dam was built at the outlet of Elbow Lake. Many cottages and year-round homes are located on Ambajejus, North Twin, South Twin, and Elbow Lakes. Extensive undeveloped stretches of Pemadumcook, Millinocket, and Jo-Mary Lakes help to preserve the scenic beauty and wilderness character of this area, which Henry David Thoreau raved about in his nineteenth-century classic, *The Maine Woods*.

The lakes of the Pemadumcook Chain make up a classic two-story fishery that supports large numbers of white perch and pickerel in its upper layer of warm water and a thriving population of salmon in the colder water below. Trolling on Pemadumcook is usually good along the lake's rocky south shore and among the islands around Nick's Gut. Early season fishing can be good where major inlets such as Sandy and Nahmakanta Streams flow into the large lakes. The area where the West Branch of the Penobscot dumps into Ambajejus Lake provides anglers with a chance to fish moving water. Each spring, salmon congregate in this area to feast on the smelts that run up the river at ice-out. Although most fish aren't huge—they average around sixteen inches—as one local angler told me, "What the salmon here lack in size, they sure make up for in numbers." This spot is particularly dear to my heart because it is where each of my three kids caught their first salmon.

Seboomook Lake and Canada Falls Lake—located near the headwaters of the Penobscot River drainage—were created as water storage reservoirs to capture snowmelt in the spring, then slowly release the water back into the river throughout the rest of the year. During late summer and into fall, these lakes serve as a critical source of water for the entire system and are sometimes drawn down nearly to their original river channels. Seboomook and Canada Falls Lakes are shallow and do not become well stratified in the summer. The drastic fluctuations in water levels makes it difficult for salmonids to thrive here. Despite these problems, both lakes provide good spring fishing for brook trout up to seventeen inches, particularly around rocky outcroppings or in the vicinity of inlets such as Gulliver and Cunningham Brooks. Trolling lures or casting with worms and spinners are the most popular ways to fish these waters, though I have had reasonable success with

Maine Folklife Center

Henry David Thoreau paid tribute to Penobscot Indian guide Joseph Attean (pictured here) in his 1853 book, **The Maine Woods.**

small streamers and dry flies, especially on Canada Falls Lake. Small boats and canoes can be launched near the dam at Canada Falls and near the east and west ends of Seboomook. Both lakes have places that contain an abundance of old stumps, so boaters should use caution in these areas.

Baxter State Park

Long before it came to be known as Baxter State Park, the rugged territory around Mount Katahdin had always been a special place to the people who lived near it. Taken from the Abnaki name *Kette-Adene*, Katahdin means "greatest mountain" and represented one of the spiritual centers of the Native American world. White men arrived here in the early 1800s and logged the area extensively for many years. By the time most of the prime timber was gone, clearcuts, roads, and camps had destroyed much of the area's original natural beauty.

Disturbed by what he saw, a young state senator named Percival Baxter introduced bills to the Maine Legislature (in 1917 and again in 1919) that proposed the creation of a state park and forest sanctuary in the Mount Katahdin area. Both bills failed decisively, as did a similar proposal promoted by Baxter in the mid-1920s when he was Governor. Determined to create a public preserve for the people of Maine, when his term of office ended Baxter took action as a private citizen and purchased 5,960 acres of land from the Great Northern Paper Company. He gave this land to the State in 1931, and in 1933 it was officially designated as Baxter State Park.

During the remainder of his life, Baxter raised enough funds to purchase thirty-two more parcels of land that totaled over two hundred thousand acres. His final gift of 7,764 acres came in 1962 and made Baxter State Park the largest privately financed public wilderness preserve in the nation. The only stipulation that

Future Maine governor and environmental benefactor Percival Baxter caught this eight-pound brook trout in 1884, which may explain why he fell in love with fishing at such an early age.

Baxter Memorial Library

Governor Baxter attached to his gifts was that the park remain "forever wild." His deep love for the land is reflected by his words inscribed on a plaque along Katahdin Stream: "Man is born to die. His works are short lived. Buildings crumble, monuments decay, wealth vanishes; but Katahdin, in all its glory, forever shall remain the mountain of the people of Maine."

Baxter State Park Trout Ponds

Most anglers visit Baxter State Park to fish for wild brook trout in remote ponds. According to Park Ranger Chris Drew, nearly 75 percent of the fishing effort is focused in the southwest corner of the park. Daicey and Kidney Ponds are popular destinations that have rental cabins and roads leading directly to them. Canoe rentals for use on these ponds as well as on outlying waters can be arranged with park personnel. Kidney is the larger of the two ponds and provides surprisingly steady fishing for trout up to fourteen inches. Shortly after ice-out, fishermen who slowly work their way around the shoreline can find good action by fishing Hornbergs and small bucktail streamers on a sink-tip line. Later in the year, fish can be caught throughout the pond during evening insect hatches. The shallow outlet cove and the point that separates the pond into two basins have been productive areas for me. Daicey Pond can yield thick-bodied trout up to fifteen inches, but is much more temperamental in terms of catch rate. Peak times in Daicey are just after ice-out and during the Green Drake hatch in early July.

More than a dozen outlying ponds can be reached from trails that begin near Kidney and Daicey Ponds. Draper, Rocky, and Lily Pad Ponds are all small fly-fishing-only gems that are within a mile walk from the road. Celia Pond often produces larger fish and can be reached by a trail that departs from the west shore of Kidney. Jackson Pond, less than a half-mile down the trail past Celia, holds trout prone to taking dry flies.

Slaughter, Polly, Windy Pitch, and Lost are area trout ponds that hold good fish, but reaching them requires a little more effort. Slaughter is a favorite of many local anglers who cast nymphs and Muddlers near springfed inlets that enter the pond on the east and northwest shorelines. September is a particularly good time to catch this pond's beautifully colored trout. Because it is just beyond Baxter State Park's western border, canoes are not maintained at Slaughter, so it can be a difficult place to fish.

Another cluster of productive trout ponds can be accessed through the Matagamon gate in the northeast corner of the park. Lower Fowler is a fly-fishing-only pond that can be reached by a two-mile trail from the Perimeter Road. Fishing opportunities also exist at Long, Round, and Billfish Ponds after several additional miles of hiking. Frost and Hudson Ponds are located north of the Perimeter Road and provide non-fly fishermen with an opportunity to catch wild, pan-sized trout.

There is also good fishing deep within the park around Russell Pond. Since this area requires about a seven-mile hike to reach, it receives much less fishing pressure than the more easily accessible ponds. Many people who come to Russell Pond set up a base camp, then spend several days taking short trips into other waters. Russell and Deep Ponds usually provide fast fishing for pan-sized trout during most of the open-water season. But according to Park Naturalist Gene Hookwater, bigger fish are more often taken in Six Ponds and the Wassataquoik Lakes. The peak period for insect activity in the Russell Pond area typically runs from mid-June through July, and during hatches fish seem to cruise everywhere. When fishing below the surface during non-hatch periods, flies such as Hornbergs, Wood Specials, and Maple Syrup Nymphs usually produce well. Wassataquoik Stream flows through this area and provides moving-water anglers with a chance to catch trout. During midsummer, miles of this stream can be

Mount Katahdin provides a scenic backdrop for fly-fishermen on Kidney Pond.

fished in shorts and sneakers from the trail along its north bank. Trout congregate below falls and pitches and in areas where brooks flow in. However, the biological productivity of Wassataquoik Stream is low, so don't expect many fish over ten inches.

Nesowadnehunk Area

Any discussion of Baxter State Park would be incomplete without mentioning Nesowadnehunk Lake, which lies just outside the park's western boundary. Nesowadnehunk is famous for producing large numbers of pink-fleshed brook trout that run between ten inches and thirteen inches. At just under fifteen hundred acres, it is one of the largest lakes in the state where trout live without competition from other species. As a result, growth rates are so good in Nesowadnehunk Lake that fisheries biologists often refer to it as a "trout factory." Despite the lake's natural advantages and designation as fly-fishing-only water, heavy pressure from a fleet of anglers in motorboats and a liberal limit (five fish per day) restrict the number of trout that reach trophy size. From ice-out until the end of the season, brook trout can be caught on bright bucktail streamers, Muddlers,

and leeches. Fish rise well during hatches, and crayfish patterns worked along the shore on a sinking line are deadly. Nesowadnehunk is a large, wind-prone lake, so fishing tends to be best early in the morning or after the breeze calms in the evening. Nearby Little Nesowadnehunk Lake is also restricted to fly-fishing only and produces nice brook trout.

Nesowadnehunk Stream begins at the lake's outlet and flows for about twelve miles before entering the West Branch of the Penobscot just below Nesowadnehunk Falls. It runs clear and fairly cold throughout the season and represents the best stream fishery in the park. Compared with other local waters, Nesowadnehunk is a fertile stream that supports healthy populations of aquatic insects and can grow trout at a reasonable rate. Adequate holding pools and cover are a problem in some stretches, however, so the average resident fish is usually less than ten inches long. Over the years, I have caught considerably larger trout where beavers have dammed the stream sections located away from the road. The best chance of catching a trophy-sized trout comes in the fall, when spawners move into the stream from Nesowadnehunk Lake.

North Woods

Wind-blown ice filled the inlet cove and made travel very difficult for these early season anglers on Allagash Lake.

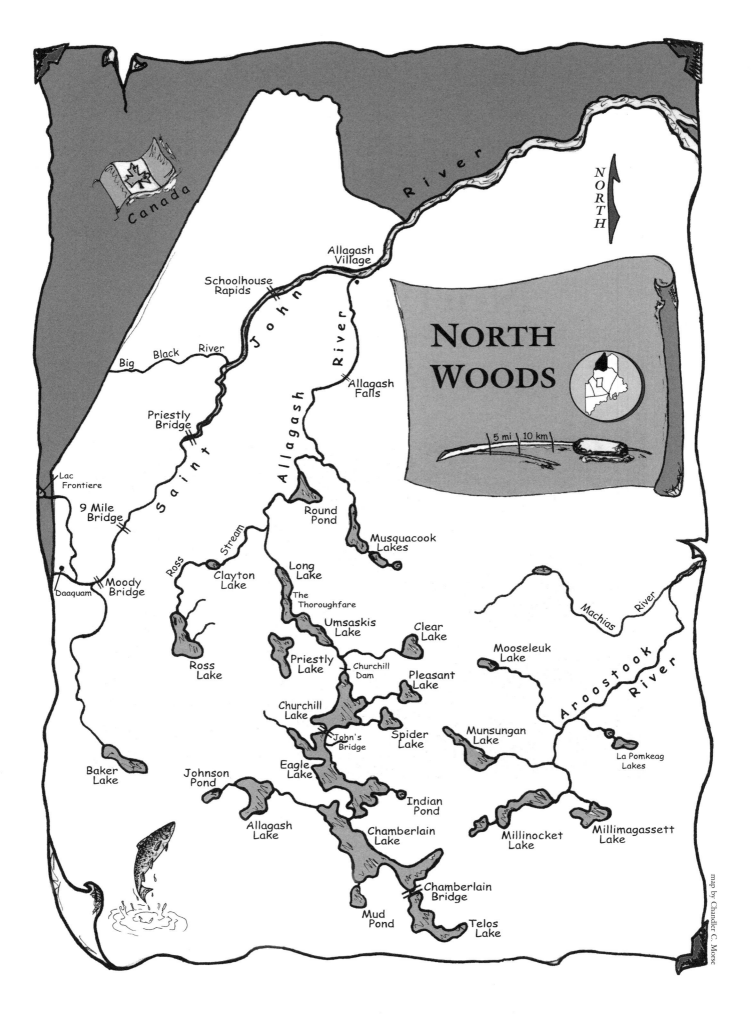

NORTH

NORTH
WOODS

5 mi | 10 km

Canada

John   River

Allagash Village

Schoolhouse
Rapids

Big   Black   River

John

Allagash   River

Allagash
Falls

Priestly
Bridge

Saint

Lac
Frontiere

9 Mile
Bridge

Ross

Stream

Round
Pond

Musquacook
Lakes

Daaquam

Moody
Bridge

Clayton
Lake

Long
Lake

The
Thoroughfare

Umsaskis
Lake

Clear
Lake

Mooseleuk
Lake

Machias   River

Ross
Lake

Priestly
Lake

Churchill
Dam

Pleasant
Lake

Aroostook   River

Churchill
Lake

John's
Bridge

Spider
Lake

Munsungan
Lake

La Pomkeag
Lakes

Baker
Lake

Johnson
Pond

Eagle
Lake

Indian
Pond

Allagash
Lake

Chamberlain
Lake

Millinocket
Lake

Millimagassett
Lake

Chamberlain
Bridge

Mud
Pond

Telos
Lake

map by Chandler C. Morse

Matt Libby

SPORTING CAMPS have been an important part of the North Woods fishing scene for as long as anglers have been coming to Maine. And Matt Libby's family has operated a set of these camps on Millinocket Lake for more than one hundred years. In the early days, getting to the camps was a two-day ordeal that began with a buckboard ride to a hotel in Oxbow and ended with a twenty-five-mile canoe trip up the Aroostook River. Once at camp, guides paddled guests— such as Teddy Roosevelt and Jack Dempsey—wherever they wanted to go, and clients often caught upward of one hundred trout a day. In the late 1940s a floatplane replaced the canoes as the main way of transporting people and supplies to Libby's. In 1968 the first road through the area was constructed.

When Matt Libby took over the operation in 1977, the North Woods had just undergone a period of explosive road building that for the first time in history provided easy access to many of the area's premier fishing spots. Matt said, "When I was a boy growing up in the mid-1960s there was no road into camp and just about the only people who fished here were sports that were staying with us. But after the Pinkham Road was built in the mid-1970s, many outstanding fisheries got fished-out almost overnight." In an attempt to help restore and preserve the type of quality fishing that he grew up with, Matt set out to change a mindset that developed when this territory was still isolated from automobiles. At times this was difficult and undoubtedly cost him business. But he lobbied hard to have bag limits reduced, and he promoted catch-and-release fishing among all his guides and clients. Matt also played an active role in the legislative process and served as a member of the Department of Inland Fisheries and Wildlife Advisory Council for many years

These days when you sit with Matt and his wife, Ellen, on the porch of their Millinocket Lake lodge and talk about the family business, you could come away with the impression that it all came easy to them. The reality is that Matt's father, Allie, died when he was four years old and his mother, Elsie, ran the operation from 1959 until Matt and Ellen took over the day after they graduated from college in 1977. Clients were scarce in the beginning, so Matt cut pulpwood and Ellen taught school to help supplement their camp income. During the past twenty years, Matt and his brothers have added a number of out-camps on remote waters, and their ever-expanding operation has developed a large and loyal base of clients. Hopefully, this will allow Matt Libby to remain a voice for conservation in the North Woods for many more years.

Maine's North Woods is one of the largest and most remote regions in the state. The majority of land comprising the North Woods is privately owned and managed for timber production. Aside from a few sporting camps that provide lodging and meals, this region is completely undeveloped. There are no paved roads or services (including gas) within this forty-five-hundred-square-mile area. First-time visitors should read the section "Planning a Trip to the North Woods" at the end of this chapter and be adequately prepared before venturing into Maine's big-timber country.

The North Woods encompasses the watersheds of the Allagash, upper St. John, and upper Aroostook Rivers. Although these rivers are geographically close to one another, fishermen who spend time on them soon discover that each has a distinct personality. The Allagash is best known for the true wilderness experience—typically via canoe trips—that it provides. Many anglers focus their attention on the moving-water section of the lower Allagash, which offers excellent spring and fall fishing for foot-long brook trout. Bigger fish are often caught in the large lakes—Allagash, Chamberlain,

Churchill, and Eagle—found in the upper half of the drainage. The upper St. John is a riverine watershed without large lakes in its headwaters, which makes it prone to periods of drought and flooding. As a result, fishing in the Upper St. John is intimately associated with spring runoff and seasonal rainfall. The upper Aroostook River contains brook trout and salmon that are catchable until the water warms in July. This watershed includes large headwater lakes typified by Munsungan, Millinocket, and Millimagassett that are productive throughout the season. Many backcountry trout ponds are located in the North Woods and can be reached from the logging roads and foot trails that crisscross this area.

Most North Woods waters have a fisheries management plan that emphasizes native brook trout and togue over salmon and other introduced species. Regional biologist Dave Baisley says, "Our [MDIF&W] goal is to provide a quality experience that gives anglers a glimpse of what fishing in northern Maine might have been like before logging, stocking, and man in general had an impact on the area." As a result, the North

Maine Folklife Center

Although dynamite was used to break apart some large logjams, the muscle of hard-working river drivers is what usually got the job done.

Woods has over one hundred different lakes, ponds, and streams where you can catch native brook trout in a pristine setting. Trout tend to grow larger here because they are not forced to compete with introduced species.

History

For thousands of years after the last ice age, tribes of Abnaki Indians traveled across Maine in annual cycles. Winters were spent on hunting grounds at the headwaters of rivers like the Allagash and St. John. When spring arrived, families in birch-bark canoes traveled down to the coast where they fished and raised crops until shortening days prompted them to return upriver to gather winter stores of nuts and berries. Everything in the Abnaki world was sacred—plants, animals, fish, and the rivers themselves—because the survival of entire families depended on the survival of everything around them.

When Europeans arrived in New England, they looked toward Maine for the natural resources—primarily flowing water and timber—that it could provide. Change began at the coast and along major rivers where mills and settlements were first built. Eventually the search for virgin timber led lumbermen to every corner of the state. They arrived in the North Woods in 1839.

The discovery of vast tracts of huge trees that stretched along the lakes and rivers of this region elicited great interest among lumber barons like Sam Veazie and Rufus Dwinel, whose mills on the lower Penobscot River were hungry for raw materials. But water was the only means of transporting logs in those days, and a major problem for mill owners was that the rivers in this region flowed northward. This meant that unless drastic action was taken, logs from the North Woods would be carried to the sawmills on the St. John River in Fredericton, New Brunswick, rather than to their own operations in Bangor.

Prior to the arrival of steamboats, rafts of logs were moved across lakes by men turning a capstan to pull the rafts along.

Motivated by the potential for huge profits, Bangor lumbermen financed the construction of a dam at the outlet of Chamberlain Lake. The goal was to raise the water level of Chamberlain Lake enough to make it flow backward into Telos and Webster Lakes. But in order to completely reverse the flow of water on the upper Allagash River, several other dikes and small dams had to be added. The project was eventually successful, and in 1842 the first logs from the North Woods were floated to Bangor.

Ten years later, all of the trees around Chamberlain had been cut and the search for timber was extended farther north. Lumbermen were again faced with the challenge of redirecting logs from the St. John to the Penobscot River drainage. The problem was solved by Eben Coe, an engineer from Salem, Massachusetts, who built a canal and lock system that allowed rafts of logs from Eagle and Churchill Lakes to be floated into Chamberlain Lake.

Steam power arrived in the North Woods at the beginning of the twentieth century and had an imme-diate impact on how work was done. Prior to 1900, rafts of logs were moved across lakes by backbreaking manual labor, but the introduction of steamboats allowed them to be towed effortlessly from place to place. Around this time, a three-thousand-foot steam-driven tramway was built that moved individual logs between Eagle and Chamberlain Lakes. Within a decade this tramway was replaced by a more efficient tank-like log hauler—designed by Alvin Lombard of Waterville, Maine—which could pull ten sleds of lumber along ice-covered roads cut through the woods.

Perhaps the most impressive chapter in the lumber-ing history of the North Woods was written between 1925 and 1927 by Edward LaCroix. This popular French Canadian built a fifteen-mile-long rail line that could haul seven thousand cords of pulp wood from Eagle Lake to Umbazookskus Lake each week. An eighteen-hundred-foot-long wooden trestle, two steam locomo-tives, and a number of other artifacts of this era can still be viewed by Allagash visitors.

Early visitors traveled upstream in canoes for several days to reach the headwaters of the Aroostook River. Today, these places are a one-hour drive from a paved highway.

The Lombard log hauler was a steam-driven, rail-less train that operated in the north woods during the 1920s.

Allagash River Watershed

The classic image of Maine fishing involves a lone angler standing in a wild river, casting a dry fly to rising trout in fading light, while a moose feeds in the nearby shallows. Such a scene can be experienced in countless places along the Allagash River and is one reason why this waterway stirs such deep emotions in the people who have traveled it. The first recorded proposal to protect the Allagash appeared in a *Portland Press Herald* editorial written by Forrest H. Colby in 1921. But it took until 1966 to pass legislation that led to the creation of the Allagash Wilderness Waterway and ensured that the "natural beauty, character and habitat of this unique area would be preserved forever." Protection of the waterway was enhanced in 1970 when it was added to the National Wild and Scenic River System. Today, this ninety-two-mile ribbon of river and lakes that winds through the heart of the North Woods stands as a monument to the foresight of conservationists who loved this territory long before today's users were born.

Day use and camping fees are collected at a number of North Maine Woods checkpoints.

Allagash Waterway Lakes

Many people who canoe the Allagash are surprised to learn that nearly half the trip is on lakes rather than on moving water. Indeed, from Telos Landing to Allagash village there are eight major lakes located on the waterway and another half-dozen connected to it. Brook trout, togue, and whitefish are found in all of these lakes, and in the winter and spring these species support popular fisheries. Angling methods are similar on these waters, so I'll provide descriptions only for the three most popular lakes.

Because these waters are part of the Allagash Wilderness Waterway, road access is limited and a number of boating and angling restrictions apply. The only hardtop boat launch is located at Chamberlain Bridge near the southern terminus of the waterway. Large boats can be launched here and used on Chamberlain and Telos Lakes. Only canoes with motors of less than ten horsepower are allowed on Eagle Lake or on any of the waters farther north. Access to Eagle and Churchill Lakes can be gained from

Good friends and good food add to the enjoyment of ice-fishing adventures throughout the North Woods.

rough launches near John's Bridge and Churchill Dam or by floating a canoe down the outlet of Indian Pond. Umsaskis Lake, Long Lake, and Round Pond can be reached from the Realty Road Thoroughfare or from the bridge on the Henderson Brook Road. Allagash Lake is the most pristine spot on the waterway. Because no motors are allowed on the lake, access is gained by either floating down or paddling up Allagash Stream or by carrying canoes and gear down a two-mile trail that leads to the south end of the lake. Information concerning the waterway is available from the Maine Bureau of Parks and Recreation, State House, Augusta, ME 04333.

ALLAGASH LAKE. Some of my fondest memories are of early season fishing trips to Allagash Lake with my wife, Cheryl, and our three kids. My first visit here was with my oldest daughter, Kristen, when she was in kindergarten. We didn't depart until the school bus brought her home at 11 AM, and I was concerned about reaching our campsite on Allagash Lake by nightfall. Despite my anxiety, we had a great time counting dozens of moose on the five-hour drive to the put-in site. After paddling across Johnson Pond and down Allagash Stream, we even managed to catch a couple of nice brook trout at the lake's inlet. Other trips provided more adventures, like the time a northwest wind filled the cove in which we were camping with floating ice. And the night smelts were running so heavily past our campsite that they startled my daughter when she shined her flashlight into the water while washing dinner dishes.

The ice usually doesn't completely clear from Allagash Lake until around mid-May, but adventurous anglers visit here as soon as any open water appears in the lake and the inlet stream is navigable. I know a number of people who have had fine togue fishing in late April. Because smelts generally run up Allagash Stream and a couple of other smaller tributaries in early May, that is when I like to fish here. By then most of the lake is ice-free, and fish can be taken by trolling streamer flies, Rapalas, or Mooselook Wobblers along the shorelines. Fish also follow spawning smelts into Allagash Stream and can be caught by casting flies and

126

lures into deep corner pools. Stream fishing is particularly good in the early morning when spawned-out smelts are floating back down to the lake. Inexperienced canoeists should use caution in the spring—cold water, high winds, and extreme isolation can be a dangerous combination.

CHAMBERLAIN LAKE. At just over thirteen miles long, Chamberlain is the largest and most popular lake on the waterway. For several weeks after ice-out, it's not unusual to count more than twenty-five trucks with trailers at the boat launch. I have a love-hate relationship with this lake: It can provide great fishing for brook trout, togue, and whitefish, but it often forces anglers to endure miserable conditions. The problem with Chamberlain Lake is that it's a long, narrow body of water surrounded by low hills; thus, when the wind blows out of the northwest—as it often does for days on end in the spring— the lake gets whipped into whitecaps and provides few places for boaters to hide. The action can be so good here, though, that people are willing to battle these elements for a chance at a trophy fish.

The keys to safety and success on Chamberlain Lake are fishing from a large boat and getting on the water early. When the weather is bad, a good alternative is to fish Round Pond or Telos Lake. Both waters are accessible from the boat launch at Chamberlain Bridge but are much smaller and more protected than the big lake. Several years ago I shared a shore-lunch at Telos Lake's High Bank campsite with a couple of guys who showed me a twenty-four-inch brook trout they caught while trolling Rapalas near Midnight Brook. Ice fishermen also catch quite a few nice brook trout and togue in Round Pond and Telos Lake, especially during January when conditions on Chamberlain are cold and miserable.

It's difficult to pinpoint the best way for open-water anglers to fish Chamberlain Lake because conditions change as the season progresses. When the smelts are running, trolling near spawning brooks can be very productive. Popular locations include the large, shallow cove where Allagash Stream dumps into the upper lake and the brook adjacent to The Arm campsite. The west shoreline between Ellis Brook and Mud Cove can also be good at this time of year.

Many brook trout are taken in early spring by trolling sewn smelts within fifteen feet of the shore. Lures like the Rapala, Mirror Minnow, and Yo-Zuri Pin Smelt or streamer flies like the Miss Sharon and Blue Smelt can be very effective. Considering the irregular and relatively shallow nature of Chamberlain Lake's shoreline, fishing close to it without getting hung up can be a challenge, especially when the wind is blowing. Depth finders are a big help, but in order to get your offerings into the fish zone you have to troll close to the rocks and risk losing a lure or two.

Togue are usually farther from shore, but they can be taken near the surface by the same methods described for brook trout. Many anglers also use lead-core line and an assortment of large dodgers, flashers, and spoons. I catch plenty of early season togue by trolling a sewn smelt or a streamer fly on a sink-tip fly line, so I generally stick to this lighter tackle. Whitefish are another popular target on Chamberlain Lake that are found offshore within fifteen feet of the bottom. Jigging in the upper lake with a Swedish Pimple, small Lead-Fish, or cut bait, is the most common way to catch these tasty fish.

Eagle Lake produces nice brook trout and togue for anglers willing to invest the extra effort it takes to fish here.

EAGLE LAKE. Eagle Lake is less than one mile north of Chamberlain and produces beautifully colored brook trout and togue. Because access is more difficult and only canoes—not boats—are allowed on the water, Eagle Lake receives much less fishing pressure than Chamberlain— MDIF&W surveys conducted in the 1980s showed that during both the open-water and ice-fishing seasons more than twice as many people fished Chamberlain Lake than Eagle Lake. Creel-census data from that period indicated that brook trout in both lakes ran around fourteen inches, but that the average Eagle Lake togue measured close to two feet—more than three inches longer than togue in Chamberlain Lake.

Eagle Lake has been surveyed several times since the 1980s, and statistics show a steady increase in the size and catch rate of both brook trout and togue. Fisheries biologist Scott Roy says, "The most likely reasons for this very encouraging trend are reduced bag limits and the introduction of smelts, which took place in the early 1960s." Today, Eagle Lake produces brook trout that can approach three pounds and togue in the five-pound range. Popular locations on the south end of the lake include the mouths of Smith and Woodman Brooks, Indian Stream, and the ledges off Pillsbury Island. Farther up the lake, Farm Island, Russell Cove, Snare Brook, and the entire east shoreline from opposite the Pump Handle to just beyond Zeigler campsite provide great spring fishing. Using light tackle to troll smelts, streamer flies, or hardware will all produce early season action. But once the smelts have stopped running and the surface water warms to around sixty degrees, many fish will abandon shoreline areas and head for deep holes that lie around Hog Island and the Narrows. Catching fish at this time of year is more difficult because it requires lead-core line or a downrigger to get offerings to the depth where fish are feeding. Because Eagle lake has a canoes-only regulation, there is the complication of fitting heavy trolling gear into a fairly small watercraft. As a result, most serious fishermen visit Eagle Lake early in the spring or during the last few weeks of September when cooling waters draw fish back near the surface.

Native brook trout are found in the vicinity of most inlet brooks along the Allagash River.

Allagash River

The moving-water section of the Allagash Wilderness Waterway is located on it lower end. This long, free-flowing stretch of river begins at Churchill Dam and, aside from minor interruptions at Umsaskis and Long Lakes and Round Pond, travels over sixty miles before entering the St. John River at Allagash Village. My first experience on the lower Allagash was a week-long canoe trip with my wife, Cheryl, in September 1981. The delightful sunny days filled with moose, loons, and brilliant autumn colors caused me to fall in love with this section of the river. Naturally, the large brook trout that we caught during the trip added to these positive feelings.

In the years since that first canoe trip, I've come to realize that brook trout over three pounds—like those my wife and I encountered—are quite unusual on the lower river. But there are a few places—the pool below Churchill Dam and the Big Eddy near the end of Chase Rapids—where large fish are occasionally taken in the spring. And each fall a few monsters can be found off the mouths of spawning tributaries such as Ross Stream. Generally, though, most of the brook trout that I catch in the moving sections of the Allagash River are less than sixteen inches long.

CHURCHILL DAM TO LONG LAKE. Some of my most enjoyable fishing on the Allagash River has taken place in the Chase Rapids section below Churchill Dam. A trail runs along much of the west bank, but you can also rock-hop your way through the pocket water on either side of the river. Although fishing is best during late spring and the fall, the Chase Rapids section holds trout throughout the season. Muddlers, Hornbergs, and a variety of nymphs will consistently draw strikes from ten-inch brookies. Al's Goldfish, Daredevles, and small Swedish Pimples also account for many of the trout taken here.

Four miles downstream, the river widens and braids into a number of channels as it approaches Umsaskis Lake. The roar of Chase Rapids is replaced by the sounds of the birds, frogs, and insects that inhabit Umsaskis Marsh. This interesting stretch of river can be reached by floating down from Churchill Dam or by motoring up Umsaskis Lake from the Realty Road Thoroughfare. Neither is a simple option, so anglers planning to fish here should spend a few days exploring the channels and runs that are formed among the grass-covered islands. Dry-fly fishing can be good in the evening, and if you hit it right the trout can run larger than average. Black flies and mosquitos can be a problem, so bring bug dope.

Umsaskis is connected to Long Lake by the three-hundred-yard-long section of moving water known in local parlance simply as the "Thoroughfare." In early spring, this section attracts smelts along with brook trout and togue from the adjoining lakes. Because it is one of the few places in the region that is ice-free, it also draws anglers eager to catch their first fish of the season. By late May the action dies down and the fishermen disperse. A few smaller trout remain in the area throughout the season and can be caught in the evening by casting dry flies off the bridge that crosses the Thoroughfare.

LONG LAKE DAM TO ALLAGASH VILLAGE. The campsite at the old Long Lake Dam serves as a central location for fishermen to sample the angling opportunities in both Long Lake and the Allagash River. A couple of miles up the lake from the campsite, trout can be found at the mouths of Ross Stream and Shepherd Brook. And there are numerous runs in the seven miles of fast water below Long Lake. Good fish are often found in the moving water adjacent to the old dam. This spot is particularly popular with anglers who are camped here and fish very early in the morning or late in the evening.

Round Pond is the last semiaccessible piece of flat water on the lower Allagash; thus, many people camp and fish here. The braided channels at the inlet and the rips at the outlet are good places to wade and fly-fish. The pond itself supports a healthy population of brook trout that can be taken on everything from dry flies to deep-trolled hardware. Round Pond looks like a place

that should produce monster trout, but I rarely catch fish longer than twelve inches. When I spoke with the local game warden about this, he thought competition from the large number of trout in the pond might be the factor that was limiting their individual size.

The eighteen miles of river from Round Pond to Allagash Falls is the most unspoiled and picturesque section of the Waterway. Fishing can be excellent around many of the brooks that enter the river in this area: just upstream from the Five Finger Brook campsite, I caught my largest Allagash brook trout. Several deep pools exist in the vicinity of the falls, but the area is a mandatory portage for all canoeists, so it is fished fairly heavily. Following a forty-foot tumble over Allagash Falls, the river flows for another twelve miles to its confluence with the St. John River. Beyond the falls, the Allagash has never been very productive for me, though I have heard stories about locals who catch plenty of trout in this piece of river.

Allagash River Headwater Lakes and Tributaries

There are many other large waters in the Allagash River watershed that have good fishing. West of the river, Ross and Priestly Lakes provide anglers with an opportunity

Allagash Falls is a mandatory portage for all canoeists.

to catch native brook trout and togue in a remote setting. With its sporting camps and road-accessible campsites, Ross typically receives more fishing pressure than Priestly. But at over three thousand acres and one hundred feet deep, Ross Lake consistently produces nice fish for anglers who endure the long trip over rough roads to get here. Smelt runs are heavy just after ice-out, and trolling the rocky east shore between Boucher and Gannett Brooks with streamers or sewn bait is usually a good bet. Ross's size and orientation make it prone to strong spring winds, so anglers fishing here should do so in a large boat.

During fall, brilliantly colored brook trout often move into Ross Stream to spawn.

Conditions are usually pleasant in the fall, and the lake's north end around Fool Brook and the outlet can offer good autumn fishing. Because of its depth, the water in Ross is slow to cool in the fall—I have been plagued by chubs on a couple of trips in September. One pleasant surprise I've encountered on this lake is the surprising number of Green Drakes that hatch sporadically throughout the summer. Maine outdoor writer Gene LeTourneau had a camp here for many years and caught countless brook trout and whitefish on Green Drake dry flies and wiggle nymphs fished in the shallows along the perimeter of the lake.

Since my passion is casting flies to rising trout in moving water, I usually spend more time fishing Ross Stream than the lake itself. I try to time my visits to coincide with the peak of mayfly activity in the stream, which usually occurs in mid-June. By this time, many streams in Maine have begun to suffer from a lack of water or from warm temperatures. But Ross Stream has a number of springs and cool tributaries that usually keep it in prime condition until the dog days of summer. This twenty-mile-long gem can be accessed from logging roads or, during high water, floated from one end to the other. The small settlement of Clayton Lake is located about midway and serves as a convenient access point. Several miles of alder-lined flats are a popular destination for anglers who motor upstream from the lake. A number of nice pools between Holmes and Harvey Brooks can be reached by bushwhacking through the woods from the road that follows the north bank. Most resident trout in Ross Stream are less than twelve inches, but larger fish that run out of the

lakes are always possible, especially on the upper and lower ends during spring and fall.

Good angling lakes also exist east of the Allagash River. Clear Lake, with its dramatic mountain backdrop and light-colored strains of brook trout and togue, is my personal favorite. But Spider, Haymock, Indian, Pleasant, Cliff, and the Musquacook Lakes all have their disciples. If you spend a couple of hours trolling with a fish finder, you will see that these lakes have plenty of fish. The problem for anglers is that the fish are so well-fed that they often refuse to bite; indeed, over the years I've seen a number of experienced fishermen get shut out. Usually, though, just when you're ready to give up, someone will catch an eye-popping four-pound brook trout—recently, I saw such a fish taken in Indian Pond on an orange Mooselook Wobbler—or land a beautiful ten-pound Haymock Lake togue. Faith restored, you find yourself returning to these remote places time and again in search of a trophy fish.

St. John River Watershed

From its humble beginnings in the tiny brooks that drain Truesdale Mountain, the upper St. John River collects water from dozens of tributaries along its one-hundred-forty-mile journey to Allagash Village. The St. John River watershed has few large lakes and limited water-storage capacity; therefore, its flow and temperature are dependent on rainfall and local weather patterns. For fishermen and canoeists this means that good timing is critical. Before making the long journey to the St. John River, visitors should obtain up-to-date information on water conditions from the North Maine Woods headquarters in Ashland. At least three thousand cfs of water are needed for good canoeing, and water temperatures around sixty degrees are ideal for fishing.

Recreationists who travel along the upper St. John River today encounter few buildings, automobiles, or people; thus, they often think that this area has always been uninhabited. In reality, French Canadians from New Brunswick traveled to the upper St. John in the 1840s in search of timber. During the eighty years that followed, a degree of of development and a rich lumbering history was established along the river. Today, all

Garrett Conover

Late May is usually a great time for a canoe trip on the upper St. John River.

of the designated campsites on the St. John are places of historical interest where logging depots or homesteads once stood. Almost every tributary that enters the river is named after a well-known woodsman or river-driver from that era.

The upper St. John is the longest free-flowing river in the eastern United States. During the energy crisis of the 1970s, the river's unique character was threatened by a massive hydroelectric development program called the Dickey-Lincoln Project, proposed by the Army Corps of Engineers. Dickey-Lincoln threatened to inundate more than forty-five miles of the St. John River and nearly eighty miles of tributary streams. Fortunately, a number of elements—economics, fisheries, and the reality that nearly all of the electricity would be sent out-of-state—contributed to the cancellation of the project in 1983. According to an Army Corps of Engineers spokesman, "It was the need to protect the Furbish Lousewort, an endangered species of plant that only grows near the banks of the St. John River, that ultimately caused the project to be dropped." This was one of the few times in the history of Maine politics that conservation defeated big business. Many people believe that the Dickey-Lincoln settlement set a precedent that contributed to other environment-friendly decisions, such as the defeat of two proposed dams on the Penobscot River (Big A and Basin's Mills) and the removal of existing dams on the Kennebec River and Souadabscook Stream. Currently, the St. John River is overseen by a resource protection committee that regulates timber harvesting and development along its entire corridor and ensures that this great river will remain a valuable resource for the people of Maine.

Upper St. John River

Because of its length, limited access, and distance from civilization, the upper St. John is one of the most difficult rivers in Maine for anglers to get to know. I have fished here on a number of occasions, yet I still feel like a novice when I venture onto a new stretch. Over the years, however, I have developed a few general rules that will improve success here. Trout are generally easiest to catch in late spring when the runoff is receding and the water temperature is around fifty-five degrees. Good fish often congregate along the edges of rapids or in quiet pools behind large boulders. The upper St. John is over one hundred fifty feet wide in many places and can be intimidating to newcomers. I find the best way to approach this river is to cast about twenty-five feet out into the current, then slowly work the offering down

and across until it ends up tight against the bank. Many strikes will occur in the slack water within five feet of shore. Traditionally, worms have been very popular on the upper St. John, but a recent survey revealed that nearly 35 percent of anglers are now fly-fishing. High-floating dry flies like grasshoppers and Stimulators or meaty-looking wet flies such as Muddlers and Woolly Worms are the most productive. Small copper-colored Mepps Spinners and roostertails can also be deadly.

Prime stretches on many of Maine's top rivers are often only a few miles long and can be quite crowded. But during spring on the upper St. John, trout can be found almost anywhere along its entire length. Another plus is that relatively few people fish here. (However, the recent introduction of muskellunge—see the following section—has caused the average number of trout per mile to decline in some areas.) Surveys show that nearly 70 percent of the trout fishing on this river is done by shore-bound anglers who venture less than one mile from their vehicles. Therefore, road-accessible places such as Poplar Island and School House Rapids tend to get the bulk of the fishing pressure. Other popular spots that require a bit more effort to reach are Longs, Big Black, and Priestly Rapids. My favorite way to fish the upper St. John is to use a motorized canoe to explore hard-to-reach areas such as Short Rapids and Seven Islands.

A big problem on the upper St. John is that in many places the riverbed is very wide and shallow. This profile results from the countless times the riverbed has been scoured by ice flows and spring floods. During low-flow periods, anglers are faced with the challenge of finding pools that provide enough depth and cover to hold fish. A lack of riparian vegetation also leaves long stretches of the riverbed exposed to the sun, which results in water temperatures that can run above seventy degrees for extended periods.

Arlo Caron grew up on the upper St. John at Ninemile Bridge and has spent the past thirty-five years guiding in this area. He says, "The key to catching good trout in the summer is finding spring holes in the riverbed or deep, sheltered pools where fish can hide." Two examples of such refuges are the ledge pool across the river from the Ninemile Bridge campsite, and the large, spring-fed corner pool a few miles below Priestly Bridge. In the old days, the prevailing thought was that most of the good trout in the upper St. John headed into the small feeder brooks when the weather got hot. According to Caron, "Years ago, this probably did occur. But with all the clearcutting that has taken place on this watershed, many of these tributaries have been laid open to the sun and don't provide the quality coldwater habitats that they once did. As a result, the bigger trout don't use them anymore." My experiences, backed by the stream surveys done in conjunction with the Dickey-Lincoln project, indicate that nowadays brook trout over ten inches long are fairly rare in most upper St. John tributaries.

St. John River Muskellunge Fishery

The muskellunge is an introduced species that entered Maine from a stocking done in Lac Frontiere, Quebec during the early 1970s. Today, though not everyone cares to acknowledge it, they are established throughout the St. John. Muskies have become so plentiful in places like Moody Bridge that during low water you can look into the river and see them holding in the deep pools.

Muskies are also found in Baker Lake—to reach this water, they traveled through more than twenty-five miles of the St. John River and its tributaries. Casting large spoons and plugs in areas where weed beds drop off into deeper water provides the best chance of catching one of these powerful fish that can weigh ten pounds. The area around the inlet on the south end of Baker Lake is popular with muskie fishermen, especially in the early morning and evening.

Some local anglers are pleased with this turn of events and have asked the state to introduce muskies into several other area lakes. However, most people place a higher priority on native brook trout and fear the eventual impact that these voracious predators will have on the trout fishery. Personally, I think that the introduction of muskies into the St. John River is a tragedy. That said, since they are established fishermen may as well take advantage of them.

The muskellunge is a recently introduced species that is loved by some Maine anglers and hated by others.

A thick-bodied Millinocket Lake salmon is too valuable to catch just once.

Upper Aroostook River Watershed

The upper Aroostook River begins at the junction of Munsungan and Millinocket streams and travels east for about thirty miles until it reaches the village of Masardis. Along the way, it receives water from tributaries such as Mooseleuk and LaPomkeag streams, then leaves the North Woods as a large river. Some great fishing is available in the watershed, but this is big, remote country that takes time and effort to figure out.

Aroostook River Headwater Lakes

Munsungan, Millinocket, and Millimagassett are large lakes that make up the headwaters of the Aroostook River. These lakes are roughly the same size and depth, and each provides opportunities for quality fishing in a wild setting. Access and boat launching facilities are limited, so many anglers stay at Libby's Camps on Millinocket Lake or at one of the sporting camps on Munsungan. I try to visit this area twice a year, and I often divide my time among the three lakes.

One of my fondest memories of this area came on a day in late September when salmon were stacked up at one of the inlets to Munsungan Lake. Although the majority of these fish were only around sixteen inches, they eagerly slashed at a small Mickey Finn or any other bright streamer I tossed at them. I probably caught more than forty salmon that day, which made it a lifetime memory. Trips to Munsungan in the spring can provide good fishing along the rocky shore between Bluffer and Reed Brooks and near the mouth of the stream flowing from Chase Lake.

Millinocket is one of the few lakes in the North Woods that contains splake. A couple of winters ago, my kids and I snowmobiled in and caught several thick-bodied fish in the eighteen-inch range. And Matt Libby told me that the sports at his camps were catching nice splake on trolled baits during the open-water season. He was particularly pleased with the fishability of these Millinocket Lake splake and said, "They act a lot more like brook trout than togue," a reference that splake are a nonreproducing hybrid of these two species.

Millimagassett is the most difficult lake in this region to reach by vehicle, so people often fish during the winter when snowmobile trails provide better access. Open-water fishing is good though, with togue being the preferred target of anglers who keep boats here. Local guide Dan LaPointe fishes this lake regularly and feels the best way to catch togue is to work large spoons with sewn bait along the bottom in the vicinity of the deep hole located south of the islands in the middle of the lake. He also told me that "some nice salmon and brook trout are taken by trolling Rapalas and tandem streamers along the northeast shoreline and around the brooks that enter on the southwest corner."

Upper Aroostook River and Tributaries

When conditions are right, the upper Aroostook can be a delightful river to fish. But since it is not a tail water with a large dam to supply cold water, many of the river's fish disappear after spring run-off subsides. Frank Frost is a biologist who, for a number of years, has studied the movements of brook trout in the Aroostook watershed. He has found that nearly all the trout here are wild fish that move into the tributaries during the summer months in search of cold water. Frost is currently trying to identify these refuges, so they can be protected from disturbance during logging and other damaging commercial operations. For the average person, though, searching for a few limited concentrations of fish among hundreds of square miles of streams, bogs, and deadwaters is like trying to find a needle in a haystack. Therefore, in a practical sense, the upper Aroostook River must be considered a seasonal fishery that is most productive in the spring and fall.

A glance at a map suggests that the Oxbow Road runs for miles along the south bank of the upper Aroostook River. This can mislead newcomers into thinking that access to this fishery is good. In reality, the river is almost always separated from the road by at least one hundred yards of thick woods. Road-accessible spots are located near the Oxbow Checkpoint and a few miles upstream where a tote road leads to an old bridge abutment near the Salmon Pool. Unless you're familiar with how to reach the best holding-water, trying to fish this river from the road can be difficult.

Fortunately, the upper Aroostook is a good river to fish from a canoe and offers a number of different floats. Bridges that cross Millinocket and Munsungan streams make good starting points for one or multiday trips that can extend all the way down to Masardis. And if you stash your walking shoes in the woods near the take-out spot, you can get back to your vehicle without having to arrange a shuttle. I have never had trouble with water levels here, but it's a good idea to check with the North Maine Woods office in Ashland before embarking on a trip.

When water temperatures are good, trout and salmon can be found in most of the upper Aroostook River's deep runs and corner pools. Hotspots include the Junction Pool area near the confluence of Millinocket and Munsungan Streams as well as the alder-lined runs around the mouths of Mooseleuk and LaPomkeag Streams. Various nymphs, Hornbergs, small Woolly Buggers, and marabou streamers have all produced fish for me. Other anglers do well with lures like Daredevles, Super-Dupers, and roostertails. This wide range of productive tackle indicates that when fish are in the river they aren't selective, which makes proper timing the key to a successful trip.

Mooseleuk Stream is an important tributary that joins the upper Aroostook about seven miles below Junction Pool. This is another seasonal fishery that is best worked from a canoe. Wading anglers can gain access at the Pinkham Road Bridge and Mooseleuk Lake Dam or by following tributaries like Smith, Middle, and Rocky Brooks down to the river. The MDIF&W thinks enough of Mooseleuk Stream to have it designated as a fly-fishing-only water with a two-fish limit. Although I have never caught any big trout here, I find Mooseleuk to be a pleasant, uncrowded stream to fish.

Another upper Aroostook tributary worth investigating is the Machais River. Several deadwaters provide fly fishermen with an opportunity to catch trout from a canoe, but during most of the year much of the upper river is too rocky and steep to float. Road access ranges from quite good in some places to nonexistent in others. I have fished here a few times early in the season and had little success. However, there are a number of pools near the mouths of cold brooks that hold trout during warm weather.

North Woods Trout Ponds

Maine has more than eleven hundred lakes and ponds that contain brook trout. Nearly five hundred of them have never been stocked, and about 20 percent of these

Despite the steady increase in fishing pressure, nice brook trout are still found in many waters throughout the North Woods.

wild fisheries are located in the North Woods. These un-stocked trout ponds are significant because in addition to providing prime habitat, each contains a genetically unique strain of fish that over centuries has become adapted to its environment. Numerous scientific stud-ies have shown that wild trout are superior to their hatchery-reared counterparts because they grow faster and live longer. Thus, when the gene pools of wild trout (such as those found in North Wood's ponds) are lost or compromised by hatchery fish, the overall via-bility of the species is diminished.

During the years since log driving was phased out on Maine rivers, hundreds of logging roads have been built throughout the North Woods. The early roads opened up vast tracts of virgin country and allowed many of the largest trout in previously inaccessible ponds to be caught and killed. As road building continued, fishing pressure in some remote ponds increased to a point that threatened the survival of these wild popu-lations. In order to protect the older, larger trout that are vital as brood stock, in 1996 MDIF&W commis-sioner Bucky Owen devised and implemented a set of "Quality Fishing Initiatives." These new regulations in-creased length restrictions and decreased bag limits on more than four hundred fifty of the state's best waters. The consensus among anglers and biologists is that these new regulations are working effectively toward making Commissioner Owen's dream of "providing all anglers in the state of Maine with a realistic chance to catch a four-pound native brook trout" into a reality.

What I like most about North Woods trout ponds is that they provide anglers with an opportunity to catch fish throughout the entire season. Over the years, ponds such as Elbow, Crescent, and Little Pleasant have provided action from ice-out until the last day of September. Area guide Mike Langley once told me, "It's not unusual for one of my clients to catch and release twenty trout from one of our local ponds during the middle of a July or August day." Of course, it helps to know—as Mike does—the location of all the spring holes. But even if you have never been to a particular pond before, you can still catch trout in the summer by following time-proven rules: fish during early morning and late evening, use fast-sinking fly lines, and concen-trate your efforts around coldwater sources and weed beds. Big, meaty-looking nymphs and Woolly Buggers are my favorite flies for North Woods pond fishing.

Planning a Trip to the North Woods

Although fishermen and other recreationists are welcome in the North Woods, this is privately owned, working forestland that is managed primarily for commercial timber harvesting. For safety reasons, no bicycles, motor-

A number of commercial sporting camps provide food and lodging for anglers traveling in the North Woods.

cycles, ATV's, horses, or oversized vehicles are allowed in this area. To control visitor access, gates are maintained at various locations throughout the North Woods. Fees are charged for road use and overnight camping.

A good way to get an idea of where you might want to fish in the North Woods is to read back copies of *The Maine Sportsman* or the *Northwoods Sporting Journal*. Both are no-nonsense monthly tabloids that employ knowledgeable local writers and are full of where-to and how-to information. Several Web sites devoted to fishing in Maine (search Maine fishing), and the home pages of the MDIF&W and the Kittery Trading Post, can provide useful information. DeLorme's *Maine Atlas and Gazetteer* is a comprehensive set of maps that shows every pond, stream, and logging road in the North Woods. The gazetteer is an essential item for anyone traveling in this area.

Once you have selected a place to fish, your lodging options are to camp or to stay at a commercial sporting camp. Campsites are typically assigned on a first-come, first-served basis as you pass through the timber company gates. Campsite reservations and general information are available at the office of North Maine Woods, P.O. Box 421, Ashland, ME 04732 or www.north-mainewoods.org

A list of sporting camps can be obtained from the Maine Sporting Camp Association, P.O. Box 89, Jay, ME 04239. American plan camps provide all of your meals in a central dining area, whereas in housekeeping camps you do your own cooking and cleanup. American plan camps are more expensive than basic housekeeping camps—the latter plan can cost as little as thirty dollars per person per day. Fishing at housekeeping camps can be good, though, which makes them a bargain. People interested in hiring a guide can get a list for the North Woods by contacting the Maine Professional Guides Association, P.O. Box 847, Augusta, ME 04332 or www.maineguides.org.

Aroostook County

The lower St. John is a large river whose water level can change dramatically with rainfall and the season. A driftboat can increase your chances for success because it allows you to fish undercut banks and deep places where currents flowing around islands meet.

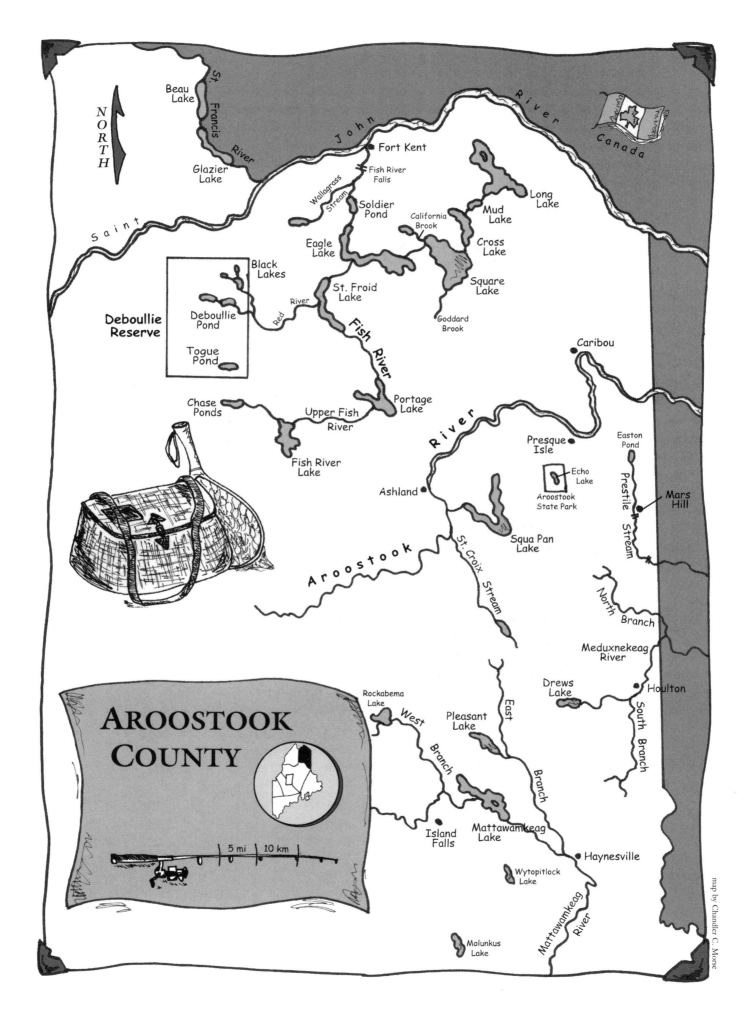

Linda Yencha

illustration by Sandra Nestlerode-Hale

YOU DON'T have to spend much time in the north-country to realize that many of the most underappreciated people on the Maine fishing scene are the women who work at remote sporting camps. Like many of the others, Linda Yencha owns a business—Loon Lodge—with her husband, Michael, and is primarily in charge of the domestic side of the operation. But even among the camp wives, Linda is unique because the first time she set foot in Maine was as a twenty-year-old newlywed who arrived at the shore of Round Pond to help clear the land on which the lodge now sits. Today she is probably the only woman left in the North Woods who, without help in the kitchen, provides meals from ice-out until the end of November.

The Yenchas also have the distinction of operating the most remote, full-service camps in Maine. It's an honest two and a half hours from the lodge to the nearest paved road, so when travelers run into any kind of problem in the area, they often end up on the Yencha's doorstep looking for help. Linda says, "We're kind of like a frontier outpost up here. Because Michael is often out guiding, I sometimes end up playing the role of nurse, auto mechanic, and even sheriff to various people who come by."

When she's not tending to lost travelers or peeling logs to build an addition onto one of the cabins, Linda's regular duties include cooking three meals a day from scratch for up to sixteen sports, then cleaning their cabins when they leave. She describes her life at the lodge as "like being a single, stay-at-home mother of triplets, except that after eighteen years they don't leave." Linda loves people, though, and says the best thing about her job is getting to know all of the guests on an individual basis.

Being isolated from family and friends for more than half of each year is more difficult for her than all the work. Linda spends what little downtime she has with her beloved dogs, Cinder and Sally, or paddling her kayak among the loons on Round Pond. Because of their location, there is no television reception or cell-phone service at the lodge—from early May through November, the only contact Linda has with loved ones is through letters and the phone calls that she makes twice a month when she goes to town for supplies. She told me, "I was here at camp when my mom passed away in 2000 and that was really tough." Then she quickly added, "But this is the life Michael and I have chosen, and we are determined to make a go of it." Fishermen throughout the North Woods are very fortunate that Linda—and other dedicated women like her—has made this decision.

It seems fitting to end this book with a chapter about Aroostook County—the "rooftop" of Maine—which differs in many ways from other parts of the state. Because of its large size, its position as one of the northernmost regions in the continental U.S., and its general isolation from the rest of Maine, the "County" has evolved as a land unto itself. New England author Charles Wilson describes it as a place that is "related to Maine, friendly to Maine, influenced by Maine, yet not wedded to her." Despite long, cold winters and an economy that sometimes runs a little behind the rest of the state, most Aroostookers love the County and take considerable pride in what has been accomplished here. The clearest evidence of the optimism and loyalty that local people feel for this region—often referred to simply as "Aroostook"—is illustrated by another passage from Charles Wilson: "Aroostook isn't merely some obscure little county in another state. It's a world unto itself, where dough will rise twice as fast as it does down Bangor way, and the land is so rich that if you leave your walking stick stuck in the ground overnight, you'll find that in the morning it will have taken root and be sprouting branches—and if you let it alone bear apples or plums by the next week!"

Historically, people in the County felt strongly about their fishing and counted on the region's lakes and rivers to supply them with sport (and food) during both the open-water and ice-fishing seasons. For many years, Aroostook waters had some of Maine's highest catch rates and produced many of its largest fish. Lately, with more leisure time available to many County residents, fishing pressure has increased and the quality of the fishing has declined. The good news is that the water quality and habitat is still in decent shape. All that's needed to restore many Aroostook County fisheries to their former glory is an adjustment in regulations that will protect smelt populations from overharvest and allow a larger percentage of legal-sized salmonids to remain in the water.

Early in the season, most Aroostook anglers use sewn smelts and streamer flies to troll the large lakes for salmon, brook trout, and togue. During late spring, when the water drops and mayflies begin to hatch, rivers become the prime destinations. The County is also well known for miles of small brooks that crisscross its landscape and provide anglers with an opportunity to catch their limit of pan-sized trout on almost any day of the open-water season. Healthy populations of bass and pickerel are found in a handful of lakes and rivers in the southern part of the County.

To make this chapter manageable, I have divided my description of the County into three distinct geographical zones. The northern zone is dominated by the Fish River chain of lakes. This includes Fish River, Portage, St. Froid, Long, Mud, Cross, Square, and Eagle Lakes and more than forty-five miles of rivers and thoroughfares. The lakes and ponds of the Deboullie Reserve and the St. John River from Allagash Village to Grand Falls are also part of this zone. The central zone's most prominent geographical feature is the lower sixty-five miles of the Aroostook River. But smaller waters like St. Croix Stream, Prestile Stream, and the Meduxnekeag River also provide good fishing. The southern zone is comprised of all the waters in the Mattawamkeag watershed and features Mattawamkeag and Pleasant Lakes as well as the East and West Branches of the Mattawamkeag River.

History

Aroostook County has a rich French heritage that dates back to the arrival of the first white settlers around 1750. Driven by the British from their homes in Port Royal, Nova Scotia, these Acadian refugees traveled up the St. John River and settled in an area near the present-day towns of Madawaska and Fort Kent. Located on fertile soil at the intersection of several major trade routes, their villages prospered and the number of Acadians living in the region quickly swelled to several thousand. These French settlements were so isolated from the rest of the world that when the first English-speaking pioneers ventured into the St. John Valley in the late 1700s, they did not know these outposts existed. Following the English settlers, large numbers of Scandinavian and Scottish immigrants also moved into the County. Despite this multicultural influence, much of this area has retained the French-Acadian flavor established by the earliest settlers.

Lumbering came to Aroostook County around 1820 when Shepard Cary and John Goddard built logging camps near Houlton. Large pines were their principle target and since there were no roads in this area, logs were transported via local rivers during spring runoff. Most of the wood was floated north into the St. John River through tributaries such as the Fish, Aroostook, and Meduxnekeag Rivers. Some logs also went south into the Penobscot River via the Mattawamkeag and several other smaller rivers. In 1838, a border dispute between Maine and New Brunswick arose over timber rights and resulted in armed militia being deployed in

Aroostook County farmers have traditionally relied on local kids to help with the potato harvest.

Maine State Archives

Years ago, winter lumber camps were established in remote areas of Aroostook County and housed dozens of men for months at a time.

Maine Folklife Center

the area. This issue was resolved four years later without a shot being fired, so it might seem like the dispute was a minor event in the overall history of the County. However, the bloodless "Aroostook War" was actually very significant to the development of the region because it led to the construction of roads and encampments, which in turn encouraged people to relocate here.

During the next forty years, the population of Aroostook County swelled from around three thousand to over fifty thousand people. Most lived on farmsteads they carved out of the wilderness several acres at a time. During these early years, the economy was diverse and included woodsmen working in lumber and cedar-shingle mills as well as farmers who produced grass seed, wool, honey, and potatoes. Over time, an increasing number of people shifted their efforts to potato production because the County's cool, wet climate and rich loamy soil favored the production of this crop.

Because potatoes couldn't be floated down rivers or effectively transported over Aroostook's rough roads, the industry didn't really boom until the arrival of the railroad. This began in 1862 when the Canadian-Pacific Railroad extended a short spur into Maine from Woodstock, New Brunswick, and culminated in the 1894 completion of the Bangor to Aroostook line. In the twenty-five years that followed, more than a thousand new potato farms were started and land under cultivation rose from less than fifteen thousand acres to more than one hundred twenty-five thousand acres. This made Aroostook County the potato capital of the world throughout most of the 1920s.

But bad weather, pests, and competition from other producers can wreak havoc on a region with a one-crop economy. And over the years, farmers in Aroostook have had their share of heartaches. Despite the ups and downs, most people maintain the type of upbeat attitude espoused by potato grower Charley Fisher after a couple of particularly tough years in the 1930s. "I've been poorer than any beggar," Fisher said. "I got no sure guarantee that I won't be again. But I like poor folks, like to help 'em when I got money—like to be amongst 'em when I don't. When folks live from the ground, poverty and riches seem to go hand in hand." Seventy years later, potato farming is still the principle industry in Aroostook County. Its importance is best evidenced by the ongoing September tradition of local high-school students getting a three-week break from school to work on the potato harvest.

Northern Zone

The Fish River watershed dominates the northern Maine landscape with a drainage area that covers more than one thousand square miles. Eight major lakes and over forty-five miles of rivers make this area a prime destination for trout and salmon anglers. In addition to this zone's lake and moving-water fisheries, I will briefly discuss the developing muskellunge fishery on the St. John River, then conclude this section with a description of the trout ponds in and around the Deboullie Reserve.

Upper Fish River Drainage

Prior to 1900 the Fish River chain of lakes was known for producing excellent catches of brook trout, togue, and whitefish. Salmon and smelts were introduced in 1895 and increased in numbers during the next twenty-five years. Large salmon and brook trout were abundant in these waters until the early 1960s when the construction of new roads and lakeside homes significantly increased the fishing pressure. The use of DDT for spruce budworm control combined with poor logging practices also took a heavy toll on this fishery. Fortunately, many of these problems have been resolved, and the future of this fishery looks bright.

FISH RIVER LAKE. Fish River Lake is the first major body of water in the upper Fish River drainage. It arises from a handful of tributaries that flow from the small ponds located to its south and west. Fish River Lake is sparsely developed and is the only lake in the chain located

Increased fishing pressure and the proliferation of landlocked salmon have reduced the number of large togue found in many Aroostook County lakes.

142

on private (paper company) land. Good access is available at a boat launch located on the northwest corner of the lake. Brook trout are the primary target at Fish River Lake and, because it is closed to ice-fishing, anglers come here early in the season—many of the largest trout of the year are taken shortly after ice-out.

I prefer to visit this area in early June, after the weather has warmed a bit and the water in the outlet stream has dropped to a wadable level. A couple of years ago, I hit it just right and caught dozens of feisty brookies on Wulffs and other easy-to-fish dry flies. During summer, most trout move into the deep hole on the south end of the lake; trolling with lead-core line and still-fishing with smelts or night crawlers are the best ways to catch them.

Good numbers of salmon are found in Fish River Lake and the outlet stream. Depending on the status of the smelt population, salmon here can vary from fairly fat to ax-handle thin. Generally, these fish are in good shape and worth pursuing with a streamer fly trolled briskly along the shoreline or cast in front of inlets such as Clayton Stream or Smith Brook. Togue are also caught occasionally, but this lake has limited deep water and isn't specifically managed for them.

PORTAGE LAKE. Portage Lake is located on Route 11 and is developed along both its east and west shores. Despite easy access, the lake experiences light angling pressure, primarily because the fishing isn't very good. With a maximum depth of only twenty-five feet, Portage Lake represents marginal coldwater habitat for salmonids. In addition, brook trout suffer from competition with perch and chubs. Despite these problems, people who fish the lake's springholes catch some nice brook trout. According to regional biologist Dave Baisley, changes in regulations that increased the size and reduced the bag limit on brook trout have helped this fishery.

ST. FROID LAKE. St. Froid is a deep, narrow lake with camps along its east and northwest shores. Because it contains plenty of cold water and supports a good pop-

Tyson O'Keefe

Winter is a popular time to fish for togue on St. Froid Lake.

ulation of large smelts, St. Froid is the best place in the Fish River chain to catch togue. Good spots to fish are the deep trough near the boat launch at the foot of the Quimby Road and on the south end of the lake around Togue Point. Anglers also troll streamers or sewn smelt on the west side of the lake near the inflows of the Red and Birch Rivers.

UPPER FISH RIVER AND NADEAU THOROUGHFARE. The upper Fish River begins at the outlet of Round Pond and travels about fifteen miles through a series of glides and deadwaters before flowing into Portage Lake. Because of its inaccessibility, this remote stretch is most often fished in the vicinity of Fish River Falls where a gravel road leads to a small camping area. When the water is receding in the spring, smelt-imitating lures and flies can produce brook trout and salmon from the rips below the falls. One way to fish this stretch is to launch a canoe below the falls and float to the bridge that crosses the river seven miles downstream.

The next section of the upper Fish River is a ten-mile stretch of flatwater that connects Portage Lake with St. Froid Lake. Limited road access and a swampy perimeter necessitates the use of a small boat. Trolling near where the river leaves or enters the lakes accounts for many of the fish taken in the spring. Some anglers also like to anchor and bait-fish in the river's corner pools and deep holes.

The final section of the upper Fish River is the three-mile-long Nadeau Thoroughfare that flows from St. Froid Lake to Eagle Lake. Route 11 crosses this scenic waterway within sight of the St. Froid outlet, making this short stretch of fast-flowing water the most accessible section of the upper Fish River. During fall, I have caught a number of good fish in the Nadeau Thoroughfare. Generally, I use bright-colored streamers such as the Cardinelle, Colonel Bates, and Pink Lady to tempt spawning salmon into aggressive strikes. If streamers fail to produce fish, small, bright-colored wet flies or single salmon-egg patterns can be effective. This area is fishable by wading along either bank, though I often use a canoe during high-water periods because it provides easier access to the best lies. Negotiating this stretch in a canoe tends to be tricky, so have a good anchor and wear a life jacket.

Timing is critical when fishing the upper river in the fall. The Fish River chain is a free-flowing system that takes considerably more rain to increase flows than rivers where fall spawning runs can be triggered simply by opening the gates on a dam at a prescribed time of year. To maximize fall-fishing success here, anglers need to keep a close eye on the weather and the calendar.

Lower Fish River Drainage

Most fish caught in the Fish River chain are taken either by spring trolling or ice-fishing on the five lakes in the lower drainage. Because angling techniques vary widely among fishermen on these waters, the bulk of this section will deal with "where and when" rather than "how-to" information. Salmonids here feed primarily on smelts, and anglers who locate concentrations of these baitfish will usually find good numbers of game fish. In the spring, trolling sewn smelt or smelt-imitating lures near smelt spawning brooks and thoroughfare inlets is usually productive. Orange Mooselook Wobblers and Rapalas or bright streamers like the Red, White, or Pink Lady can also be effective when the water is murky. Fishing in the thoroughfares can be productive for anglers working the edges of the current during low-light periods in the morning and evening. The best results on the lakes themselves occur after the wind has raised a bit of a chop on the water. Salmonids move deeper when the water warms; thus, during July and August experienced anglers use lead-core line and downriggers. Still-fishing with live smelts in deep holes is another technique that is widely employed in the summer. A surprising number of opportunities for fly-fishing are available in shallow mud-bottomed coves on calm evenings during the Green Drake hatch.

Omer Lebel

In 1987, Omer Lebel of Van Buren set the world record for a brook trout taken through the ice with this eight-pound, four-ounce beauty that he caught in Long Lake.

LONG LAKE. Long Lake is the largest and northernmost lake in the lower Fish River drainage. With the village of St. Agatha on the upper end and Route 162 running the length of the western shore, it is one of the more developed lakes in Aroostook County. Yet despite the fishing pressure, Long Lake is one of the best places in Maine to catch a "wall-hanger." Each year, salmon that approach ten pounds are taken from this lake's cold, clear waters. In 1992, Omer Lebel of Van Buren set the ice-fishing world record for brook trout when he caught an eight pounder on a Swedish Pimple. Hardtop boat launches are located a couple of miles south of St. Agatha on Route 162 and at the foot of the lake in the village of Sinclair.

Pinpointing precisely where to catch salmon here is difficult because fish can be spread throughout the water column and turn on and off abruptly. For topwater trolling in the spring, the south shore of Sinclair Cove is usually a good bet because of several smelt spawning brooks that dump into the lake at that point. Van Buren Cove and the east shore of the lake in the vicinity of Paulette Brook are also popular areas to fish. These places produce best when there is a moderate chop on the water. A wide array of lures and baits are fished in Long Lake—some of the most effective are sewn smelts on a plain hook or behind a dodger, Yo-Zuri Smelts, Rapalas, and streamers like the Gray Ghost, Blue Smelt, and Barnes Special.

MUD LAKE. Mud is the sleeper among the lakes of the lower Fish River drainage. Relatively small and shallow, Mud doesn't receive half the fishing pressure experienced by the other lakes, yet creel-census data indicate that the catch rates here can be as good as those of other local waters. One reason for Mud Lake's angler neglect is its lack of a boat launch—to get here, anglers must either float down from Long Lake or motor up the thoroughfare from the village of Guerette. Mud is the only lake in the area that is closed to ice-fishing;

anglers who fish just after ice-out are often rewarded for the extra effort it takes to get here. Good trolling routes run from the mouth of the outlet thoroughfare up to Harris Brook and from the inlet to the small cove on the south side of the lake. Making a few passes across the middle of the lake can also be productive, especially if it's early enough in the season to work your offerings along the edge of the receding ice sheet.

CROSS LAKE. Cross Lake has a well-maintained boat launch located about one mile from Route 161. Spring trollers can look for trout in the shallow area across the lake from the boat landing around the mouth of Black Brook and in the vicinity of the brooks that flow into the north end of the lake. Salmon can be taken virtually anywhere, but a good place to start is north of the boat launch about seventy-five yards off the east shore. My favorite early season spot is the outlet thoroughfare. I usually motor down to the first large corner pool, then slowly troll a Rapala, Flash King, or streamer fly back upstream against the current. Strikes often occur in the area where the thoroughfare exits the lake. Try to hold your boat steady in the current so that your offerings work back and forth with little forward movement.

SQUARE LAKE. Most lakes in the Fish River chain are narrow and are sheltered by surrounding ridges. Square Lake, however, is shaped like a bowl and lies completely exposed to the north wind that can quickly whip it into a froth. I had a bad experience here several years ago when I took a small boat across the lake to do some late September fly-fishing in the salmon pool near the head of the outlet thoroughfare. When I left the boat landing the day was warm and sunny. But when I emerged from the thoroughfare for the return trip, wind had trans-

Each spring, many quality salmon are taken by anglers trolling on Cross Lake.

Bangor and Aroostook Railroad

Square Lake has been producing fine brook trout like this for many years.

formed the lake into a sea of whitecaps. In order to get back to the landing, I had to wait until after dark for the lake to calm enough for me to cross. Safety must always be your primary concern on big, remote lakes.

Despite its propensity for wind and waves, many anglers rate Square Lake their favorite in the Fish River chain because it is a consistent producer of quality salmon and brook trout. Square is also special because its low-relief topography and lightly developed shorelines provide a wide-open feeling that is not available on many other Maine lakes. A boat launch on the northeast end of the lake can be reached by a five-mile-long access road that runs south off Route 161. Because this road can be muddy in the spring, some people boat into Square through the thoroughfares from Cross and Eagle Lakes.

The smelts on Square often begin to run before the ice has cleared from the lake. To avoid missing any early season action, some hardcore fishermen use snowmobiles to haul canoes across the ice in the winter, then store them in the woods near the mouths of smelt spawning brooks. When the current opens patches of water in front of the brooks, they have private access to the fish that often congregate near the mouth. Casting smelt-imitating streamers on a sinking line is the method of choice for many anglers, but lures and live bait can also be effective. A less ambitious early season alternative is to fish a live smelt or worm at the mouth of the thoroughfare that flows in from Cross Lake.

Once the ice clears completely, fish spread out and surface trolling dominates the scene. Prime locations include the area from the boat landing to Rocky Point, the shoreline between Barstow and Limestone Points, and the drop-offs just beyond the mouths of most inlet brooks. However, when the fish are biting, they can be caught in most locations. Later in the season, fly-fishing can be good on calm evenings when fish are feeding on mayflies in Goddard Cove or in the vicinity of California and Dimock Brooks.

EAGLE LAKE. The village of Eagle Lake is located about halfway down the lake itself and divides the heavily developed west basin from the Maine Public Reserve Land that surrounds the east basin. (Note that this is a different body of water from the Eagle Lake described in the North Woods chapter.) Because there are many camps on this lake, you are likely to see people fishing almost anywhere. A couple of productive early season fishing spots in the west basin are found along the shoreline between Brown's Point and Gilmore Brook and in the area near the lake's outlet. Good places to fish in the east basin include Three Brooks Cove, the mouths of the Nadeau and Square Lake thoroughfares, and the rocky shoreline on the easternmost end of the lake.

Although good-sized salmon, brook trout, and togue were historically available in Eagle Lake, around 1990 the size of fish began to decline. By 1998 it was difficult to catch a legal fourteen-inch salmon on Eagle Lake. When I asked regional biologist Dave Baisley about the situation, he said there simply were too many predatory salmonids in the lake and not enough smelt to feed them. He explained that "many lakes with good spawning habitat and potential for high rates of natural reproduction suffer periodic declines in fish size due to occasional overabundances of juveniles, which develop after several consecutive years of prolific spawning." He also noted that "these cyclic patterns among predators and prey are common in nature" and that maintaining the ideal number of smelts needed to produce robust, fast-growing fish is one of the most challenging aspects of his job. To increase the size of Eagle Lake fish, in 2000 the MDIF&W suspended the stocking of togue and salmon, reduced the size limit on salmon to twelve inches, and stocked smelt eggs in the lake's feeder brooks. Preliminary reports indicate that game fish populations are improving and that the future of salmon fishing on Eagle Lake looks bright.

Nice salmon can be taken in the lower Fish River between the outlet of Eagle Lake and Soldier Pond.

THOROUGHFARES. The thoroughfares that connect the five lower Fish River Lakes are shorter but generally more productive than those in the upper drainage. All of them can be navigated at moderate water levels with boats up to sixteen feet long. However, because a number of obstructions are present in these waters, newcomers should seek navigational advice from local anglers. I have the most trouble navigating the thoroughfares when I am salmon fishing in September because, unless it has been a wet fall, at several locations there is barely enough water to float a boat. The long, rocky run that leads into the Salmon Pool on the Square Lake Thoroughfare is particularly nasty—on several occasions I have had to drag my boat out after dark because the water was too shallow to run an outboard motor.

With the exception of the three-and-a-half-mile stretch between Eagle and Square Lakes, the thoroughfares in this area are fairly short and easy for fishermen to read. All contain a few deep pools where fish congregate. Trolling is popular in the spring, but "plunk fishing" the deep holes with worms or live bait is common. During heavy runoff, floating debris can make fishing difficult here. After the water level drops, insect hatches in riffle areas provide fly fishermen with opportunities to catch good fish in the evenings, at least until midsummer. My favorite time to visit these thoroughfares is in September when streamside hardwoods are ablaze with fall color. I have spent memorable days casting bright marabou streamers and wet flies to salmon that were best measured in pounds rather than inches. Lately, however, the size of the average fish has declined. Hopefully, changes in regulations and an increase in voluntary catch-and-release fishing will restore these waters to their full potential.

LOWER FISH RIVER. The final section of the Fish River begins at the outlet of Eagle Lake and flows for ten miles before entering the St. John River at Fort Kent. Water levels fluctuate drastically with the seasons and dictate the approach that anglers must use to fish here. In the spring, casting or trolling

Many pools in the Fish River thoroughfares can be fished from boats and, during the fall, are popular places for salmon fishermen to gather.

from a small boat is popular because high water washes out most pools and makes wading nearly impossible. Boats can be launched near the bridge that crosses the river in the village of Soldier Pond, and from there you can travel either upstream or downstream. I have spent several delightful days in late May exploring the four miles of river above Soldier Pond, and on each outing I caught more than a dozen brook trout and salmon. All these fish were taken on wet flies like the Picket Pin and Hornberg and small bucktail streamers either cast or trolled with a sinking fly line. And although no monsters turned up in my catch, fish in the three-pound range are taken here regularly.

Downstream from Soldier Pond the lower Fish River becomes more turbulent, so newcomers who fish from a boat should use caution when approaching the unfamiliar rapids. At optimal water levels all but the worst places can be negotiated by experienced boaters. Most people are better advised to fish a spot where they can carry a small boat into a defined section of the river instead of trying to float the whole thing. A couple of

such places are the braided islands on the outskirts of Fort Kent and the area around Fish River Falls. Casting directly off the bridge that crosses the river at Soldier Pond can also be productive.

Once the water drops and begins to warm, the pools and glides of the lower Fish River are fun to explore with a canoe. I know of anglers who floated the lower Fish River with inner tubes and managed to catch trout along the way. I prefer to fish this stretch in the fall when trout and salmon are concentrated in the deeper pools and at the mouths of inflowing brooks.

Lower St. John River

The fifty-mile section of the lower St. John River that I will describe here flows from Allagash Village to the dam at Grand Falls. Because there are no large water-storage impoundments above this stretch of the St. John, the river exhibits a large seasonal variation in flow and temperature and is heavily influenced by local run-off and rainfall. Madawaska angler George Bragdon once described the lower St. John as "an impossibly large freestone stream," which is a good way to visualize it. Traditionally, brook trout have been the principle target for most anglers, and when conditions are right fish up to seventeen inches can be taken. A few salmon also drop into the lower St. John from the Fish River. Streamers, nymphs, small spinners, and worms are all used here. Decent insect hatches—thus, dry-fly fishing—are also available for anglers who are present at the right place and time. Because of the river's size, many people use small boats to maneuver among its numerous islands and braided channels. A paved road follows the river for many miles and provides shore anglers with good access. Mid-June through early July is usually a productive time to fish this river, though a heavy rain or an unseasonable hot spell can cause the fish to disappear overnight. It is wise to check local conditions before making a trip to the St. John.

In the last decade, trout fishing in the lower St. John has suffered a serious setback from the muskellunge that were, as I mentioned in the North Woods

chapter, introduced into the watershed from Lac Frontiere, Quebec. A number of twenty-pound muskies have been taken from Glazier Lake, which is connected to the St. John via the St. Francis River. In fact, during the winter of 2000 the state record for muskellunge was broken twice in the same month by fish taken in Glazier Lake. Muskies have also been caught in many other places on the lower St. John including the headpond above Grand Falls and at the base of Fish River Falls.

If muskies make their way over Fish River Falls, the world-class salmonid fishery in the Fish River chain will be severely impacted. The destruction of coldwater fisheries by more competitive exotic species is the biggest problem that Maine fisheries face in the new millennium. But in a state the size of Maine, with its diverse and remote waters, illegal introductions of fish are virtually impossible for law enforcement personnel to prevent. The worst thing about exotic species is that once they are established, eradication is usually not bio-

Island Pond anglers often use a dry line to cast flies to passing trout.

logically or economically feasible. In real terms, there is nothing the MDIF&W can do about muskies in the lower St. John River except to regulate and manage them.

Deboullie Reserve

Deboullie is a one-hundred-fifty-square-mile public land reserve located about ten miles east of St. Froid Lake. It contains numerous hiking trails and is a great place to relax and get away from the hassles of everyday life. When I visit the Deboullie Reserve, though, I come to fly-fish for brook trout in the ponds that are located throughout the area. There are inviting campsites on a number of ponds. I usually stay at Red River Camps on Island Pond because, along with good food and accommodations, they have locked canoes stashed on all the outlying waters.

Stink, Upper, Denny, and the Little Blacks are all fly-fishing-only ponds that hold good-sized trout. Each pond has a unique character; thus, it takes time to learn how to fish them effectively. Galilee and North are two other fly-fishing-only ponds in the area. Both require a bit of a hike to reach and contain smaller trout, but they are ideal places to fish with a float tube. Gardner, Deboullie, and Pushineer Ponds are larger waters that have special regulations but are not restricted to fly-fishing only. In addition to larger-than-average brook trout, these three ponds contain fishable populations of blueback trout, a rare species whose range in Maine is limited to several dozen waters.

Despite this diversity of opportunities, many people who travel to Deboullie stay at Red River Camps and spend a good deal of time fishing on Island Pond. In part, that's due to its convenience, but this pretty pond also contains a large supply of fat twelve-inch brook trout that are usually willing to smother a passing Muddler or rise to a dry fly.

Northern Aroostook County is home to a number of other fine trout ponds located near but outside the Deboullie Reserve. These include Hunnewell, Deer, Dickwood, and Ben Lakes, which are west of the Fish River, and Blake and Third Sly Brook Lakes, which are east of the river.

Central Zone

The Aroostook River is the most prominent geographical feature in the central zone. It originates at the confluence of Millinocket and Munsungan Streams and flows in a northeasterly direction for about one hundred miles before joining the St. John River just beyond the New Brunswick border. The western half of this waterway flows through miles of remote timberland and was covered in the North Woods chapter. Here, I will focus on the section of the Aroostook River that drains the forests and farmland located east of the village of Masardis. I will also describe trout fishing in several of the central zone's smaller waters, namely, St. Croix and Prestile Streams and the Meduxnekeag River.

Aroostook River

Most trout fishing in the Aroostook River takes place from mid-May through June as high water recedes. During this period, fish spread throughout the river and feed actively on minnows, crayfish, and assorted invertebrates. Trolling is the method of choice for most anglers, who use everything from worms to tandem streamers. Bright-colored lures like Daredevles, Al's Goldfish, and Rapalas are popular, but Cecil's Smelts and Flash Kings catch their share of fish. Early in the season, trolling slowly along back eddies found near large boulders and islands is the best way to entice trout to bite. As the river begins to warm and clear, imitations fished near the tailouts of rips and around inlet brooks also produce well.

Ten maintained boat launches, in addition to numerous turnouts off farm roads, offer Aroostook River anglers a variety of fishing-trip options, which range from short jaunts around Caribou or Presque Isle to an all-day float between Masardis and Ashland. A couple of popular spots are the islands in the Castle Hill section of the river and the run between Parkhurst and Maysville. When conditions are good, many places on this river can be productive. I became convinced of this recently when I put my boat in at the launch located just off Route 11 behind the Aroostook Fish and Game Club in Ashland and began the day trolling a Black Ghost upstream past the mouth of the Machais River. Although I caught a number of trout of up to twelve inches, to prove a point I abandoned this stretch and headed downstream to try my luck in the vicinity of the Little Machais River. In short order, I began to catch trout here as well. Although most of the fish I caught that day were fairly small, reports from local anglers indicate that trout up to sixteen inches, as well as occasional salmon, are taken here.

For many people, the fishing season on the Aroostook River ends when the water level drops below the point that allows them to troll. However, during mid-summer trout concentrate near the mouths of cool inlets and springholes and can provide fast action for wading anglers. Sporadic hatches of mayflies and caddis occur on many evenings—even when the fish aren't rising, fly fishermen can still do well with nymphs, wet flies, and small streamers like the Little Brook Trout and Banded-Leg Muddler. The key to summertime success on this river is finding areas where significant numbers of fish are concentrated. In the Caribou area worthwhile places to explore are rips and runs located just north of the city and the mouths of local tributaries such as Spring and Gray Brooks.

St. Croix Stream

The St. Croix is a rather small, lightly fished stream that flows into the Aroostook River near the village of Masardis. Aside from a few rough four-wheel-drive roads, the only vehicular access to this twenty-mile-long waterway are just above the mouth at the Route

11 bridge and twelve miles upstream at St. Croix crossing. Because of this limited access, most people fish the stream by using a small boat or canoe to either motor up from Masardis or float down from the upper bridge.

Prior to Memorial Day, the best fishing occurs in the deadwater areas in the middle section of the stream between Cranberry and Matherson Brooks and in the upper reaches near St. Croix Lake. Trolling with small spoons and flies or casting worm and spinner rigs into pockets behind rocks will usually produce enough pan-sized brookies to complement a meal of fresh fiddle-head ferns, which are abundant in this area. As the water warms, most trout will move from the deadwaters into the more highly oxygenated riffle areas. The lower rips in the vicinity of Blackwater Stream and the broken water near St. Croix crossing generally produce best at this time of year.

Anglers who enjoy catching pan-sized brookies in a remote setting will quickly become fond of this off-the-beaten-path stream. Local guide Dan LaPointe says

Fiddlehead ferns are a prized, springtime delicacy gathered from low-lying areas of the Aroostook River.

Matt Libby

Nice, native brook trout can still be found in Prestile Stream and the Meduxnekeag River.

that trout in the fourteen-inch range are occasionally taken here. On my last visit, however, I averaged at least ten chubs for every trout that I caught. So for maximum enjoyment of this delightful little stream be sure to have realistic expectations of success.

Prestile Stream

The Prestile is a relatively small stream that begins near Easton and flows for about twenty-five miles before crossing the Canadian border. It is a popular spot for local fishermen because trout can be taken here from opening day until the end of the season. Early in the year, most fishing is centered around easy-to-reach places where overwintering trout are concentrated. The pools below the dams in Mars Hill and Robinsons are a couple of places where Aroostook anglers catch trout on opening day. Water temperatures below forty degrees cause fish to be sluggish, so worms bounced along the bottom or plunked into a back eddy are the best ways to catch trout at this time of year. A bit later, Buckley's Deadwater and the small headponds behind the dams can also provide good fishing.

Trout spread out in the stream as insects become active, and when conditions are prime in June wading anglers can find fish in nearly every run and riffle. Numerous farm roads, bridges, and an abandoned right-of-way from the Bangor and Aroostook railroad provide access to Prestile Stream. Popular spots are the riffles and pools between Westfield and Mars Hill and the deep hole where Whitney Brook enters the stream. When I fish Prestile Stream I like to get off on my own, so I usually pull on a pair of hip boots and wade down the middle of the stream, using a grasshopper or Slim Jim to pull trout from likely looking pockets.

The Prestile is a biologically productive stream because of its limestone substrate. Therefore, good hatches of Hendricksons, Blue-Wing Olives, and assorted other mayflies and caddis are often encountered here. Prestile trout are small—they average around nine inches— because most of the fish caught are killed rather than released. A few trout up to sixteen inches are available here, and your best chance to catch them is at dawn or dusk.

Meduxnekeag River

The Meduxnekeag River is another waterway that benefits from the limestone substrates found in this area. Brook trout and brown trout grow to respectable sizes

Both the East and West Branches of the Mattawamkeag River provide anglers with solitude and the opportunity to catch native brook trout.

in this fertile water, and decent mayfly and caddisfly hatches make the Meduxnekeag a good river for dry-fly fishermen to practice their craft. This waterway is comprised of several distinct sections whose character and fishability vary considerably.

The North Branch of the Meduxnekeag flows through the village of Monticello and has good fishing a few miles northwest of town where the West Road crosses the river. The best opportunities for fly-casting are available above the bridge. However, because pan-sized brookies are found throughout this area, ambitious anglers can follow the river for miles in either direction.

The South Branch of the river has better access and contains both brookies and browns. Fish tend to run larger here, so angling pressure is a bit heavier. The South Branch is divided in half by a small flow-through lake near Hodgdon that provides good spring fishing. Most trout move to springholes or the mouths of cool brooks when the water warms in the summer.

The mainstem of the Meduxnekeag River begins at the outlet of Drews Lake and travels for about twenty miles before crossing into New Brunswick. The city of Houlton divides the river into two distinct sections. The upper mainstem river has deep pools that can hold fish over two pounds. Spin-fishing is the angling method of choice because much of the upper river is fairly narrow and lined with trees. A number of farm roads provide good access. A productive, easy-to-reach pool is located below the mouth of the South Branch near Carys Mills. Drews and Nickerson are two lakes in the area that can provide excellent fishing. Brookies, browns, togue, and a variety of warmwater species usually provide fast action during both the open-water and ice-fishing seasons.

Below Houlton, the lower mainstem Meduxnekeag widens and flows through a broad agricultural valley. Road access to some pools is possible but often involves the difficult task of picking your way along a series of private, unmarked roads that wander through potato fields. Given that hassle, some anglers prefer to float this river in a canoe. Many of the pools on the lower Meduxnekeag are long, slow glides that offer fish ample opportunities to compare your artificial flies to the naturals floating by. This type of fishing is challenging for some anglers and frustrating for others. During the summer months, browns can be so difficult to catch here that many people fish for them only at night. Favored local methods involve skittering large

flies like Wulffs and Muddlers across the moonlit surface of deep pools. There are a number of stocked trout ponds in the area—Conroy, Carry, Number Nine, and Timoney Ponds provide better-than-average fisheries.

Southern Zone

The southern zone is composed of waters in the Mattawamkeag watershed. Coldwater fisheries in this part of the County are largely confined to the East and West Branches of the Mattawamkeag River, Pleasant and Mattawamkeag Lakes, and a number of smaller brooks and beaver flowages. Smallmouth bass are widely distributed in these waters, in a number of other area lakes, and in the mainstem of the Mattawamkeag River.

Mattawamkeag River

Upstream from Interstate 95, both the East and West Branches of the Mattawamkeag River are relatively small streams that flow through remote country. Road access is better along the upper West Branch, and fishing can be good at Warren Falls, Stair Falls, and Jackson Sluice. I like to visit these places as soon as spring run-off recedes because flows become low during midsummer. However, some brook trout are present throughout July and August, and I have had reasonable success by casting worms or weighted nymphs directly into the frothing pools found beneath small waterfalls and by working the relatively deep holes in spring-fed tributaries.

Below Interstate 95, the East Branch widens and becomes navigable with a canoe or a small boat. Early in the year, the area around Red Bridge is a popular place to troll or cast a worm and spinner into a foaming back eddy or corner pool. Later in the season, this spot has good insect hatches and offers productive fly-fishing. The West Branch provides an opportunity to catch both brook trout and salmon—there are several pools right in the town of Island Falls where you can catch these fish. Some West Branch anglers focus their attention on the ten-mile stretch of river that flows from the outlet of Mattawamkeag Lake to Haynesville. When you hit it right, fishing with flies or spinning gear can provide steady action for decent-sized salmon and small brook trout that average ten inches. The river in this area alternates between rocky pools and riffles and can be tough to wade when the water is up. Access here is limited, but shore anglers can find good fishing in the middle section of the river by following a gravel road off Route 2A north of Haynesville. Driving to most other areas on the lower West Branch is very difficult, so I typically use a canoe when I fish here. The East and West Branches merge at Haynesville to form the main-stem of the Mattawamkeag River. Aside from a few coldwater pools in the vicinity of the Mattawamkeag Wilderness Park that hold trout, fishing here is primar-ily for smallmouth bass, pickerel, and perch.

Southern Zone Lakes

Pleasant Lake is a scenic spot that provides patient anglers with a chance to catch nice salmon and brook trout during both the open-water and ice-fishing sea-sons. A healthy population of large smelts allows these salmonids to grow fat and sassy and also provides a popular food fishery. Because of the abundance of bait-fish, salmon are often finicky and can be difficult to catch. A thriving population of smallmouth bass also inhabits the rocky shelves and shorelines of this lake and are usually more cooperative than the picky salmon. These hard-fighting bronzebacks are a favorite early summer target for fly fishermen using popping bugs.

Nearby Mattawamkeag Lake provides even better warmwater fishing. People with camps on the lake say that catching twenty bass a day is a regular occurrence throughout the summer. Heavy weed growth on the shallow flats found throughout the upper basin pro-vides good cover for baitfish and leeches and allows anglers to do well fishing everything from bucktail jigs to plastic baits. Many of the islands, points, and sub-merged rock piles in the lower basin are favorite targets for local bass fishermen. The lower basin also supports a limited salmonid fishery focused in the deep hole found between Big Island and Black Point. Macwahoc, Wytopitlock, and Molunkus are other lakes in the area that provide good fishing for warmwater species.